STATUS OF WOMEN IN MODERN SOCIETY

STATUS OF WOMEN IN MODERN SOCIETY

Sharat Dwivedi

CYBER TECH PUBLICATIONS
4264/3, Ansari Road, Daryaganj, New Delhi-110002 (India)
Ph.: 011-23244078, 011-43559448 Fax: 011-23280028
E-Mail: cyberpublicationsdelhi@yahoo.com
Website: www.cybertechpublications.com

STATUS OF WOMEN IN MODERN SOCIETY

Sharat Dwivedi

First Edition 2010

Asian Offset Printers

Published by :

G.S. Rawat for **Cyber Tech Publications**
4264/3, Ansari Road, Daryaganj, New Delhi-110002 (India)
Ph.: 011-23244078, 011-43559448 Fax: 011-23280028
E-Mail: cyberpublicationsdelhi@yahoo.com
Website: www.cybertechpublications.com

Preface

Status of Women' is a pretty worn-out theme. Much has been written and much has been spoken on the subject and yet one has to go on harping on the same theme for a simple reason that the woman has not attained her full status and its necessary to remind her of it so that she may continue her efforts till the goal is reached. The term 'status' signifies the sum total of the various culturally ascribed roles one has to play and the rights and duties inherent in a social position. Besides the ascribed status, there is also the 'achieved status' which results from one's efforts and personal achievements. The concept of status is used to indicate the ordering of individuals in terms of attributes such as, level of education, occupation, income, perception of one's status within the home and in the community, decision-making role, number of restrictions imposed on one's activities, freedom and so on.

There is a great upsurge in awareness about women's rights among all sections of society. The developmental programmes and policies give emphasis to improving women's social status. In spite of urbanization and industrialization our culture and economy are predominantly agrarian, rural based. So empowering women, who are the backbone of our agrarian economy, is a sure path to achieve major economic gains. Our development efforts have yielded creditable benefits for women in doubling their life expectancy over the lat fifty years, and considerably reducing female infant mortality and child mortality rates. Women have a crucial role to play in the modern society. This book has been designed to meet a long-felt need and locate the enormous variety of women images, identify the ideological inspiration as well as under pinnings behind these images and comprehend the manners and processes through which these images affects, shape and even determine the reality of women's status in society.

—Author

CONTENTS

Preface

1. Introduction 1
2. Introduction: the Rhetoric of Television, Criticism, and Theory 42
3. Advancing the Status of Women 69
4. Politics of Diversity in the Present Society 73
5. Status of Women in Islam 79
6. Status of Women in the Rural Khasi Society of Meghalaya 94
7. Women's Studies and Research in Iran and Muslim Countries 104
8. The Role of Women in America 109
9. Modern-Day Slavery 138
10. The Task of Woman in the Modern World 171
11. Woman's Future Position in the World 190
12. Women's Empowerment 201
13. International Conference on Population and Development 237

Bibliography 271

Index 272

CONTENTS

1. Introduction

1

INTRODUCTION

Nowadays women empowerment has been increasing so rapidly all over the world and women are starting their own business to seek greater control over their personal and professional lives. In Pakistan, women do not enjoy the same opportunities as men. The segregation of gender starts early and becomes a way of life. However, economic necessity is forcing more and more women to engage in economic activities-employment or entrepreneurship.

Economic Census of Pakistan finds women entrepreneurship in Pakistan at the lowest ebb among the developing countries; it is estimated that women entrepreneurs presently comprise about 3 percent of the total 3.2 million entrepreneurs in the country and an estimated 33 percent of women are in rural areas.

These women are engaged in crafts such as embroidery, tailoring, carpet or durree making, shawl making, leatherwork, pottery, ceramics and food processing having incredible skills and potential.

This research would cover the rural areas of Bahawalpur and we will identify the problems or barriers and their relevant impact on women entrepreneurial activities. Another aspect of this research is that we want to identify to what extent the variables i.e. finance, access to technology, information, managerial skills, mobility, networking and trust building, education, experience etc. are affecting the women entrepreneurial activities in rural areas.

OBJECTIVES

Our main objective to conduct the research is to identify the problems or barriers which are faced by women in conducting entrepreneurial activities in rural areas. To measure the extent to which each variables has an impact on women entrepreneurial activities in rural areas.

How women respond to these barriers. How women cope with these barriers.

Problems faced by women entrepreneurs in rural areas of Bahawalpur are in compliance with the problems faced by women entrepreneurs in other rural areas of Pakistan. And to know in which activities women of Bahawalpur in rural areas are mostly engaged.

VARIABLES

1. Dependent variable
   - Women Entrepreneurial Activities in Rural Areas
2. Independent variable
   - Finance
   - Access To Technology
   - Skill Development
   - Networking And Trust Building
   - Expensive Raw Material
   - Quality Control
   - Working Environment
   - Mobility
   - Communication Skills
   - Training
   - Mentoring
   - Socio cultural Constraints
3. MODERATING VARIABLE
   - Education
   - Experience

4. Intervening variable
   - Socio cultural constraints

Research Methodology

These particular areas are important for the proper execution of proposed research project.

1. Collection of Secondary data.
2. Collection of primary data.
3. Data Analysis Technique.

Collection of Primary Data

Primary data was collected through pilot survey and well structured questionnaire.

- Basti Dera Izzat
- Basti Tiba Badr Sher
- Samma Satta
- Mele wali gali chowk himatian

COLLECTION OF SECONDARY DATA

Secondary data was collected through internet websites. Some articles on the research topic were also taken in consideration and data was also gathered from different business research books.

Questionnaire

For this research purpose we will prepare a questionnaire. And this questionnaire will approximately contain 20 to 30 questions relating to concern problem. Nature of questionnaire will be self expletory while keeping in mind that questionnaire should be motivated in nature.

Hypothesis

Ho: adequate education of women in rural areas has no significant impact on their business related skills.

HA: adequate education of women in rural areas has a significant impact on their business related skills.

Sampling

Sample Size

It is calculated as

n = (z * s) 2/E2

Where,

Z = Level of significance

S = Standard deviation

E = Allowable Error

Sampling Techniques

As our target population is entrepreneur/self employed rural women, so we will do Simple random sampling.

Target population

- All entrepreneur/self employed women in rural areas of Bahawalpur.

Sampled population

- Women doing embroidery work
- Women having their own Beauty parlor
- Women who are running schools in rural areas

NATURE OF THE FINAL REPORT

This report will explore all the barriers or problems faced by women in order to develop entrepreneurial environment in rural areas.

Not only it will identify the barriers in establishing business by rural women but also it will find the extent to which each problem will effect adversely in establishing business.

Report Format

The format of the final report will be such that it will be helpful for the concerning company to have answers of their questions easily and will be effective as well.

Final report will include the following items:

- Title Page

- Preface
- Acknowledgement
- Table of Contents
- Management Summary
- Description of Methodology
  1. Research Design
  2. Data Collection
  3. Sampling
- Analysis of data and interpretation.
  1. Percentages
  2. Cross tabulation
  3. Chi-Square
  4. Correlation
- Findings
- Conclusion and recommendations.
- Appendix.

QUALIFICATION OF RESERACHERS

TROPICAL TRACKERS is a team of highly competent and qualified personnel which was established in January, 2000.

he name of Tropical trackers is a symbol of quality, trust and reliability in he business world of Pakistan. This is all because of members who have a broad based academic and research background. The detail of each member's research background is as under:

Aisha Akram

She is a resident of Bahawalpur. She is a Student of BBA-6th in the department of management sciences,The Islamia University of Bahawalpur also. She has done her Fsc Pre-medical from FG College Bahawalpur.

She has conducted research on the topics of

- Establish a Business in china.
- Industry analysis- sweets and bakery

- Cost- analysis and financial statements analysis – Barket industry and co (Rohi Bread)
- Monetary policy of Pakistan

Fehmida Akram

She is resident of Bahawalpur. She is a student of BBA-6th in the Department of Management Sciences, IUB. She has done her Fsc Pre-medical from FG College Bahawalpur.

She has conducted research on the following topics:

- Establish a Business in norvey .
- Industry analysis- sweets and bakery
- Cost- analysis and financial statements analysis – Barket industry and co (Rohi Bread)
- NIFT

Madiha Jabeen

She is resident of Bahawalpur. She is a student of BBA-6th in the Department of Management Sciences, IUB. she has done her fsc pre medical from Govt.Sadiq Degree College Bahawalpur.

She has conducted research on topics like:

- Business in Egypt .
- Industry analysis- sweets and bakery
- Cost- analysis and financial statements analysis – Barket industry and co (Rohi Bread)
- Monetary policy of Pakistan

Madiha latif: She is a resident of Bahawalpur. she is a Student of BBA-6th in the Department of Management Sciences, IUB. She has done her f.Sc from Govt. Sadiq degree college, Bahawalpur. She has conducted research on topics:

- Business in Canada.
- Industry analysis- sweets and bakery
- Cost- analysis and financial statements analysis – Barket industry and co (Rohi Bread)
- Monetary policy of Pakistan

BUDGET

Cost

Total cost of the research is Rs. 16200/-

Cost of research includes following expenses

1. Cost of Proposal	Rs. 200/-
2. Cost of primary data collection	Rs. 600/-
3. Cost of Printing	Rs. 2000/-
4. Cost of Photostat	Rs. 500/-
5. Fees of Consultants	Rs. 10000/-
6. Expenses of Traveling	Rs. 2000/-
7. Telephone expenses	Rs. 500/-
8. Binding and Report	Rs. 500/-
Total Cost RS.	Rs. 16200/-

Terms of Payments

- 30% of the cost will be received at the time of signing the contract.
- 20% of the cost will be received at the end of January.
- Remaining 50% of the cost will be received at the time of presenting final report of research to you.

SHEDULE

Time Frame

• Research Proposal	15 days
• Secondary data collection	7 days
• Interview questions Design	3 days
• Primary Data Collection	15 days
• Data Analysis	5 days
• Preparation of Final Report	
1. Composing and printing.	10 days
2. Binding.	2 days
3. Submission of final report	3 days
Total Estimated Time	60 days

Grantt Chart

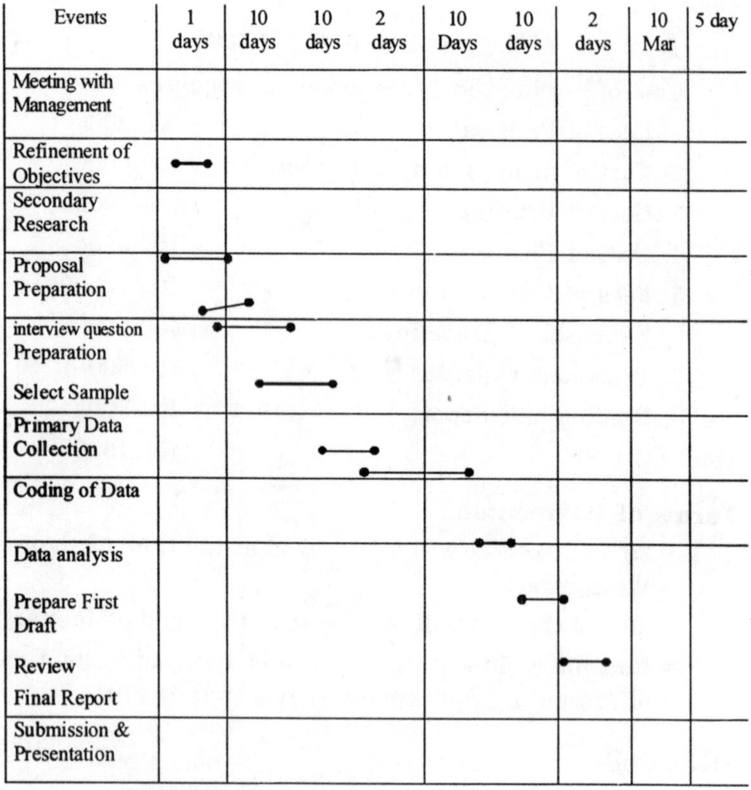

INTRODUCTION

Problem Studied

Why The Entrepreneurial Activities In Women In Rural Areas Are Not Flourishing? What are the problems along with socio cultural constraints that are affecting women entrepreneurial activities in rural areas?

Background Information

Nowadays women empowerment has been increasing so rapidly all over the world and women are starting their own business to seek greater control over their personal and professional lives. In Pakistan, women do not enjoy the same opportunities as men. The segregation of gender starts early and becomes a way of life. However, economic necessity is forcing more and more women to engage in economic activities-employment or entrepreneurship. Economic Census of Pakistan finds women entrepreneurship in Pakistan at the lowest ebb among the developing countries; it is estimated that women entrepreneurs presently comprise about 3 percent of the total 3.2 million entrepreneurs in the country and an estimated 33 percent of women are in rural areas. These women are engaged in crafts such as embroidery, tailoring, carpet or durree making, shawl making, leatherwork, pottery, ceramics and food processing having incredible skills and potential.

This research would cover the rural areas of Bahawal Pur and we will identify the problems or barriers and their relevant impact on women entrepreneurial activities. Another aspect of this research is that we want to identify to what extent the variables i.e. finance, access to technology, information, managerial skills, mobility, networking and trust building, education, experience etc. are affecting the women entrepreneurial activities in rural areas.

Research Goals

- Our main objective to conduct the research is to identify the problems or barriers which are faced by women in conducting entrepreneurial act Our main objective to conduct the research is to identify the problems or barriers which are faced by women in conducting entrepreneurial activities in rural areas.

Other purposes of research are as under:

- To measure the extent of each variables impact on women entrepreneurial activities in rural areas.
- How women respond to these barriers.
- How women cope with these barriers.
- Problems faced by women entrepreneurs in rural areas of Bahawalpur are in compliance with the problems faced by women entrepreneurs in other rural areas of Pakistan.

- In which activities women of Bahawalpur in rural areas are mostly engaged.
- To find the proper solutions of these problems.
- To create awareness in women about their efforts and role in the society

LITERATURE SURVEY

Entrepreneurship

Entrepreneurship is the process of creating something new and assuming the risks and rewards. It is the process of creating something new with value by devoting the necessary time and effort, assuming the accompanying financial, psychic and social risks, and receiving the resulting rewards of monetary and personal satisfaction and independence.

Rules of Entrepreneurship

Starting a business requires discipline and discipline requires rules, some fundamental business advice—simple, straight forward and easy to implement.

1. Find a need—be ahead of your time.

   Find a niche where the Giants won't bother to go.
2. Identify your market and learn all about it.

   You have to know everything about your business at the start.
3. Prepare a business plan...yes you have to.

   No bank will take you seriously without a plan for profits.
4. Have adequate financing to start and to stay.

   Success does not happen overnight, so be sure you're financially fit.
5. Pay for the best professional advice.

   Lawyers, accountants, insurers do work on an as needed, fee basis.
6. Keep your overhead low and your standards high.

   Work from home or at a low cost, convenient location.

7. Establish a clearly defined distribution network.

   Whatever your product or service, how will you present and sell it?

8. Be creative—your new idea does count.

   Depend on marketing strategies rather than costly advertising to grow.

9. Seek and hire the most qualified people.

   From the first employee, look for someone who knows more than you.

10. Know your competition and work to win.

    Be persistent, focused and flexible...anything can happen.

11. Learn from the success and failure of others.

    Read, watch trends, and observe what is "hot" in your industry.

12. Use technology as a tool for building your business.

    From computers to telecommunications to the Web-use them all.

13. Don't be sensitive and don't take it personally.

    Be prepared for rejection, but never give up your dream.

14. Never underestimate the power of passion.

    You will need to take risks and believe when no one else does.

But you must clearly identify your goals and live by them. Use these rules as a road map to your success.

An entrepreneur is a person who has possession over a new enterprise or venture and assumes full accountability for the inherent risks and the outcome. The term is from French and was first defined by the Irish economist Richard Cantillon.

- Women entrepreneurs

The term Women Entrepreneur refers to a woman who is running her own or family own business. A female entrepreneur is sometimes known as an entrepreneuse.

Characteristics

The society of women is the foundation of good manners; of course a pre-requisite to achieve brilliant results especially for success in business. The increasing trend developed among the women to be self-employed suggests that time is not far away when women factor would also have an important role in the economic growth of the country. Possessing the natural gift of politeness, women entrepreneurs, and if provided the level ground, are expected to bring new milestones to this country. Women entrepreneurs in the developing world make a large and often unrecognized contribution to their countries' economic development. They employ other people, provide valuable services, and play a vital role in the development of emerging market economies worldwide. In the developing economies WEs is a diverse group ranging from those who manage large conglomerates to those who operate roadside restaurants.

Barriers, some real, some perceived and some self-imposed, confront women entrepreneurs. In the area of international business obstacles include limited international business experience, inadequate business education and lack of access to international networks. Societal, cultural and religious attitudes also impede women in business. Other challenges faced by all enterprises and women in particular are; financing, globalization of social and economic environments, marketing, and management. Transition economies can pose difficult hurdles such as banking, legal aspects, political contacts, customs tariffs, bureaucracy that daily invents new mechanisms for the simplest procedures, and extortion.

Characteristics reflected in research of women entrepreneurs show a woman who is highly motivated, initiates action and activity without direction has a high internal locus of control, and propensity toward achievement. Women's decision processes indicate a highly personal, subjective process. Studies reveal that there are multiple general individual characteristics of women business owners that promote their creativity and generate new ideas and ways of doing things.

Background

In most countries, regions and sectors, the majority of business owner/managers are male (from 65% to 75%). However, there is increasing evidence that more and more women are becoming interested in small business ownership and/or actually starting up in business. In addition, rates of self employment among women are increasing in several Asian countries. Although there are no official statistics relating businesses to the gender of their owner/manager, there is a good deal of evidence to suggest a significant increase in female entrepreneurship. One consequence of this is that women are a relatively new group of entrepreneurs compared with men, which means that they are more likely to run younger businesses. This in turn has some implications for the problems they face and their ability to deal with them.

Challenges Faced by Women

In Pakistan, as in many other developing countries, women are handicapped in society. Therefore they face many challenges, as they do not enjoy the same opportunities as men. The segregation of the sexes starts early and becomes a way of life. They are not only deprived of financial resources but also lack access to basic needs such as education, health, clean drinking water and proper sanitation. Limited access to the essentials of life undermines their capabilities, limits their ability to secure gainful employment, and results in income, poverty and social exclusion. Their ambitions and aspirations are suppressed.

The crude activity rate (% of labor force in total population) for women in rural areas is 10.7% and 6.3% in urban areas) and the refined activity rate (% of labor force in population of persons having 10 years of age and above) is for women in rural areas is 16% and 8.8% in urban areas. Women businesses in Pakistan are typically characterized thus:

- Most women-headed businesses operate from home, and financial matters are taken care of by male family members.
- Women entrepreneurs are seen in subordinate roles; with low levels of education and technical skills; low

exposure to business; lacking role models; lacking peer support and business associations; low incomes and poor investment capacity.

Gradually things are improving for women, which have been caused by their tremendous determination and courage. They are entering in the field of education, health, engineering, IT and active participation is seen in the sports and politics arena.

About 60% of women entrepreneurs in Pakistan have opted for traditional business such as parlors, bakeries, boutiques, but the largest number is employed in the garments and handicrafts sector. In general, urban women are better placed in terms of accessing information than those operating in the rural areas.

However, improvements need to be realized in the rural areas where women still lag behind due to the lack of awareness to engage themselves in other activities. In rural areas even where top positions are filled by women entrepreneurs most of the opportunities are diverted towards enhancing the skills of men. Women are essentially performing house-hold chores and helping their family in the fields.

This hampers their growth, as there is no time due to domestic chores taking precedence over anything else. Many women are learning skills such as embroidery, sewing, and knitting for income generation, but lack conducive environment to embark on such a journey of developing their career. This is because of the restrictions placed on them by the society which does not allow them to receive formal training and to enter the market place. They not only lack the financial resources but also lack awareness for facilities available to develop their skills.

However, economic necessity is forcing more and more women to engage in some sort of employment, without relieving them of their traditional roles. There is a potential envisaged to develop the handicrafts sector and create income generation measures for these women as they possess the talents and aptitude for entrepreneurial development.

Key Issue

A key issue is whether women entrepreneurs face specific problems in Start up the businesses that are different from those faced by male-owned businesses.

Problems Faced by Women

Some of the basic problems a highlighted by various research studies undertaken by women entrepreneurs are:

- Lack of information
- Lack of Micro Financing Schemes
- Lack of Skill Development
- Lack of Entrepreneurship/Business Skills
- Lack of Marketing Facilities
- Lack of Product Designs
- Lack of Networking and Trust Building
- Expensive Raw Material
- Low Quality Control
- Non-Conducive Working Environment

Women may have particular problems with raising finance and may have had less chance than most men to accumulate the confidence, skills and contacts necessary to start and run a successful business.

In addition, gender discrimination by finance and support providers, customers or employees may be an issue. Some previous research has suggested that it is more difficult for women to raise start-up and recurrent business finance than men and that women are more likely to encounter credibility problems when dealing with bankers (Carter and Cannon, 1992).

There are four areas of financing that can pose particular problems for women. Firstly, women may be disadvantaged in their ability to raise start-up finance. Second, guarantees required for external finance may be beyond the scope of most women's personal assets and credit track record. Third, once a business is established, finance may be more difficult for female entrepreneurs to raise than for their male counterparts, because of the greater difficulties that women face in penetrating informal financial networks.

Finally, the relationship between female entrepreneurs and bankers may suffer from discrimination. Certainly, recent evidence suggests that female entrepreneurs use substantially less capital at start-up than male owners, although intra-sectoral similarities demonstrate that gender was only one of a number of variables affecting the business financing process.

The Lack of Access to information especial information relating to Business and Technology poses a major hindrance in the progress of women owned enterprises in Pakistan. Women, in Pakistan, have limited access to technology and information, which leads to many problems.

Their access to information is mainly limited because of the restraint on their mobility and communication due to socio-cultural factors. Lack of access to information hinders women entrepreneurs in many ways.

A new start-up is never an easy job and it is made more difficult when access to information regarding laws and regulations is limited. Also women entrepreneurs, due to their limited resources and limited accessibility usually do not have information about supplies; middles men and lack know how about working out the feasibility of their start-ups.

The lack of access to information and technology also leads to certain marketing problems, such as packaging and designing. With better access to business and technical information women entrepreneurs could also avail the opportunity of marketing and selling through the World Wide Web.

'Lack of management skills or training' was felt to be a problem for women entrepreneurs because of their lower propensity to have had previous business experience. Although difficulties in accessing business advice or support appears to be a minor rather than major problem for women entrepreneurs, while difficulties with language caused problems for their clients or members.

Difficulties with access to markets and/or lack of marketing skills are rated highly as problems.

So lack of sales and marketing skills was the most commonly reported problem faced by female entrepreneurs, after finance.

Other issues include:

- Lack of availability of child care;
- Society's attitude towards women entrepreneurs;
- Unequal opportunities between men and women;
- Lack of confidence on the part of women.

Variables:

- Information
- Finance
- Discrimination By Finance Providers
- Access To Technology
- Skill Development
- Managerial Skills
- Marketing Facilities
- Product Designs
- Networking And Trust Building
- Expensive Raw Material
- Quality Control
- Working Environment
- Education
- Experience
- Mobility
- Communication Skills
- Training
- Mentoring
- Advocacy
- Socio cultural Constraints

THEORATICAL FRAMEWORK

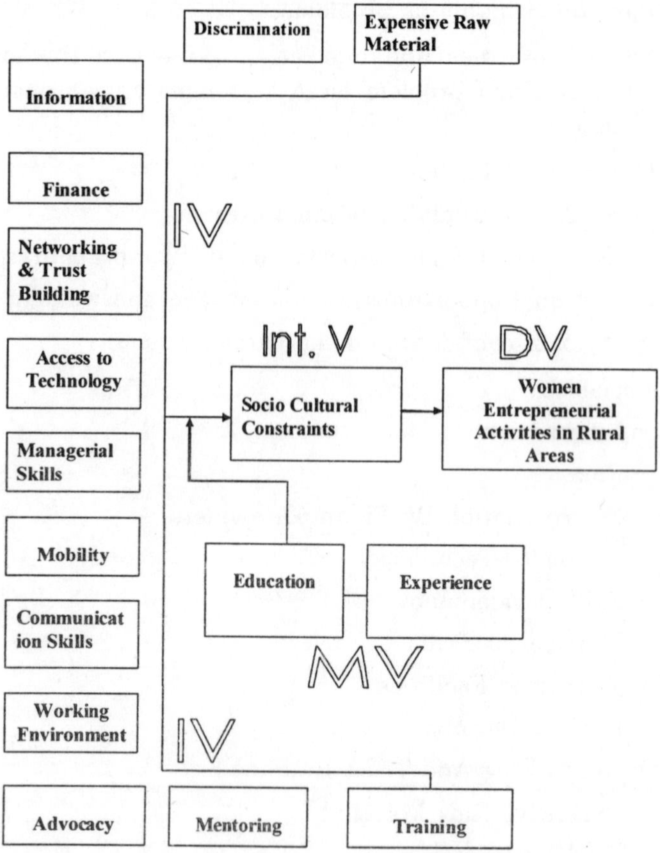

Formulated Hypothesis

Hypothesis

No.1

Ho: age has not a significant impact on experience of women entrepreneurial/self employed activities in rural areas.

HA: age has a significant impact on experience of women entrepreneurial/self employed activities in rural areas.

No.2

Ho: adequate education of women in rural areas has no significant impact on their business related skills.

HA: adequate education of women in rural areas has a significant impact on their business related skills.

No.3

H0: there is no relationship between mobility and type of transportation used by women entrepreneurs in rural areas.

HA: there is a relationship between mobility and type of transportation used by women entrepreneurs in rural areas.

No.4

H0: there is no relationship between the availability of finance and the use of low quality raw material.

HA: there is a relationship between the availability of finance and the use of low quality raw material.

No. 5

H0: the entrepreneurs/self employed rural women whose families are not supportive are easily managing their work and personal life.

HA: entrepreneurs/self employed rural women whose families are supportive are easily managing their work and personal life.

No.6

H0: mostly the rural women are not engaging in entrepreneurial activities to fulfill their household expenditures.

HA: mostly the rural women are engaging in entrepreneurial activities to fulfill their household expenditures

No.7

H0: there is no relationship between training and business related skills.

HA: there is a relationship between training and business related skills.

No. 8

H0: Those women entrepreneurs who are more educated are not having good interpersonal communication skills.

HA: Those women entrepreneurs who are more educated are having good interpersonal communication skills.

RESEARCH DESIGN

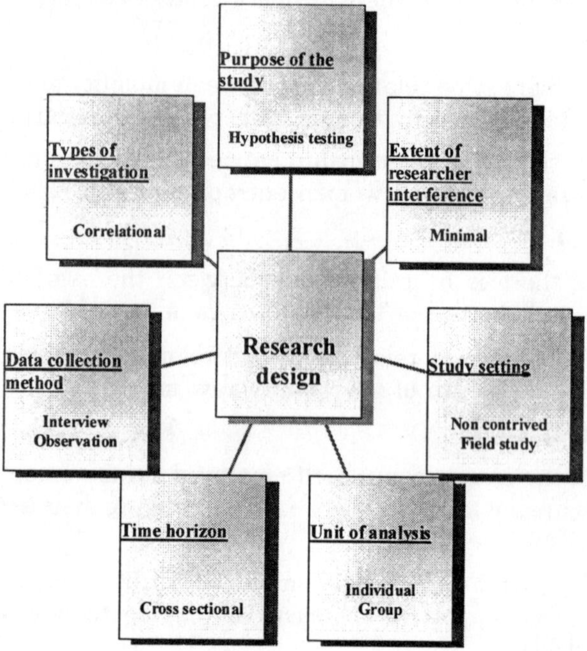

PURPOSE OF THE STUDY

It is hypothesis testing as much is known about the problem at hand and we are concerned to study that whether the variance in the determined independent variables is affecting the success of women entrepreneurial activities in the rural areas.

Type of Investigation

In this research we have established a correlation between different variables affecting the women entrepreneurial activities in the rural areas.

Extent of Researcher Interference

Here researcher interference will be minimal because correlation study is conducted in the natural environment (normal work flow) of the organization because we are only concerned with the influence of one variable with the other variable.

Type of Study

It is a non contrived setting because the research will done in the natural environment of the organization where work proceeds normally and mostly correlational studies are conducted in non contrived setting and correlational studies done in organizations are called field studies.

Unit of Analysis

In this unit of analysis will be individual as well as group unit of analysis because we will talk to individual woman as well as women working in groups.

Time Horizon

As we have gathered data just once in order to answer a research question, so it is called one-shot or cross sectional analysis.

Data Collection Techniques

Data collection technique that we have used is survey.

- Tool:
  - o questionnaire
  - o Observation
- Secondary Data:

For every researcher, secondary data is very important, without it one thrash out one's project. It also gives the background, overview and guidelines for the research. In our research, it has got much importance. Major sources of our data are articles on the internet, web and different books related to our topic.

- Primary Data:

We collected our primary data from the interview conducted through survey and we have also come to know very practical information which reveals much more things.

- Basti Dera Izzat
- Basti Tiba Badr Sher
- Samma Satta
- Mele Wali Gali Hamatiyan Chowk

Data analysis techniques: The statistical tool that we will use for our study is the Statistical Package for Social Sciences (SPSS) technique. Data collected from above mentioned organizations will be analyzed by following methods.

- Frequency distribution
- Chi-square method.
- Correlation.

SAMPLE DESIGN

- Target Population:

All the entrepreneurs/self employed women of rural areas of Bahawalpur.

- Sampled Population:

AREA

* Basti Dera Izzat
* Basti Tiba Badr Sher
* Samma Satta
* Mele Wali Gali Hamatiyan Chowk

Sampled Business Categories

- Women doing embroidery work
- Women having their own Beauty parlor.
- Women who are running schools in rural areas

Sampling Frame

Infinite population: As our population is infinite so it is difficult to identify all the population and to draw a sampling frame.

Sampling Method

Probability sampling

Sampling technique:

Simple random sampling

FORMULA: population size/sample size

Sample size: n = (z * s) 2/E2

Through this formula we have determined the sample size of 60.

Field Work

To gain our purpose we have surveyed the rural areas of Bahawalpur and filled our questionnaire from our sampled population.

Data Analysis Techniques

* Frequency distribution
* Chi-square method
* Cross Tabulation

DATA ANALYSIS

Frequency Distribution

FREQUENCY AND PERCENTAGES

a) Age Category:

		Frequency	Percent	Valid Percent	Cumulative Percent
Valid	Below 18	2	3.3	3.3	3.3
	18-25	18	30.0	30.0	33.3
	26-35	13	21.7	21.7	55.0
	36-45	7	11.7	11.7	66.7
	46-55	15	25.0	25.0	91.7
	55 and above	5	8.3	8.3	100.0
	Total	60	100.0	100.0	

Age Category

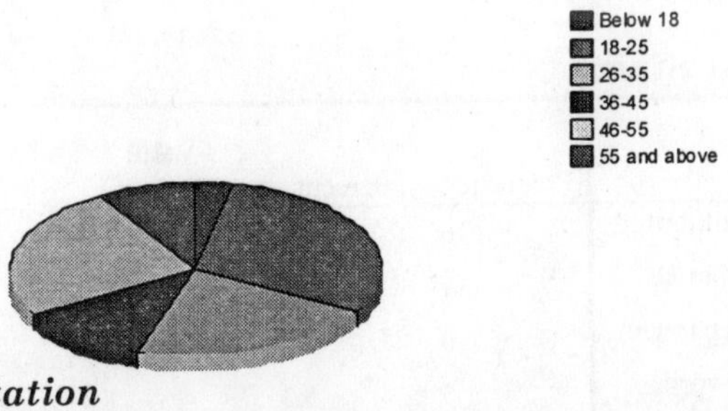

Interpretation

This Question is designed to get the personal information about the age of self employed or women entrepreneurs. Most of the women lie in the age group of 18-25 years i.e. 30%.

b) Your age when you start this business:

		Frequency	Percent	Valid Percent	Cumulative Percent
Valid	below 18	11	18.3	18.3	18.3
	18-25	22	36.7	36.7	55.0
	26-35	7	11.7	11.7	66.7
	36-45	16	26.7	26.7	93.3
	46-55	4	6.7	6.7	100.0
	Total	60	100.0	100.0	

Your age when you start this business

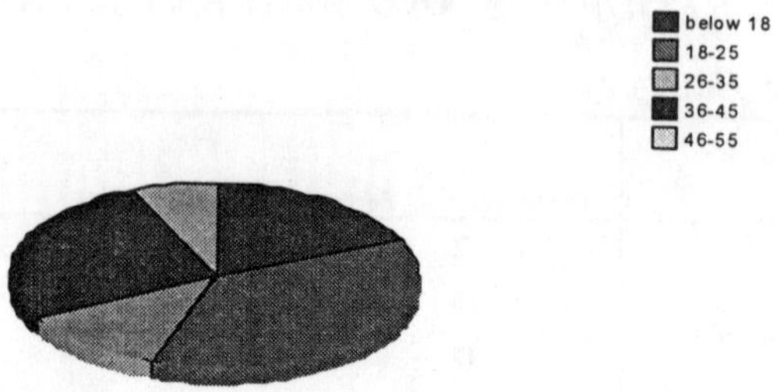

Interpretation

This question is designed to know that at what age mostly women involve in the entrepreneurial activities and from this we got to know that most of the women start their own business at the age of 18-25 years.

2. Marital Status

		Frequency	Percent	Valid Percent	Cumulative Percent
Valid	unmarried	16	26.7	26.7	26.7
	married	31	51.7	51.7	78.3
	separated	6	10.0	10.0	88.3
	divorce	5	8.3	8.3	96.7
	widow	2	3.3	3.3	100.0
	Total	60	100.0	100.0	

Marital Status

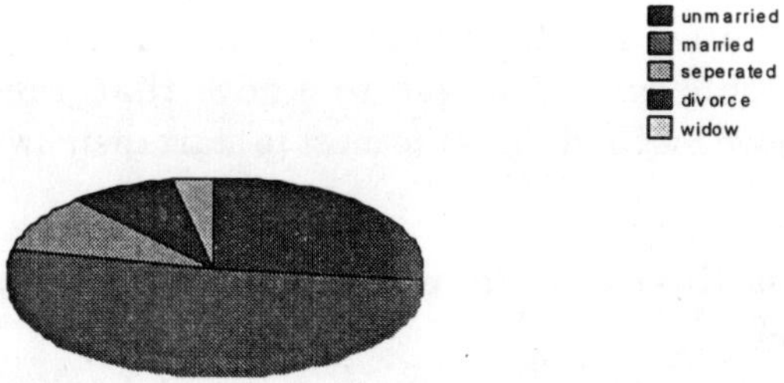

Interpretation

This question is designed to know that how many women entrepreneurs are married or unmarried, separated or divorced and widowed. Thus, we got to know that majority of the women entrepreneurs are married i.e. 52%.

3. Which person inspires you to do your own work?

		Frequency	Percent	Valid Percent	Cumulative Percent
Valid	family member	30	50.0	50.0	50.0
	friend	6	10.0	10.0	60.0
	neighbours	3	5.0	5.0	65.0
	any other	21	35.0	35.0	100.0
	Total	60	100.0	100.0	

Which person inspires you to do your own work?

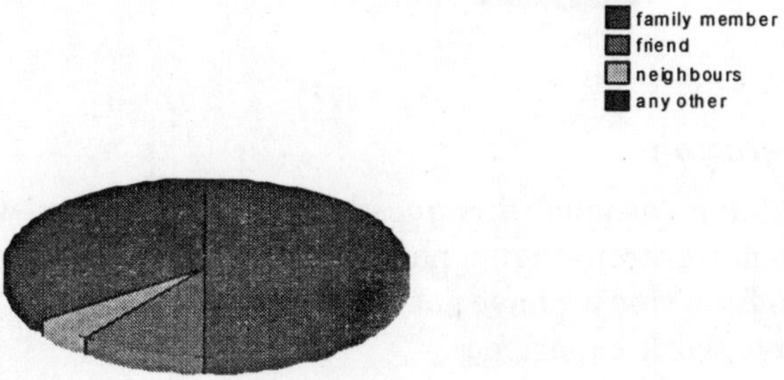

Interpretation

We have designed this question to know that what is the major inspiration for the women to start their own business and from this we have got to know that their family members have inspired them the most to start their own business i.e. 50%.

4. Do you have any experience of working before anywhere?

		Frequency	Percent	Valid Percent	Cumulative Percent
Valid	not at all	25	41.7	41.7	41.7
	some what	11	18.3	18.3	60.0
	moderately	20	33.3	33.3	93.3
	very much	4	6.7	6.7	100.0
	Total	60	100.0	100.0	

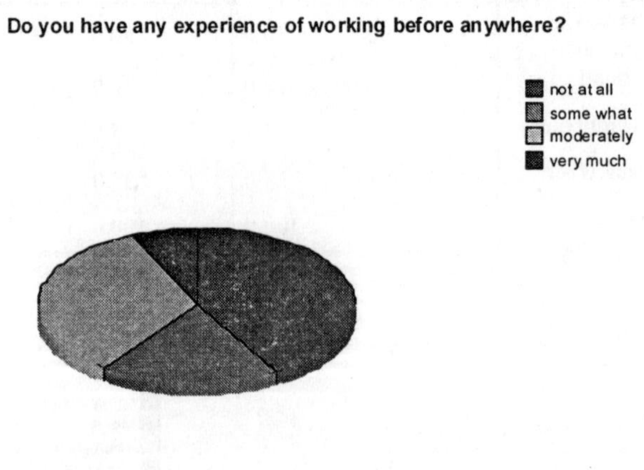

Interpretation

We have designed this question mainly to know whether these women entrepreneurs have any previous work experience and thus from this we have got to know that most of the women don't have work experience.

5. How you can well define the purpose of your job?

		Frequency	Percent	Valid Percent	Cumulative Percent
Valid	satisfy financial needs	33	55.0	55.0	55.0
	Desire to enjoy the job for its own rewards	10	16.7	16.7	71.7
	To prove yourself	3	5.0	5.0	76.7
	To become independent	14	23.3	23.3	100.0
	Total	60	100.0	100.0	

How you can well define the purpose of your job?

Interpretation

This question is designed to know about what is the main purpose for the women entrepreneurs to start this business and we found that mostly women start for satisfaction of their financial needs.

6. Do the people in the society criticize upon you for doing this work?

		Frequency	Percent	Valid Percent	Cumulative Percent
Valid	not at all	1	1.7	1.7	1.7
	some what	19	31.7	31.7	33.3
	moderately	23	38.3	38.3	71.7
	very much	17	28.3	28.3	100.0
	Total	60	100.0	100.0	

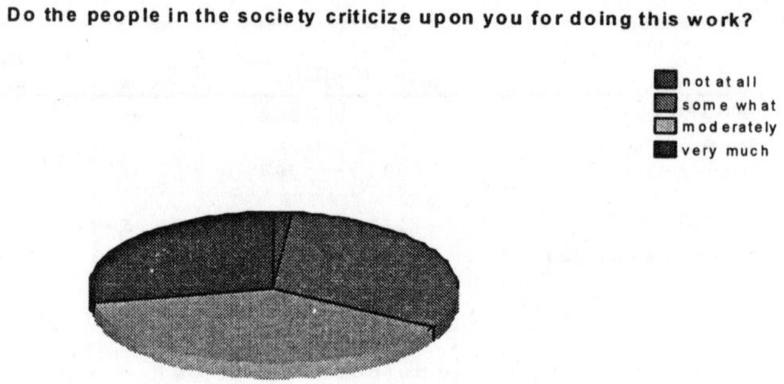

Interpretation

We have designed this question mainly to know whether the women who are doing their own business face any criticism from the society and thus we have got to know these socio cultural constraints are the major problem women are facing nowadays.

7. Are you taking any of the following steps to enhance your skills?

		Frequency	Percent	Valid Percent	Cumulative Percent
Valid	Getting education	18	30.0	30.0	30.0
	Getting computer training	5	8.3	8.3	38.3
	Getting training in the required field	7	11.7	11.7	50.0
	Seeking advice from some experienced person	30	50.0	50.0	100.0
	Total	60	100.0	100.0	

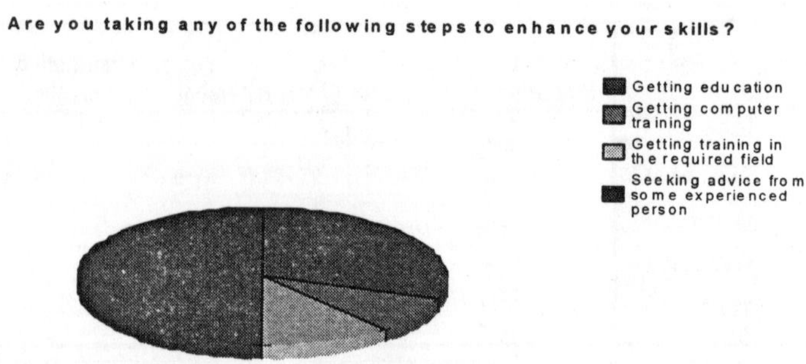

Interpretation

We have got to know that mostly entrepreneurs are getting training in the required to further enhance their skills, while only some of them are getting education but only a small percentage is focusing to get the computer training.

8. Is your family supporting you in your activities?

		Frequency	Percent	Valid Percent	Cumulative Percent
Valid	not at all	5	8.3	8.3	8.3
	some what	18	30.0	30.0	38.3
	moderately	30	50.0	50.0	88.3
	very much	7	11.7	11.7	100.0
	Total	60	100.0	100.0	

Is your family supporting you in your activities?

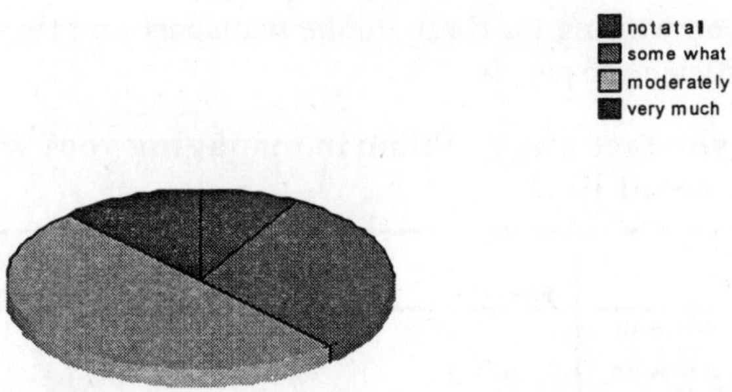

Interpretation

Finding of this question is that most of the families of these women entrepreneurs are supporting to some extent.

9. What are your modes of transportation?

		Frequency	Percent	Valid Percent	Cumulative Percent
Valid	public	32	53.3	53.3	53.3
	private	28	46.7	46.7	100.0
	Total	60	100.0	100.0	

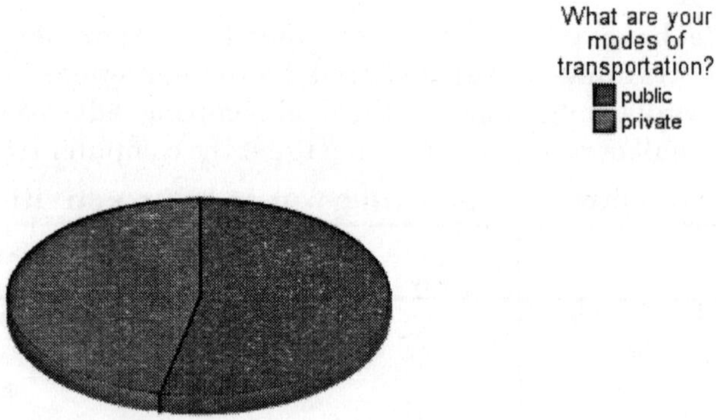

Interpretation

In this question we come to know that mostly women use public transport and this is major difficulty for these women that they don't have their own transport and lot of time is wasted on waiting for these public transport and they have to face criticism of people.

10. Do you face any problem in managing your work and the personal life?

		Frequency	Percent	Valid Percent	Cumulative Percent
Valid	noa at all	8	13.3	13.3	13.3
	a little bit	22	36.7	36.7	50.0
	moderate	24	40.0	40.0	90.0
	a lot of	6	10.0	10.0	100.0
	Total	60	100.0	100.0	

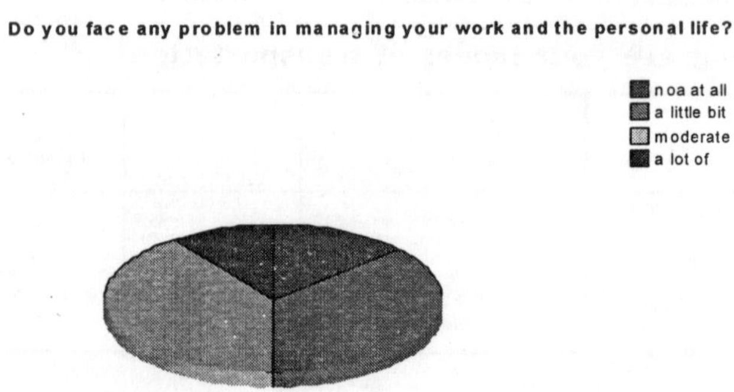

Interpretation

This question is designed to know whether these women face any difficulty in managing their work and personal life. And we come to know that these women face moderate difficulties in managing all this i.e. 41%.

11. You compromise on the quality of raw material in case you lack finance?

		Frequency	Percent	Valid Percent	Cumulative Percent
Valid	strongly disagree	16	26.7	26.7	26.7
	disagree	13	21.7	21.7	48.3
	neither agree nor disagree	1	1.7	1.7	50.0
	agree	25	41.7	41.7	91.7
	strongly agree	5	8.3	8.3	100.0
	Total	60	100.0	100.0	

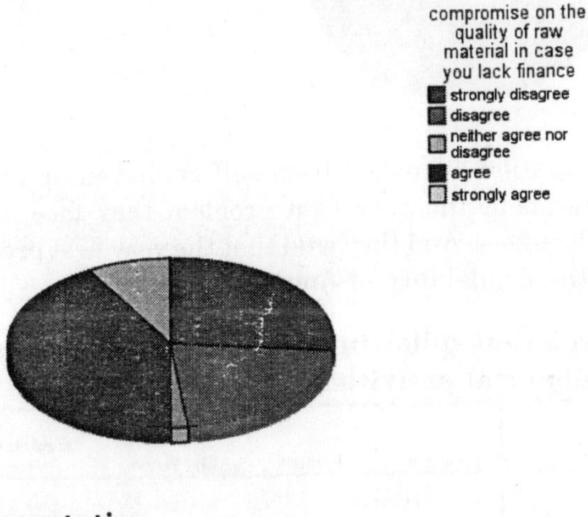

Interpretation

This question is designed to know whether these women compromise on the quality of raw material in flourishing their entrepreneurial activities. And we come to know that most of the women agreed on low quality material in case they lack finance.

12. What was the very first problem that you face while starting your business?

		Frequency	Percent	Valid Percent	Cumulative Percent
Valid	finance	30	50.0	50.0	50.0
	social support	11	18.3	18.3	68.3
	experience	12	20.0	20.0	88.3
	mentor	5	8.3	8.3	96.7
	any other	2	3.3	3.3	100.0
	Total	60	100.0	100.0	

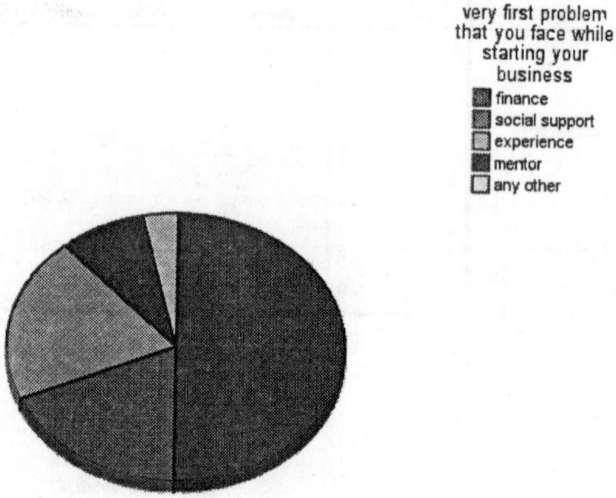

Interpretatio

In this question we asked from self employed or women entrepreneurs about the very first problem they face at the start of their business. And they said that the very first problem they face is the availability of finance i.e. 50%.

13. How do you rank following in the order of importance for entrepreneurial activities?

		Frequency	Percent	Valid Percent	Cumulative Percent
Valid	finance	31	51.7	51.7	51.7
	Communication	3	5.0	5.0	56.7
	training	12	20.0	20.0	76.7
	mobility	5	8.3	8.3	85.0
	social support	9	15.0	15.0	100.0
	Total	60	100.0	100.0	

rank following in the order of importance for entrepreneurial activities

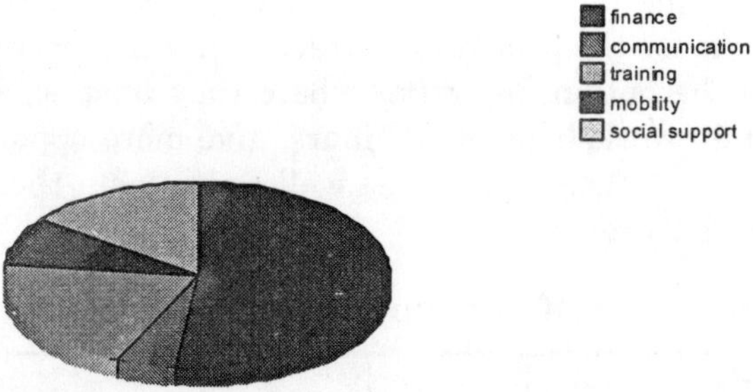

Interpretation

In this question we asked about the importance of these things in their entrepreneurial or self employed activities i.e. which thing is most important and which is least. Here we come to know that finance is most important and then training, social support, mobility and communication respectively.

14. What do you think govt. should do to promote women entrepreneurial activities?

		Frequency	Percent	Valid Percent	Cumulative Percent
Valid	open vocational inst.	13	21.7	21.7	21.7
	relaxation in terms of microfinance	19	31.7	31.7	53.3
	any other	28	46.7	46.7	100.0
	Total	60	100.0	100.0	

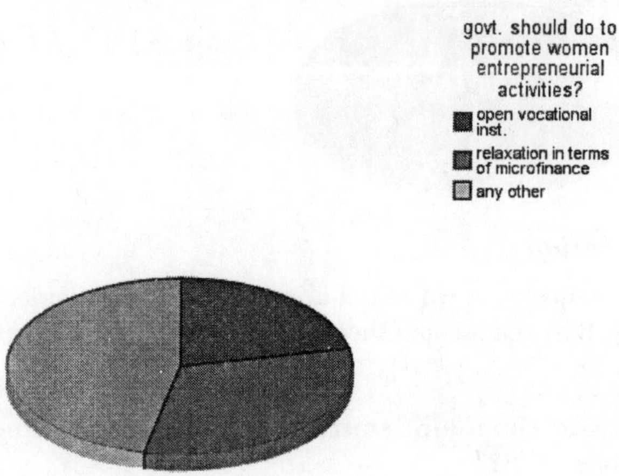

Interpretation

This question is designed to know that what the government should do for the promotion of these activities. Here they have chosen the option any other where they have said that they should do workshops or seminars, give more opportunities or privileges to these women as well as promote their attempts of this venture.

15. What type of enterprise are you engaged in?

		Frequency	Percent	Valid Percent	Cumulative Percent
Valid	trade	2	3.3	3.3	3.3
	services	36	60.0	60.0	63.3
	manufacturing	21	35.0	35.0	98.3
	any other	1	1.7	1.7	100.0
	Total	60	100.0	100.0	

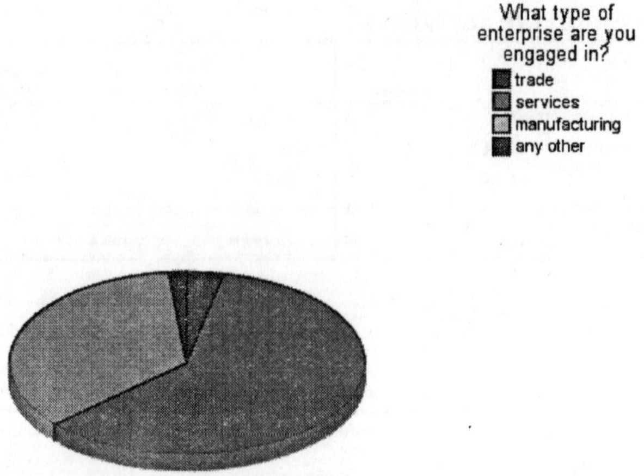

Interpretation

In this question we asked about the type of business they are engaged in and most of these women are engaged in services i.e. 60%.

16. What was the major source of money you started this enterprise with?

		Frequency	Percent	Valid Percent	Cumulative Percent
Valid	Borrowed/got loan from financial institution	8	13.3	13.3	13.3
	Savings over a period of time	4	6.7	6.7	20.0
	Savings from other enterprise/business	16	26.7	26.7	46.7
	Borrowed from a friend/relative	5	8.3	8.3	55.0
	Help from friend/relative	11	18.3	18.3	73.3
	any other	16	26.7	26.7	100.0
	Total	60	100.0	100.0	

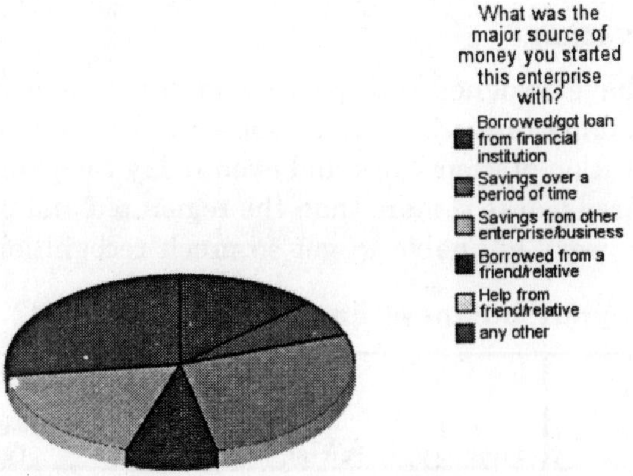

Interpretation

In this question we are mainly concerned to know about that from where mostly women entrepreneurs arrange for their start up finance and thus from this we have to know that the main sources they employ are the savings over a period of time and help from friend/relative.

17. Is the enterprise registered?

		Frequency	Percent	Valid Percent	Cumulative Percent
Valid	yes	25	41.7	41.7	41.7
	no	35	58.3	58.3	100.0
	Total	60	100.0	100.0	

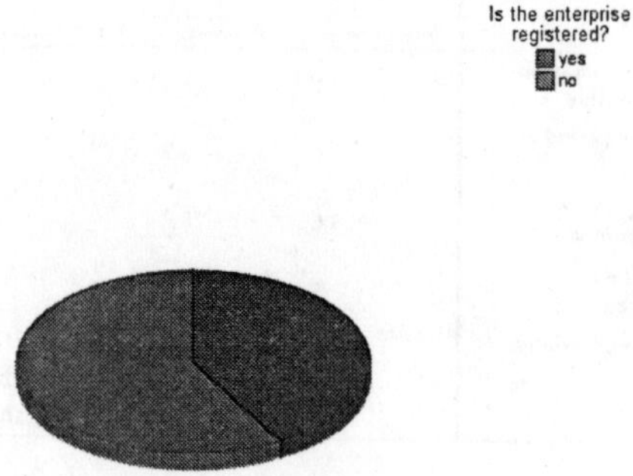

Interpretation

We have designed this question mainly to address one of the most important issues that women are facing because of no registration of their work and even today the percentage of unregistered works is more than the registered and because of this their work is unable to get so much recognition.

18. Does your business have a bank account?

		Frequency	Percent	Valid Percent	Cumulative Percent
Valid	yes	20	33.3	33.3	33.3
	no	40	66.7	66.7	100.0
	Total	60	100.0	100.0	

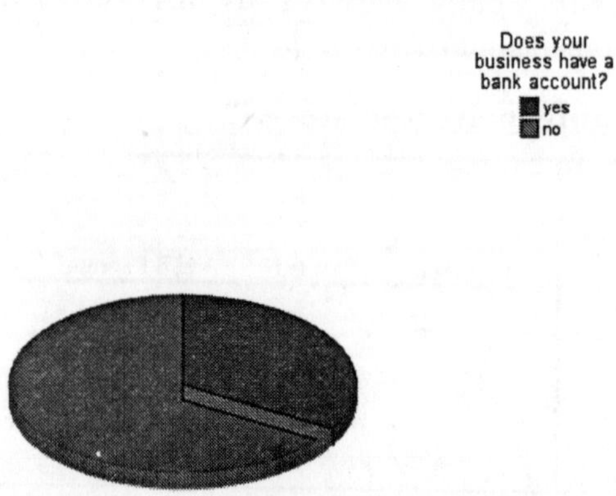

Interpretation

We have designed this question mainly to know weather the women who are doing their own business have any bank account of their own business and thus we have found that majority of these businesses do not have any bank account.

19. Do you contribute money from your business towards household expenditure?

		Frequency	Percent	Valid Percent	Cumulative Percent
Valid	somewhat	3	5.0	5.0	5.0
	moderate	22	36.7	36.7	41.7
	very much	35	58.3	58.3	100.0
	Total	60	100.0	100.0	

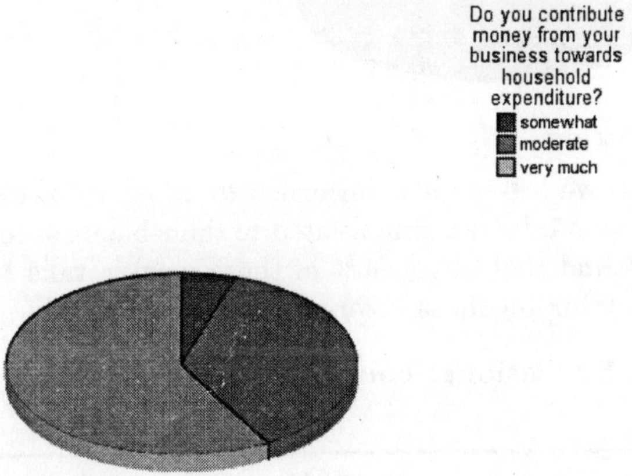

Interpretation

In this question we are mainly concerned to know that whether these self employed women spend their money in their household expenditures or not and thus we have found that most of these spend their money in household expenditures i.e. 58%.

20. Have you take any type of training before or after the start of this business?

		Frequency	Percent	Valid Percent	Cumulative Percent
Valid	training before start of business	42	70.0	70.0	70.0
	training after start of business	12	20.0	20.0	90.0
	no training	6	10.0	10.0	100.0
	Total	60	100.0	100.0	

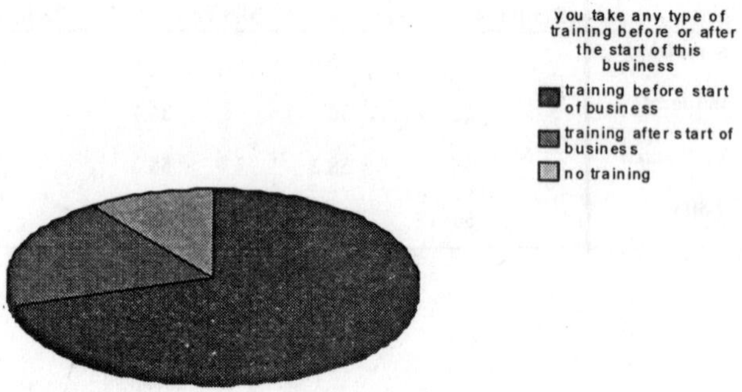

Interpretation

In this we are mainly concerned to know about the %age of women who take training related to their business and thus we have found that about 80% of these women take training related to their business before starting it.

21. What Educational background do you have?

		Frequency	Percent	Valid Percent	Cumulative Percent
Valid	primary	31	51.7	51.7	51.7
	secondary	14	23.3	23.3	75.0
	diploma	8	13.3	13.3	88.3
	bachelors	7	11.7	11.7	100.0
	Total	60	100.0	100.0	

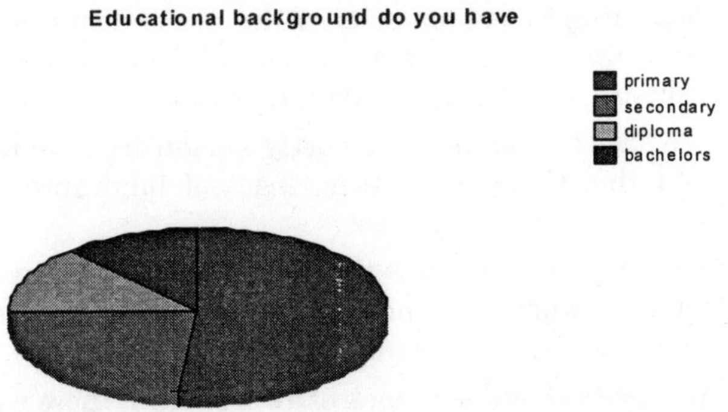

Interpretation

We have basically designed this questionnaire to know about the education of these women entrepreneurs/self employed in rural areas as education have significant impact on the success of any business.

FINDINGS AND CONCLUSIONS

We are highly thankful to the God Almighty who enabled us to accomplish such an important task with due care. We tried our best to complete this task to the best of our abilities. We are thankful to our Research Instructor who showed confidence in us and assign us a research on the "Problems faced by entrepreneur/self employed rural women ". In order to achieve our objectives we conducted a research in the Bahawalpur city and used "Survey" method to collect the data. The finding of this research is obtained after applying the statistical test like Z-Test to the result of the collected data and chi-square test. We are confident that our results are statistical significant. The details of the findings are as follows:

Findings

- After conducting the survey, we find that most of the respondents believe that they are facing a lot of problems regarding their entrepreneurial/self employed activities.
- After this research we have come to know that most of these women are involved in handmade embroidery work.

- According to the majority of the respondents the most important problems are finance and then training, social support, mobility and communication respectively.
- We have also found that mostly women are not educated and this thing is creating a lot of hindrance in the success of their business.
- We also come to know that most of the businesses run by these women are not registered and they also do not have any bank account.
- We found that due to lack of awareness of these women, they are unable to avail the opportunities being provided by the govt.
- We also find that these self employed women are facing a lot of socio cultural constraints.

SUGGESTIONS

Recommendations

1. Government should arrange exhibitions on quarterly, semiannually or annual basis to promote the work of women entrepreneurs in the rural areas as this will provide them a platform where they can bring their work on scene.
2. Government should train the employees who work in the micro financial institutions as to how to deal with the customers and tell them the benefits of the scheme.
3. Government should do extensive ad campaigns to promote the work of these women not only within the country but also at the international level.
4. Awareness should be created among these women as to how they can gain success in their business by getting proper education and getting required skills.
5. There should be relaxations in the terms of micro finance so that they can easily start their own business.
6. Society should not only support but also encourage such women who are source of pride for the nation.
7. Special buses should be run for females so that they do not face any kind of problem while traveling.

The purpose of this part is just to find out the specific weaknesses that may affect the findings of the study. During this research we face a number of problems due to which the internal as well as external validity of our Research findings are affected.

These are as follows

1. Most of the women are not educated so they are not able to understand some questions.
2. Some of the women of beauty parlors were not cooperative.
3. The target market we are focusing is from rural areas so we have to face some difficulties in tracing their homes.
4. Some family members of illiterate women don't allow them to meet with us.
5. Due to lack of education of these women we are also facing communication problem i.e. some women are not able to understand Urdu language.
6. Due to social pressure many women know what problems they are facing but they are not allowed to tell that.
7. We felt difficulty in operating SPSS software.
8. Lab was not frequently available which a main problem for us.

2

INTRODUCTION: THE RHETORIC OF TELEVISION, CRITICISM, AND THEORY

Academic television criticism has come a long way in the past two decades if you date its birth, as I do, with the publication of Horace Newcomb's *TV: The Most Popular Art* in 1974. Its increasing theoretical sophistication is evident, and is made most clear, perhaps, by the metacriticism that has developed to interrogate the assumptions of critical practice. Television criticism has become an increasingly self-conscious and self-reflexive activity that requires definitions, explanations of perspective, and defense of positions before a critic can even begin to engage with a text (a term that also cannot be taken at face value).

This chapter is my attempt to situate this project within the myriad perspectives that constitute television study. In that process, I engage with debates that I will not resolve: my primary concern here is to explain why I approach the texts that I analyze in the way that I do, as well as to explain what I see as the merits of that approach. I organize this discussion around a series of key terms—*criticism, text, audience* and *theory*—that I will use repeatedly in this book and which I view as central to the practice of television criticism at this point in time. I begin with an explanation of my view of what criticism, both broadly and with regard to television, is about; specifically, I offer my perspective on its social, theoretical, and political functions. In the following sections on text, audience, and theory,

I discuss some current debates over these concepts as I sketch my own position relative to those issues. Related to my discussion in the Preface, what emerges from this discussion is my view of television as a rhetorical medium and my belief that television criticism is a rhetorical activity.

TELEVISION AND CRITICISM

Criticism is a social activity because it is written for an audience. As Said writes, "there is always an Other; and this other willy nilly turns interpretation into a social activity, albeit with unforeseen consequences, audiences, constituencies and so on" (1983, p. 137). For example, I view myself as addressing several audiences simultaneously in this book: television critics, feminist critics, fans of the programming I study, students. Each of these communities will no doubt have different uses for and reactions to various parts of this book. I expect and welcome that. One can never, as Said indicates, be cognizant of all of the ways one's work might be received.

Even so, this discussion of my views of criticism is designed to sketch some parameters for how I would prefer my criticism to be understood. It is, in a sense, my contract with imagined and potential readers, intended to tell them what to expect from me and my work. The expectations that readers have of the criticism they read is a central, but rarely articulated, concern to television critics. For example, at one level, the debates within television studies over the relative values of studying texts (or content) versus studying audiences (or reception) and the validity of the conclusions derived from studying either often seem to me to be linked to the issue of expectations.

The growth of attention to reception in studying television has given television scholars new questions to consider as they study television's role in making meaning for audiences. Although I do not do reception study myself, I find it interesting and useful, particularly because it has expanded the possibilities for television study and because it produces a *different* kind of knowledge from that produced by textual analysis of television. However, to say that reception study is valuable because it produces a different kind of knowledge is not the same as saying that it produces better or more valid knowledge, an unfortunate conclusion that can be inferred from reading some of the work on reception theory. Textual analysis, it is sometimes implied, cannot tell us what we *really* need to know: what actually goes on in the minds of viewers (as opposed to what the textual critic *speculates* goes on in their minds). As Charlotte Brunsdon puts it, "the pursuit of the audience" can be characterized "as a search for authenticity, for an anchoring moment in a sea of signification" (1990, p. 68).

The most powerful claim of audience studies has been that "real" viewers often resist the dominant messages of television and interpret programming in ways that suit their own interests, a claim that has cast suspicion on the claims that textual critics make for the oppressive or hegemonic function of texts (or for any predictable function of texts). Intentional or not, such judgments cast the differences between approaches within the framework of a zero-sum game in which only one party can be right, making the other automatically wrong. [1]

What troubles me most about this kind of thinking is that it assumes that it is proper to expect television study to reveal the "truth" of how texts work to produce various effects upon their receivers. Disagreements over how "open" texts are, how "active" audiences are, and how possible it is for viewers to "resist" the hegemonic message of a text are issues we must settle on our way to discovering how to access that truth. There are problems with this assumption at various levels, many of which I discuss later in this chapter. What I question at this point, however, is why critics feel the need to ground the value of criticism on "truth" in the first place.

Linked to my background in rhetorical studies, I view criticism as a species of *argument* rather than as a quest for truth, and I view skeptically any assurance of greater truth value derived from method. Moreover, linked to my awareness of feminist critiques of science and knowledge production, I view criticism as a kind of argument that, whatever its value to the reader, articulates the interests of the arguer first. This does not mean that all criticism is ultimately solipsistic or self-centered; however, it does mean that it is always the product of socially situated persons who make arguments that are enabled but also limited by their experiences and perspectives.

However, there is no such thing as the totally isolated, individualistic, idiosyncratic reading of a text. Because all critics are socially situated members of communities, their interpretations of texts are the product of social life. Membership in a community is always partially linguistic (anyone who tries to read works on postmodernism without first learning the jargon has lived this realization) and to the extent that you speak or write so that others can understand you, you are acting socially. Criticism is a particular kind of writing, one that I view as fundamentally rhetorical. By rhetorical, I mean that it assumes an audience, that it attempts to persuade, and that its "truths" are social, reflecting what we agree to believe, based on the evidence and our interpretation of it, at a particular point in time. Because of the wealth of things that a critic might write about and the wealth of things that might be said about them, any access to knowledge provided by the critical act is necessarily partial and contingent.

Moreover, because the critic must make choices, his or her work is rhetorical. Criticism "takes up a text and re-circulates it, that is, 'says' or "does" that text differently, and asks the listener or reader to reunderstand and re-evaluate the text, to see and judge it in new ways suggested by the critic" (Nothstine, Blair, and Copeland, 1994, p. 3). Given this perspective, criticism is not about discovering or reporting the meaning in texts. Rather, it becomes a performative activity that is, in some sense, dedicated to creating meaning. This distinction is particularly important for feminist criticism, given that

> a fully politicized feminist criticism has seldom been content to ascertain old meanings and . . . take the measure of already constituted subjectivities; it has aimed, rather, at bringing into being *new* meanings and *new* subjectivities. . . . In this respect it may be said to have a performative dimension—i.e., to be doing something beyond restating already existent ideas and views, wherever these might happen to reside. (Modleski, 1991, p. 49)

This perspective assumes that texts are *polysemous*—that is, they can mean in different ways at different times. However, my use of polysemy here differs from its current meaning in cultural studies, in which it is used to refer to the possibility that audiences can decode texts in varying ways (Fiske, 1986). Rather, I use the term as it applies to critical activity as opposed to audience activity. In his *Anatomy of Criticism* (1957), literary critic Northrop Frye explained the necessity for critics to accept that there are manifold critical approaches to a text by arguing that the alternative was to choose a school of critical thought "and then try to prove that all the others are less legitimate. The former is the way of scholarship and leads to the advancement of learning; the latter is the way of pedantry" (1957, p. 72).

Certainly, undiscriminating pluralism has its limits, and not all criticism is equally valuable. A work of criticism can be poorly supported, poorly argued, or simply unconvincing. However, the motive for diversity in critical approaches should not be a search for the holy grail of truth but an exploration, with unavoidable twists and turns, toward the many, sometimes contradictory, possibilities of understanding. This perspective does not see criticism as an attempt to provide the most accurate retelling of how a text is received or as an attempt to account for the widest variety of interpretations; rather, it views criticism as an argumentative activity in which the goal is to persuade the audience that their knowledge of a text will be enriched if they choose to see a text as the critic does, while never assuming that that particular "way of seeing" is the only or the best way to see that text (or that all audiences do, in fact, see it that way). Thus, even when a critic writes as though s/he is "discovering" or "revealing" a meaning in a text (and I often find myself using such language), what s/he has "discovered" is the *possibility* of meaning rather than its certainty. This perspective is not a maneuver to avoid standing behind the arguments we make as critics or a descent into endless relativism; instead, it is a responsible position that acknowledges the contingency of the claims that we as humans make about any human activity.

As a critic, then, I argue for the possibility and the usefulness of understanding a text in a particular fashion. The power of the arguments I make depends upon how well they interpret the text, the strength of their evidence and theoretical underpinnings (which I address more specifically later), and, ultimately, their heuristic value. The heuristic value of criticism, in my view, is both theoretical and political. In theoretical terms, it means that the argument should, in addition to revealing something interesting and useful about the text itself, reveal something interesting and useful about the *kind* of symbolic activity that the text represents, whether it is music, literature, or television programming. That is, given the recombinance of symbolic activity (which is especially true for television), arguments that help to explain Mary Tyler Moore might also help to explain rhetorical processes in other sitcoms, or in other programming that deals with feminism. I view the kind of grounded theory that arises from and can be used for the study of concrete texts as the most useful kind.

Politically, the heuristic value of criticism, specifically the feminist criticism that I practice, is its capacity to engage our thinking about the political implications of discursive practice. To the extent that criticism teaches us something about television and how it works, it tells us something about the world and how it works. The poststructuralist insight that everything is discourse, and that we therefore cannot separate discursive practice from "real life," is quite useful here. Whether or not television "reflects" reality outside the tube is beside the point: we watch television and it is therefore part of life. Rather than existing in some autonomous realm outside of political life, media is part of it. What criticism can do is to accentuate the importance of that realization and offer specific arguments for its meaning.

In this book, for example, I argue that one of the ways that programs such as Mary Tyler Moore and Murphy Brown function politically is that they offer visions of what feminism "means." They are fictional, to be sure, and to some extent we are aware of their artificiality. However, to deny that they influence our thinking about women, women's roles, and the impact of social change is, it seems to me, to be dangerously naive. It is possible for television to be acknowledged as fiction and yet be experienced as realistic in its characterization or treatment of issues (Deming, 1990, p. 41). As I discuss in Chapter 5, the controversy engendered by then-Vice-PresidentDan Quayle's attack on Murphy Brown's decision to have a baby out of wedlock is a vivid illustration of the symbolic possibilities that can reside in a fictional character. As a feminist critic, the political task that I see for my work is to give presence to such possibilities, to articulate them in a way that can provide some insight into the world in which we all live and which shapes us in myriad ways. Feminist literary critic Annette Kolodny calls this the "altered reading attentiveness" (1985, p. 158) that a feminist critic can bring to a text:

> All the feminist is asserting, then, is her own equivalent right to liberate new (and perhaps different) significance from these same texts: and, at the same time, her right to choose which features of a text she takes as relevant because she is, after all, asking new and different questions of it. In the process she claims neither definitiveness nor structural completeness for her different readings and reading systems, but only their . . . applicability in conscientiously decoding woman as sign. (1985, p. 160)

Finally, at the most basic level, this work is intended to continue the conversation about feminism—what it has meant and can mean—because the more talk there is about it, the more likely it is to live on as a viable, dynamic, and fertile set of ideas and practices. As Modleski writes, "It remains importantly the case that feminist critical writing is committed writing, a writing committed to the future of women" (1991, p. 47).

TELEVISION AS RHETORICAL TEXT

At this point, if not earlier, the term *text*, as I use it, deserves some attention. Already, I have used "text" in the broad sense that many critics use it—to refer to the artifact, or the "thing" to be analyzed. However, because television programming, unlike a poem or a speech (at least as we traditionally understand them), is capable of being divided or "textualized" in so many ways, it makes sense to be specific. All of the television series that I analyze in this book—*The Mary Tyler Moore Show, One Day at a Time, Murphy Brown, Designing Women,* and *Dr. Quinn, Medicine Woman*-constitute what I consider my primary texts.

I make arguments that explain what I see as patterns occurring within each series and which give each series a distinctive rhetorical function in defining feminism. Generally, then, I define "text" at the level of the series, rather than the episode. Because it is my contention, which I treat in more detail in Chapter 1, that texts are interpreted in relation to other texts, my analysis also treats as "texts" a variety of other kinds of discourse. For example, I use what John Fiske (1987a, p. 85) has called "secondary texts"—journalistic criticism, reviews, advertisements, promos, interviews with stars and producers—to argue for the way that treatment of programming in mass media can both enable and constrain interpretation (see also Allen, 1992, p. 132). On a broader level, I will also discuss the interaction of these television texts with other culturally produced "texts" about feminism found in press coverage of the movement and its effects.

In short, my approach to the specific television texts I analyze is to place them within a context that I believe sheds light on how they might be understood. Given my contention that television draws from and contributes to the larger cultural conversation about feminism, a major part of my approach to these texts is based on contextual concerns. Much as rhetorical critics view speeches as responses to specific situations and as affected by audience expectations regarding genre and occasion, I view television discourse about feminism as situated and constrained by its relationship to other forms of cultural discourse about feminism, to previous televisual representations, to secondary texts, to industry practice and commercial demands, and to the expectations attached to established televisual genres. I view all of these factors as constraints that work to channel the messages that television presents (and that viewers receive) about feminism in particular directions.

I believe that it is a mistake to treat texts as ahistorical entities that can be abstracted out of their historical/cultural milieux and given timeless meanings. It is particularly a mistake for my purposes in this book. Because my purpose is to discuss the interaction of television and feminism at different points in time since 1970, I treat these texts as products of their time, directed at audiences in their time and contributing to the cultural conversation about feminism in their time. Although I certainly cannot avoid bringing my historical hindsight, as a critic writing in 1995, to a text like Mary Tyler Moore, which went off prime-time in 1977, my case study of the program attempts, as much as possible, to create an understanding of its feminist discourse as a product of the 1970s. As Celeste Condit has argued, such an approach leads away from simplistic praise or blame of programming and toward a calibrated understanding of the particular role [programming] played in introducing certain limited pieces of information to different ranges of audiences at different times. Critical analysis should therefore, at least at times, be rhetorical; it should be tied to the particularity of occasion; specific audiences, with specific codes or knowledges, addressed by specific programs or episodes. (1989, p. 115)

Underlying Condit's perspective, and my own, is a conception of television texts as rhetorical entities that can be interpreted as performing particular functions at particular times. These are *persuasive* functions that work to make some ideas, positions, and alternatives more attractive, accessible, and powerful to audiences than others. Particularly when television programming is studied with an eye toward its role in social change, it is useful to view it as rhetorical discourse that works to accomplish some end(s).

Kenneth Burke (1973, p.1) notes that we can think of "any work of critical or imaginative cast as the adopting of various strategies for the encompassing of situations." Thus, all artistic work can be approached as "the *functioning* of a structure" that is designed to accomplish something (Burke, 1973, p. 74). If we assume that a work is designed to "do something" for its audience, then "we can make the most relevant observations about its design by considering the poem [or creative work] as the embodiment of this act" (Burke, 1973, p. 89). Within such a rhetorical perspective, works of art are "strategies for selecting enemies and allies, for socializing losses, for warding off evil eye [sic], for purification, propitiation, and desanctification, consolation and vengeance, admonition and exhortation, implicit commands or instructions of one sort or another" (Burke, 1973, p. 304).

A rhetorical perspective, then, assumes that symbolic acts function to accomplish an end, and that they do so through the employment of strategies that influence audiences. However, this is not a one-way process in which texts impose meaning upon audiences. As Burke indicates, rhetorical discourse is strategic because of its ability to interact with, draw from, and respond to the context in which it occurs and in which its audiences are situated (1973, pp. 1-3).

Within this general perspective, there are still a variety of ways to analyze or interrogate a text. The angle that I take on the texts I examine in this study is directed at their role in negotiating the meaning of social change wrought by feminism. The meanings offered by television are rarely direct, often contradictory, and never final. Certainly, it is the central dynamic of series television to rework the same problematic over and over. Thus, the persuasive function of television is not so much to provide solutions to cultural conflicts but, rather, to negotiate the parameters for the debate. This is why, for example, one of the central concerns of this project is not so much an evaluation of the success or the failure of television's feminist visions but, rather, an understanding of how entertainment programming has functioned to influence cultural perceptions of feminism.

My view is consonant with that of critics who claim that those who produce television programming function as "cultural interpreters" (Newcomb and Hirsch, 1987, p. 458), and that television acts to "*articulate* the main lines of the cultural consensus about the nature of reality" (Fiske and Hartley, 1987, p. 602). The interpretation and articulation that occur in television entertainment involve choices at many levels. Thus, the rhetorical critic of television is interested in such questions as why an artist chose to deal with certain topics (and not others); why the artistic elements chosen were structured as they were (and not some other way); why certain characteristics of the medium . . . are emphasized (and others are not emphasized); what purpose, among all those possible, seems to be governing hese choices; and to what audience the work addresses itself with what potential effect. (Medhurst and Benson, 1984, p. x)

Such questions do not require a determination of intent. Any work can have effects beyond those for which it was designed. A rhetorical critic is concerned with the purpose, strategies, and functions that can be discerned from an understanding of the television text and its potential interaction with audiences.

TELEVISION AND AUDIENCES

Although, as I said above, I do not wish to engage in a contest over the truth-seeking potential of criticism, there are several good reasons to revisit the issues involved in debates over audience activity and textual power. The most important reason is that such debates force critics to consider, to articulate, and, ultimately, to make more precise our always present but often implicit *arguments* about how texts and audiences interact. Indeed, it is my contention that the best way to deal with this issue is to treat it as a collection of arguments that use different types (and strengths) of evidence and reasoning to support different positions. And, because arguments are always susceptible to fallacies, my organization of this section is based on a discussion of the various manifestations of what I see as a recurring fallacy in this species of argument: the false choice.

To provide a quick overview, here are some of the troublesome dichotomies that I see at work in what, for lack of a better term, I call the powerful text/active audience debates: hegemony versus polysemy (of the text), passive versus active viewing (by audiences), critics versus audiences (as the makers of meanings), and dominant culture versus subculture (as the major determinant of social subjectivity). [3] I also discuss another dichotomy that I believe should be strengthened rather than dissolved: that between culture and politics.

To begin at the top, the concept of hegemony, based on the writings of Italian Marxist Antonio Gramsci, refers to "the myriad ways in which the institutions of civil society operate to shape, directly or indirectly, the cognitive and affective structures through which men [and women] perceive and evaluate problematic social reality" (Femia, 1981, p. 24). The ideological function of this process is made clearer by Becker, who describes it as "the cultural, intellectual, and moral direction exercised by the dominant classes over other classes. In part, hegemony is the imposition of one or more classes' ideology on other classes" (1984, p. 69). Media's role in the maintenance and reproduction of hegemony has been the topic of much cultural studies research, including that produced by British scholars such as Stuart Hall (1982) and other members of the Birmingham group, as well as that produced in the United States by scholars such as Todd Gitlin (1980, 1982). For example, Gitlin has argued that, in television entertainment, major social conflicts are transported *into* the cultural system, where the hegemonic system frames them, form and content both, into compatibility with dominant systems of meaning. Alternative material is routinely *incorporated*: brought into the body of cultural production. Occasionally oppositional material may succeed in being indigestible; that material is excluded from the media discourse and returned to the cultural margins from which it came; while *elements* of it are incorporated into the dominant forms. (1982, p. 527)

Scholars critical of this perspective argue that it presents texts as closed, as offering only the possibility of absorption of the ideology offered, and thus positioning the audience as passive receivers. In contrast, it is the textual critic who actively makes meaning from the text by articulating its structures of domination (and assuming these strategies are usually invisible to the audience). Given this framework, the dominant ideology as disseminated through media, education, religion, and so on (what Althusser [1971] would call the "ideological state apparatuses"), has an enormous amount of power to mold the subjectivity of audiences so that they are persuaded to think and behave in ways that are not necessarily in their interests as defined by their social experience (or, as it is often expressed, as defined by their subcultural identities as, for example, workers, women, members of oppressed racial or ethnic groups, gays, or lesbians, to name a few hardly distinct categories).

As John Fiske has put it, such an account makes hegemony appear "almost irresistible" (1987a, p. 40). Or, as another writer recently explained her decision to disregard Marxist-influenced analyses of popular culture: "To embrace the Frankfurt school position on the hegemony of state capitalism, for instance, is necessarily to see the television viewer as a figure essentially passive, held captive by the communications apparatus of the capitalist interests, at best a prisoner of false consciousness" (Tichi, 1991, p. 9).

On the other side of this series of dichotomies are those who argue for the polysemy of the text—that is, its capacity to invite different meanings from different viewers. From this perspective, viewers are actively making meanings as they watch television, and these meanings do not necessarily reflect those "preferred" by the text. Audiences, rather than critics, are thus makers of meaning. Finally, the subjectivities of active audiences (that is, the way they see themselves and the relations through which they operate in the world) are much more determined by their specific (again, often termed "subcultural") social experience than by the ideological operations of the dominant culture. The implication of this perspective, again in the words of John Fiske, is that textual studies of television now have to stop treating it as a closed text, that is, as one where the dominant ideology exerts considerable, if not total, influence over its ideological structure and therefore over its reader. Analysis has to pay less attention to the textual strategies of preference or closure and more to the gaps and spaces that open television up to meanings not preferred by the textual structure but that result from the social experience of the reader. (1987a, p. 64)

This quotation, in fact, efficiently expresses the distance that at least some see between the dichotomies I have suggested.

Having established, albeit briefly, the substance of these positions, I would like to mediate between them, blurring their boundaries while carving out my own position on the relationship between texts and audiences. Although I explore a variety of issues, it is for the purpose of coming back to where I began, with a rationale for an essentially *rhetorical* approach to television study. Generally, my position throughout this discussion is that critics' understanding and employment of the concepts of hegemony and polysemy (and the terms and concepts that radiate from these central ideas) would benefit from more nuanced explanation of our motives and reasoning for employing them in particular situations at particular times for particular purposes.

For example, those critics who work with the concept of hegemony are accused of adhering to the position that television viewers are passive cultural dupes who are caught up in the static, totalistic, and inescapable web of ideology emanating from commercial television. Tichi's illustrative comment is that "the resistant figure . . . has no legitimate place in [the] Frankfurt school [of] thought" (1991, p. 9). If we look past Tichi's unfortunate tendency to lump all Marxist cultural analysis under the aegis of the Frankfurt school, the most crucial oversight in this view is that it discounts the fact that hegemony theory *assumes* oppositional thinking; that is why the hegemonic process must be dynamic, flexible, and "leaky" (Gitlin, 1982, p. 526). As Gitlin rather emphatically points out in what has become a central work on hegemony and television: "One point should be clear: the hegemonic system is not cut-and-dried, not definitive. It has continually to be reproduced, continually superimposed, continually to be negotiated and managed, in order to override the alternative, and, occasionally, the oppositional forms" (1982, p. 527). Moreover, even the Frankfurt school perhaps has been judged more harshly than necessary, as Thomas Streeter argues: " Horkheimer and Adorno did not arrive at their pessimistic views because they failed to take into account social difference, plurality, and resistance. Their despair should not be taken for an orthodox, mechanistic understanding of social domination. On the contrary, their fear was that plurality and difference has [sic] been thoroughly accommodated to the modern order" (1989, p. 16, quoted in Rapping, 1992, p. xxx).

The question becomes, then, not whether or not resistance or oppositional thinking exists—hegemony theorists have always assumed that-but how powerful or effective they are relative to the hegemonic process and, moreover, what role the media play in facilitating them. This question goes to the heart of arguments about the polysemy of texts. While some researchers have claimed that the television text is an "'empty vessel' that can be all things to all people" (Barkin and Gurevitch, 1987, p. 18), the position advanced by John Fiske is more representative of claims for the "open" text. Fiske describes the television text "as a structured polysemy, as a potential of unequal meanings, some of which are preferred over, or proffered more strongly than, others, and which can only be activated by socially situated viewers in a process of negotiation between the text and their social situation" (1987a, p. 65).

Although Fiske admits that the "dominant" ideology at work in a television text can usually be discerned (1987a, pp. 51 - 52), there is no guarantee that audiences will receive the text in the intended fashion; instead, "the dominant ideology . . . can be resisted, evaded, or negotiated with, in varying degrees by differently socially situated readers" (1987a, p. 41). Generally, it is impossible to disagree with this position. The fact that feminist critics can and do perform feminist readings of patriarchal texts means that there is no reasonable way to claim that a text is closed. However, the power of the dominant ideology, or preferred meaning, of the text is visible in Fiske's formulation, given that every possibility he offers is a *reaction to the preferred meaning*. In short, resistance or opposition assumes that the viewer "gets" the preferred meaning of the text (to the extent that there is ever only one preferred meaning) prior to resisting it (Evans, 1990, p. 150).

For example, when I watch a program, such as the NBC drama Law and Order, that is often deeply at odds with my politics (although I consider the program superbly done and eminently watchable), I often find myself verbally resi[illegible] (I talk back to the set and deconstruct certain characterizations).

I think of myself, at these times, not as making a different meaning from that intended by the program, but, rather, of evaluating the preferred meaning negatively. What I experience, in short, is more akin to what Celeste Condit has called *polyvalence*—the process through which audiences *receive* essentially similar meanings from television texts but may *evaluate* those meanings differently depending upon their value systems. She notes that "different respondents may similarly understand the messages that a text seeks to convey. They may, however, see the text as rhetorical—as urging positions upon them—and make their own selections among and evaluations of those persuasive messages" (Condit, 1989, pp. 107-108).

Condit's analysis of the limits of polysemy is instructive in a number of ways. She urges critics to consider the possibilities of polysemy and resistance in a social context, stressing the differential resources and efforts necessary to construct truly oppositional or resistant meanings. Part of the power of the ideology offered by television is that "it *relays* and *reproduces*, and *processes* and *packages*, and *focuses* ideology" that is at work elsewhere in society as well (Gitlin, 1982, p. 510). A "preferred" reading does not happen in isolation and does not rely solely on the power of the text; it partakes of the competencies and discursive codes that are reinforced throughout the different areas of social life (not to mention those, like genre, narrative pattern, and intertextuality, that are learned from television itself). In short, even if we agree that viewers negotiate the meanings of television, "their definitions do not match the discursive power of a centralized storytelling institution" (Carragee, 1990, p. 88).

Condit points out that "oppositional and negotiated readings require more work of viewers than do dominant readings" (1989, p. 109), and, moreover, that the possibility of these nonpreferred decodings is dependent upon the codes available to the viewer. So, for example, while television viewers (assuming they are moderate consumers of media) can easily acquire the codes necessary for preferred readings, the acquisition of codes for negotiated or oppositional readings is more difficult and less common (Budd, Entman, and Steinman, 1990, p. 177). The likelihood of counterreadings may have been exaggerated, Condit argues, because audience researchers have tended to study groups that have access to oppositional codes (1989, pp. 110 - 112). [4] In the end, "it is not the case that all human beings are equally skilled in responding to persuasive messages with countermessages. The masses may not be cultural dupes, but they are not necessarily skilled rhetors" (1989, p. 111). [5]

Of course, audience researchers have claimed that oftentimes it is the social experience of viewers, as members of subcultures or interpretive communities, that provides them with the resources to resist television's hegemonic messages. For example, as Fiske explains this position, "the actual television viewer is a primarily social subject. This social subjectivity is more influential in the construction of meanings than the textually produced subjectivity which exists only at the moment of reading" (1987a, p. 62). Two assumptions in this position trouble me. First, it posits the social subjectivity of the viewer (linked to membership in a subculture or interpretive community) as autonomous from, rather than overlapping with, and substantially affected by, media subjectivity (see Budd, Entman, and Steinman, 1990, p. 174). Second, it overlooks the strong possibility that television texts, because of their repetitive nature and their participation in a wide-ranging system of cultural hegemony, produce a subjectivity that is hardly momentary and isolated from other sources of reinforcement.

Membership in a subculture may indeed provide a strong sense of subjectivity that can be used to combat the insinuations of the dominant culture. However, it seems a mistake to assume that all viewers are members of coherent subcultures or, for that matter, that all subcultures are critical. As Budd, Entman, and Steinman note, "Subcultures can be reactionary or accept most elements of the status quo" (1900, p. 175). Let us say, however, that we decide to grant that subcultures do routinely provide viewers with the resources to interpret television against the grain. Then, staying with the theme of placing claims for audience resistance within a wider social context, the next

. question that seems natural to ask is, to what end does this interpretation occur? What does it mean, if anything?

If we celebrate the active audience to prove that viewers are not dominated by cultural hegemony, then what have we proven when their resistance does not go beyond negotiating with the messages of television? Or, as Elayne Rapping puts it, while we seem to have established that people can watch television in different ways, "we have not been asking how they watch it in similar ways, or, more to the point, how they receive and use it in ways similar enough to lead to potential changes in power relations" (1992, p. xxvi). This is a serious gap if we are to take audience research as having political implications (which is clearly the hope of scholars like John Fiske [see 1986, p. 394], for instance). Budd, Entman, and Steinman succinctly summarize this problem: "Researchers have yet to demonstrate that the active thinking and resistance to hegemonic principles that may accompany the viewing of TV entertainment spills over into direct thinking about and behavior in politics" (1990, p. 178). In the end, there is still a power structure that benefits a few people; the people who make television programming continue to get richer, and, of particular concern to me, women continue to live in patriarchy.

A summary of the arguments articulated thus far is useful at this point. First, hegemony, rather than assuming an all powerful, closed text, presumes the possibility of resistance and opposition. Moreover, this position is not inconsistent with Fiske's claim that the hegemony of the text is never total. . . . The meanings within the text are structured by the differential distribution of textual power in the same way that social groups are related according to the differential distribution of social power. All meanings are not equal, nor equally easily activated, but all exist in relations of subordination or opposition to the dominant meanings proposed by the text. (1987a, p. 93 ; see also Fiske, 1992, pp. 291-292)

However, as I have argued, it is possible that what critics have called polysemy is, in many cases, polyvalence—that is, the possibility of viewers creating different *evaluations* of a text, rather than different meanings.

Another argument I have offered here is that it is a misnomer to call viewers passive if we believe they accept the ideology of a text and active if we believe they resist it. Decoding is always work and always requires competence from audiences, denying the label of "dupes." Our concern should, rather, be with the resources available for decoding and with the *kind* of decoding we wish to analyze (Evans, 1990, p. 150). This position also carries caution about our assumptions regarding the distance between what textual critics do and what audience researchers do. In the end, we are all making arguments based on the evidence we choose to examine.

For critics stressing hegemony, that evidence consists of the text and the codes of the dominant culture. For audience researchers, that evidence is the behavior and discourse of audiences, to which we give meaning based, oftentimes, on subcultural codes or the competencies of interpretive communities. This realization, I suggest, dissolves the dichotomy between critics and audiences as meaning makers in different types of studies. In both textual studies and audience studies, the act of interpretation and argument by the researcher (whether ethnographer or critic) is paramount.

Finally, given the evidence of the world around us, we should be careful about the extent to which we claim that the influence of subcultural codes necessarily overrides dominant cultural codes or is critical of or resistant to them. Also imbricated in this issue is the need to recognize that television has codes of its own, that, as George Gerbner has said, "People are now born into the symbolic environment of television and live with its repetitive lessons throughout life. . . . Living with television means growing up in a symbolic environment" (quoted in Tichi, 1991, p. 3). This environment is not separate from the social experience of a subculture or a dominant culture but interacts with, affects, and is affected by, both.

Ultimately, what I have suggested is that positions that have at times been taken to be dichotomous can, rather, be characterized as sharing some of the same strengths and weaknesses. As I said earlier, I am troubled by the drawing of differences between textual criticism and audience research, or between the hegemony or polysemy of the text, that cast the two activities or perspectives as opposing players in a zero-sum game: that is, if one kind of activity is "right," the other must be "wrong." This kind of thinking is implicit, for example, in a quotation from John Fiske I used above, in which he asserts that "textual studies of television now *have to* stop treating it as a closed text. . . . Analysis *has to* pay less attention to the textual strategies of preference or closure and more to the gaps and spaces that open television up" (1987a, p. 64 ; my emphasis). Obviously, Fiske is not suggesting that critics have to become audience researchers, although he uses the conclusions of audience research to support his claims about the polysemy of the text. However, he is suggesting that there is no question that analyzing the polysemic potential or the "gaps and spaces" in a text is more valuable, more useful, and, I suspect, more "accurate" in terms of how texts are used than is analysis of the hegemonic functions of texts.

At this point, it seems to me, we verge into a dangerous area that is hardly supportive of critical pluralism. At the point that we assert that one kind of work is more worthy than another, we must ask on what basis that evaluation is made. As the arguments reviewed above indicate, the basis for claiming greater access to truth through interpretive audience research is rather shaky. Those arguments also suggest that texts have both hegemonic and polysemic dimensions and that the articulation of either is largely a function of the choices and the emphasis of the researcher.

This state of affairs should not leave us at a relativistic impasse, however. Instead, I suggest that it underscores the importance of examining and articulating the motives, purposes, and possible consequences of whatever kind of television analysis we attempt to do. That is, we should choose our approach to the objects we study because of what we want to find out, because of the problem(s) that we want to solve, rather than because we are convinced that one approach leads to truth and the other to conjecture. At the same time, we must always realize that we cannot solve *all* of the problems or explore *all* of the possibilities that the text (whether it is a television program or audience discourse *about* a television program) presents.

TELEVISION AND THEORY

The division of topic implied by a new heading is rather artificial at this point, particularly because "theory" has been an implicit or explicit presence in everything I have discussed thus far. However, I wish to make some broad statements about the uses of theory as well as to continue explicating my approach to the texts in this study. Because, as a rhetorical critic, my aim is always to make an argument about how a text can be understood, I value theory most for its explanatory potential and for the vocabulary or set of assumptions it provides to make sense of symbolic processes, to solve the "problem" that a text, or group of texts, presents. Critics always situate their arguments within implicit or explicit theoretical constructs, although to differing degrees. The more foregrounded the theory, the more likely it is that the artifact illustrates the theory. Conversely, the more foregrounded the artifact, the more likely it is that the theory helps understand the artifact. Recognizing that a bit of both of these scenarios is true in every piece of good criticism, I tend toward the latter.

However, it is also clear by this point that I am working with some broad assumptions about how television texts function as part of cultural discourse. I find it necessary, then, to articulate my theoretical assumptions at two levels. First, I reiterate my broad assumptions about how television texts function as a part of cultural hegemonic processes, explaining my motives, as a critic and a feminist, for choosing this framework. Second, I explain my essentially inductive approach to the individual texts I analyze in the case studies to follow. This move is not as contradictory as it seems. Although I am working with hegemony theory as a broad rubric, I suggest that each of these texts illustrates unique rhetorical strategies and deserves considered critical attention on its own terms. Each series reproduces hegemonic assumptions about women and feminism, yet each does so in different ways and to different degrees.

TELEVISION AND CULTURAL HEGEMONY

As is no doubt evident by this point, I tend to favor a view of the text as powerful in its potential to persuade viewers to perform preferred readings. I believe in hegemony because the evidence for its power is, in my experience, quite good. The problems that I am trying to solve in my study of these texts is a product, then, of my social experience as a feminist and a teacher and of my purposes as a critic. As a bridge to further explication of my motives, it is useful to review Todd Gitlin's explanation of why Antonio Gramsci was led to develop hegemony theory. According to Gitlin, Gramsci was stimulated by the desire to understand why the working class in Italy, given its social experience, was not revolutionary and, instead, yielded to fascism (1982, pp. 507-508). Hegemony, the "bourgeois domination of the thought, the common sense, the life-ways and everyday assumptions of the working class," provided an explanation for Gramsci of the failure of the working-class movement (Gitlin, 1982, p. 508).

At a general level, hegemony makes sense to me, as a feminist, in a similar fashion. For example, it allows me to understand and to analyze why women themselves have historically been the most powerful enemies vconclude that culture or pleasure *is* politics. Culture is mistaken for politics only by default—only in a society stripped of opportunities for serious politics. . . . Scholastic radicalism, in other words, serves the theorist as a shield against practical resignation" (1990, p. 192). Elayne Rapping has a similar concern about romanticizing individual resistance to the extent that we end up "redefining the word political to fit these inherently noninstrumental views of cultural use" (1992, p. xxiv). This does not mean that audience research that stresses resistance by viewers is not meaningful and useful; it simply means that we should be judicious about our claims for its implications. The same, of course, is true for our claims about the power of the text. As an academic feminist critic, my belief that culture is political is an underlying premise of my work. Yet, as a woman who lives in "white supremacist capitalist patriarchy" (hooks, 1994), I also believe that collapsing culture and politics is short-sighted and naive. I do not rely on hegemony theory in this project because I believe that viewers are victims of an inescapable ideology to which I am immune and therefore capable of explicating. Instead, my motivation is rhetorical and pragmatic: I believe that the concept of hegemony is useful in interpreting the specific phenomenon that I wish to examine: the construction of feminism, as a set of beliefs, practices, and effects, in selected U.S. popular prime-time television programs since 1970. I am interested in elucidating a set of dominant discourse practices that I argue were shared by prime-time television and other forms of cultural discourse. I will be relying on the premise that viewers are likely to interpret television according to the dominant codes available to them as members of American society and as consumers of American media. This perspective assumes that viewers outside the white, middle-class, heterosexual "mainstream" to whom television aiways presumes it is speaking still understand the "rules" for preferred readings, even as they might work to deconstruct them.

Thus, I focus my analysis of the potential function of these texts on what is shared by viewers rather than what is not. This is consistent with my rhetorical perspective; rhetorical critics traditionally are concerned with how people are persuaded to adhere to positions as members of a public with common beliefs, attitudes, and values. This perspective is useful for understanding television because television's political functions are not confined to its address to the pleasures of individuals. In addition, television "makes present" particular codings in the public space. Once such codings gain legitimacy they can be employed in forming public law, policy, and behavior. Even if they are not universally accepted, their presence gives them presumption (the right to participate in formulations, and even the need for others to take account of them in their policy formulations). . . . Hence, television, or any mass medium, can do oppressive work solely by addressing the dominant audience that also constitutes the public. (Condit, 1989, p. 112; see also Rapping, 1992, p. xxxi)

This perspective does not mean that television discourse is always and only reflective of dominant interests. The gaps, spaces, and contradictions that interest resistance theorists are also present, and their presence is always a qualification of claims for the hegemonic functions of a text. As John Fiske (1986) has rightly argued, such polysemic potential is what makes television watchable by so many people and what allows its popularity. However, what I am maintaining here is that it is as legitimate and useful to emphasize the function of television as dominant, public discourse as it is to study the gaps and spaces it contains that may facilitate differential private decodings.

The very premise of this project belies a vision of hegemony as totalistic and static. To claim, as I do, that feminist ideology has been manifested in television entertainment in a variety of ways over the past twenty-five years is to presume the flexibility and adaptability of hegemonic practice and to acknowledge its inability to contain completely the possibilities of social change. If nothing else, the (tele)visions of feminism that I analyze here demonstrate the television industry's willingness to engage with (some of) the questions that feminism has raised in American society. It is not my intent, either, to discuss television's treatment of feminism only to argue for the many ways in which feminist ideology as been coopted and depoliticized to serve dominant interests. I address these processes at length, but I also address the ways in which, despite efforts to contain it, feminism has established a presence on American television that has not just changed but often progressed over time.

Because I view the (tele)visions of feminism that I analyze as contributions to the evolution of cultural debate about feminism, I am interested in, to use Fredric Jameson's terms, both the "ideological" and the "utopian" dimensions of their role in the "transformational work" of mass culture (1979, pp. 144, 141). Jameson posits that mass culture texts possess intersecting ideological and utopian (or transcendent) dimensions; the ideological dimension encompasses the ways in which a text facilitates "legitimation of the existing order" (1979, p. 144) and functions hegemonically. Jameson also maintains, however, that texts have a simultaneous utopian dimension that "remains implicitly, and no matter how faintly, negative or critical of the social order from which, as a product and a commodity, it springs" (1979, p. 144). For Jameson, then, "social and political anxieties or fantasies" must "have some effective presence in the mass cultural text in order subsequently to be 'managed' or repressed" (1979, p. 141). Once that "presence" is established, it cannot be totally erased; it has become part of cultural discourse.

Ultimately, one of the biggest challenges to commercial television entertainment, which I will return to throughout this book, is the need to respond to social change and the desire of audiences for representations of "the new woman" (as she is defined at different moments in time) while working within perceived economic and institutional constraints. The situation I described in the Preface regarding the place of women within television's economic context obviously invites analysis that emphasizes the hegemonic processes of television; that is, that focuses on the set of practices in which oppositional or alternative ideology is packaged or framed to limit, undermine, or contradict its power. However, given the contradictions that exist both within and across television discourse, through both programming and advertising, its hegemonic function can never be complete.

THE RHETORICAL UNIQUENESS OF THE TELEVISION TEXT

Up to this point, I have been detailing the broad assumptions under which I am working because of my overall purpose in this book. Beyond those assumptions and the general worldview developed through my training as a rhetorical critic, I do not consider myself to be working at all times within a given theoretical tradition, such as psychoanalytic criticism or even cultural studies (which represent quite a large umbrella in the first place).

Thus, although I bring with me some broad assumptions about how television does its cultural work, I also assume that the strategies through which that work is accomplished *differ* across programming. That is, I can assume that television operates hegemonically at a broad level and yet still assume that different examples of television discourse will manifest hegemonic functions in distinct ways. This is particularly true for this project because I argue that television representations of feminism change over time, just as the conversation about feminism in other areas of cultural life changes over time.

At the level of analyzing individual texts, then, my approach is inductive rather than deductive. I begin with the programming that I wish to understand and to explain, and I gain a thorough familiarity with it. For example, I have been a long-time viewer of all the programming discussed in this book. In the case of programs such as The Mary Tyler Moore Show, Murphy Brown, Designing Women, and One Day at a Time, not only was I a faithful viewer during their lives on prime-time, but I have had continued exposure during their "afterlives" in syndication. Indeed, the popularity of all of these sitcoms in syndication is one of the factors that attracted me to them as potential case studies. In the case of more recent and short-lived programming, such as Dr. Quinn, Medicine Woman, I have followed the series since its debut.

My experience with the text itself governs the approach I will take to it, reflecting the belief that "working out from the particular (rather than applying ready-formed analytical systems) gets critics closer to the subject *before* deciding which analytical systems are appropriate and with what limitations" (Deming, 1990, p. 48). Thus, while I have an overarching purpose in this book to explore the ways in which programming constructs feminism over time, the critical tools that enable my discussion of each unique text differ because each text functions differently. This is why, for example, my analysis of Designing Women relies heavily on theories of women's use of language and conversation, while my analysis of Murphy Brown pays a great deal of attention to intertextuality.

This inductive approach leads to the case study organization of this book in which I perform close analysis of relatively few examples of programming. I prefer to study television at the level of the series. When a series becomes an artifact for a critic, it becomes possible to do the kind of close reading that reveals patterns of plot and character, recurring rhetorical strategies, and, ultimately, repetitive rhetorical function, that I find interesting and useful. This focus on what Caren Deming calls "concrete particularity" means "resisting, or at least suspending, the manly inclination to argue deductively from principles assumed to apply to all television equally" (1990, p. 59).

Generally, my concern is with understanding the functions of this programming as part of cultural debates about feminism, rather than with using these texts to promote a new way of understanding television. Following Kenneth Burke's (1973) admonition to "use all there is to use," I attempt to integrate the insights offered by theorists and critics that will help me to make the arguments that I wish to make about the programming that I discuss. To the extent that the case studies reveal continuity between strategies of representation of feminism over time (as I believe they do), I am hopeful that this book produces a kind of grounded, historically situated theory that can be helpful to scholars studying the uses of feminism in popular culture.

3

ADVANCING THE STATUS OF WOMEN

"The emancipation of women, the achievement of full equality between the sexes, is one of the most important, though less acknowledged prerequisites of peace. The denial of such equality perpetrates an injustice against one half of the world's population and promotes in men harmful attitudes and habits that are carried from the family to the workplace, to political life, and ultimately to international relations.

There are no grounds, moral, practical, or biological, upon which such denial can be justified. Only as women are welcomed into full partnership in all fields of human endeavor will the moral and psychological climate be created in which international peace can emerge."

This position, taken from a statement on peace written by the Universal House of Justice in 1985, reiterates the teaching of Bahá'u'lláh that society must reorganize its life to give practical expression to the principle of equality between women and men. Since its inception nearly one hundred and fifty years ago, the Bahá'í Faith has taught the equality of the sexes. Indeed, the Bahá'í Faith is the only independent world religion whose Founder has stated unequivocally that women and men are equal.

"Women and men have been and will always be equal in the sight of God," said Bahá'u'lláh.

In accordance with this teaching, the worldwide Bahá'í community has been at the forefront of the movement to advance the rights of women for more than a century. And the Bahá'í approach, which advocates full equality and a firm sense of partnership between women and men, is increasingly recognized as being on the cutting edge of women's issues worldwide.

Bahá'ís understand, for example, that the values which women bring to human interaction are necessary to the proper functioning and advancement of modern society, and that qualities that have formerly been associated with the feminine sides of our natures—such as compassion, nurturing, cooperation and empathy—will be increasingly important in creating a peaceful, just, and sustainable world civilization.

Bahá'í institutions around the world promote various educational efforts for women, and work to raise the consciousness of both women and men about this fundamental equality. Many of its schools, learning centers, and grassroots social and economic development projects specifically include the promotion of women's advancement into their curricula or agendas.

Women compose approximately 30 percent of elected leadership in Bahá'í councils at the national level, comparing favorably to national parliaments, which average 10 percent women worldwide.

Bahá'í women have long been active in the struggle to promote women's equality. The Bahá'í Faith was founded in 1844 in Iran and among its early followers was Tahirih , a Persian poet and scholar. In 1852, she laid down her life in defense of her beliefs, which included her right to lay aside the veil and to work for the complete emancipation of women.

Laura Dreyfus-Barney, a member of the first Bahá'í community in Europe, was among the leading figures in promoting the advancement of women in the early years of this century. In the years after World War I, she focused her attention on mobilizing women for peace. She represented the International Council of Women (ICW) in the League of Nations and was President of ICW's Peace and Arbitration Commission.

After World War II, Ms. Dreyfus-Barney played an important role in the development of the relationship between the United Nations International Children's Emergency Fund (UNICEF) and non-governmental organizations (NGOs).

Martha Root, an American journalist from Pennsylvania, circled the globe several times in the 1920s and 1930s to promote the cause of women's equality—along with the other progressive principles of the Bahá'í Faith. With a unique facility for approaching high dignitaries, she took the Bahá'í message of interdependence and oneness to kings, queens, presidents, ministers, statesmen, professors, clergymen and poets in Europe, Asia, Africa and Australia.

Since the Bahá'í International Community (BIC) obtained consultative status with the United Nations Economic and Social Council (ECOSOC) in 1970, it has cooperated officially with the United Nations in its work to improve the status of women throughout the world.

The Bahá'í International Community has worked directly with the United Nations Commission on the Status of Women and its Secretariat, the UN Division for the Advancement of Women. In addition, the BIC has established close, cooperative relationships with other international non-governmental organizations at the United Nations that seek to promote the advancement of women.

Initially the BIC contributed to the work of the United Nations by submitting statements to United Nations bodies, and in particular the Commission on the Status of Women, on various aspects of equality. Such statements have addressed the education of girls, the importance of elevating the status of women as mothers, the relevance of women's participation at local, national and international levels to the establishment of world peace. As part of International Women's Year in 1975, the BIC participated in the first World Conference on Women, held in Mexico City. Two Bahá'í representatives were officially accredited to attend the Conference and nine representatives attended the NGO (Non-Governmental Organization) Tribune, the parallel meeting for non-governmental organizations.

During the next ten years, designated the United Nations Decade for Women, the Bahá'í International Community developed a solid reputation for its work promoting the advancement of women. BIC representatives served on NGO committees on the Status of Women in New York, Geneva and Vienna and participated in the World Conferences on Women held in Copenhagen, Denmark in l980, in Nairobi, Kenya in 1985, and in Beijing, China in 1995 .

The Community's representatives have also been involved in planning parallel activities for NGOs at these meetings. Relationships were established with major organizations worldwide whose focus is also the promotion of the advancement of women.

The BIC collaborates on an increasing basis with UN agencies such as the United Nations Children's Fund (UNICEF) the United Nations Development Fund for Women (UNIFEM); the United Nations Development Program (UNDP); and the United Nations Fund for Population Activities (UNFPA).

4

POLITICS OF DIVERSITY IN THE PRESENT SOCIETY

Zuzana Kulašíková, free lanced expert on gender issues, Bratislava, Slovakia At the 20century there is a tendency of an actual renewal of the theoretical problematic of societal justice and equality, which is determined by new societal processes and interlink ages, which are connected with efforts newly establish the ideal of modern society and to include into it, groups of citizens with societal status, which have been not accepted on the base of various aspects. Such ongoing social process in post modern societies is the sociologist Z. Bauman labeling as „fluid Modern". The adjective „fluid"is indicating change in the majority of areas of societal life. Changes are arising under the influence of global aspects, having negative and also positive impact to the private sphere (family, relationships) and public sphere (labor market, public life).

One of the relevant processes of the present is along with intensive demographical trends, determining feminization of elder ness and poverty, migration and global economical trends also the process of "individualization" which is manifesting itself on micro and macro levels – in family and in politics. Opinions on individualization are different. According to some it is the decision making something positive out of these process, the escape of the individual, mainly women from preliminary defined rules and the raise up of their personal freedom in the decision making process (e.g. in the area of reproduction rights, utilization of contraception), access to new possibilities, personal selection and freedom, which is today appreciated as the highest value. Ulrich Beck, Professor of Sociology at the London School of Economics, is contributing with an original view to individualization and elaborating his long term impact in a differentiating way to women and men. According to his opinion *„individualization is the first reduction and secondly the change of individual society life forms by others, in which the individual should create his life story by himself."* As of Beck ideas it is clear that the traditional concept of the role of women and her identity in the sense of dominant appreciation in the home sphere is in the era of postindustrial society unsatisfactory and is requiring a reevaluation. This is based not only in full socialization of the women and her integration into all spheres of the society but also in the fulfillment of a basic condition of this integration as an owner of self identity. This is contributing to a transfer of new forms of families, new partnerships, new life strategies etc.

In this context are developing movements for human rights, whereby the movement for human women rights is to be created. The goal is to secure equal treatment with both genders and the elimination of the discrimination in all spheres of the society. This isn't possible to be realized without the fact, that the whole society, men and women will be aware of the necessity of a change and actively participating on this goal through civic society.

Equal opportunities on the base of gender are one of the main principles of the EU, which by this declared the necessity to integrate this principle into activities of public policies of each country. Under the influence of the EU, the politics of gender equality has opened, e.g. measurements for the change of gender relationships in the sense of equality. For each EU member state there are typical specific conditions and good practices, which each country utilized and is utilizing in accordance with specific cultural and social conditions. An important factor of their creation was the basic framework, given by the EU, which was step by step created by primary and secondary European legislation and with recommend tools and methods. The Report on Equality of the EU as of 2004 is in this context mentioning: "in the last ten years there is an obvious tendency towards equality between men and women. Changes didn't come automatically but have been caused by initiatives of strategic policy to the support of equality between women and men on the EU and also on the national level".

The process of „individualization" is in the mentioned lines visible also in Slovakia, but the linkages are more complicated, due to the impact which are citizens giving to the family. In 2007 the Slovak National Centre for Human Rights realized a research „Appreciation of Human Rights and Principles of Equal Treatment within the Adult Population, which defined the opinions of Slovak public, which areas of the society they are considering as the most important – to which bigger attention should be given. Responses of Slovak respondents showed that human rights do not belong to these aspects of society which are considered as the most important; out of six areas they have been placed on the last but one place, whereby the last was the area of national minorities. As regards the question in this research according to which it is necessary at the most to follow the keeping of human rights, the respondents preferred „family and children" and at least preferred „sexual minorities" and „penitentiary". (Report from the Research, SNCHR, Bratislava 2007, p. 16, 19, 20). In this connection it is necessary to support the discourse of the new understanding of family in connection with self-realization of women and the division of partner duties among both genders, together with the overall understanding of an equal status of women in the society. In the Slovak reality this is initiated mainly by individual ideas of citizens men and women - represented by women NGOs and independent research institutions. In a smaller amount it is created through state bodies, international structures – as the EU, international human rights organizations. The achievement of consensus about forms and contextual content of the gender policy was a part of a decade long term process accompanied with more intense and practical discussions among these subjects. Their main part was the search of common stand points within the solution of principal questions of these politics, which have been affecting mainly the taboo areas of the latent character as: gender discrimination at the labor market, violence committed on women, women trafficking, reproducing rights of women, etc.

Women nongovernmental organizations and network of experts in a considerable manner participated on the presentation of the interest of the society in the area of gender equality. „In this connection according to the research of IVO, „Women, men and equal opportunities" some of the action lines to be mentioned. There are mainly activities oriented to the raise up of gender sensitivity and the excitation of gender stereotypes, which the Slovak NGOs are quite often realizing in cooperation with teachers. The second line was the establishment of a common platform „Possibility of a Choice", which repeatedly showed the intent of some of the NGOs to stand against trials about reduction of reproductive rights of women. Third – and maybe the most important line was lobbying and successful introduction of amendments of legal norms linked towards elimination of domestic violence. Extraordinary have been also activities of NGOs in the area of participation of women in public policy." Further from actual global social processes, having impact on the status of citizens in the society are migration processes and in connection with them the raising diversity, which is determining the raising multiethnic character and cultural variety of the society. Acceptance of this fact is conditioned with the securing of equal opportunities on a race base. The goal is to achieve a more tolerant approach towards differences, which would the equal status of citizens not implicitly link with the acceptance of hegemony norms of the given society.

Norm is for example a white heterosexual woman of middle class. Solution of multiplicity discrimination of women is at the present an actual call of the multicultural feminism which is trying „the acceptance of difference". The goal is to achieve a more tolerant approach to differences.

The mentioned process has in an increased manner impact also on the Slovak Republic, whereby the number of migrants is raising as well as of asylums seekers. In the last period there was an increase of legal migrants. Since 1993 the raise of the numbers was seven times, and therefore the security of women which are subordinated to multiply discrimination (as women and as representatives of other races) is actual. At the present there are in Slovakia mainly migrants from Asia and Near East, and former Russia and this mainly in connection with war conflicts or instable political and economical situation in countries of their origin. In this connection the opinions of the Slovak public are relevant, resulting from the already mentioned research of the SNCHR. Their opinions on the measurement of the potential „social distance", e.g. acceptability of social groups are as follows: drug dependent, Roma, citizens with deviant behavior, Moslems, homosexuals and immigrants. In the responses of the respondents there is also the prevailing fear from economic and social impacts of immigration, more than 40 percent is of the opinion that they are taking the jobs of people which have been born here. (Final Report from the Research, pp. 24-23). Inevitable are activities which could be a part of prevention, respectively elimination of repeated discrimination.

The status of Roma minority in the Slovak Republic is a good example how gender issues are transformed into all problems of the society. As a positive example of Slovak activities mainly of the civic society there is a possibility to mention a program which is trying to utilize the potential of Roma women, who are subordinated to discrimination as woman, as Roma and eventually as elderly Roma. If there will be offered to the girls and women sufficient opportunities, education awareness and health care, it could strengthen their status within the community and respectively it could mean also the improvement of the Roma minority as a whole.

One of the responses how to manage some of the indicated present social processes is the policy of equal opportunities and anti discriminatory politics. The European Year of Equal Opportunities for all, showed mainly serious problems resulting from repeated discrimination; therefore even the European policy of equal opportunities stated as policy of gender equality at the present that it is important to understand gender as a multiple category within which a complex of „gender", „race" and „class" relationships is acting. Therefore questions of non discrimination and equality should be „clearly represented"in an overall scale of European policies and to be further implemented into the life of the society. One of the ways is the process of „individualization", appearing in the policy: deepening of citizenship and his activities.

Civic society in the Slovak Republic was created and is proceeding different as it was in France and Italy. At the present there is a need for an inevitable „narrowing" dialogue between organizations of civic society and other key involved subjects on the inter state level. As the utmost important in this area we are considering the necessity to find the optimal form of effective communication of all involved subjects within the creation and execution of anti discriminatory policies.

Slovak researches are showing similar problems as the overall EU has. The Report of the EC on Equality and Non discrimination in 2005 showed that main obstacles for the application of anti discriminatory regulations is the duration of anti discriminatory attitudes and behavior (68 %), not completed acts (59 %) and not satisfactory information and awareness about rights and obligations (48 %). The Slovak context is also indicating the need of fight against prejudice and stereotypes, which is in a majority realized through subjects of civic society. As regards their activities the majority of citizens of the Slovak Republic is considering them according to the research of SNCHR as positive and do agree with the opinion that their existence is contributing to quality of democracy. The share of respondents which expressed positively themselves towards NGOs was higher in categories with higher education. The intensive linkage of the civic public and bodies of state administration is for the policy of equal opportunities inevitable.

5

STATUS OF WOMEN IN ISLAM

INTRODUCTION

The status of women in society is neither a new issue nor is it a fully settled one.

The position of Islam on this issue has been among the subjects presented to the Western reader with the least objectivity.

This paper is intended to provide a brief and authentic exposition of what Islam stands for in this regard. The teachings of Islam are based essentially on the Qur'an (God's revelation) and Hadeeth (elaboration by Prophet Muhammad).

The Qur'an and the Hadeeth, properly and unbiasedly understood, provide the basic source of authentication for any position or view which is attributed to Islam.

The paper starts with a brief survey of the status of women in the pre-Islamic era. It then focuses on these major questions: What is the position of Islam regarding the status of woman in society? How similar or different is that position from "the spirit of the time," which was dominant when Islam was revealed? How would this compare with the "rights" which were finally gained by woman in recent decades?

HISTORICAL PERSPECTIVES

One major objective of this paper is to provide a fair evaluation of what Islam contributed (or failed to contribute) toward the restoration of woman's dignity and rights. In order to achieve this objective, it may be useful to review briefly how women were treated in general in previous civilizations and religions, especially those which preceded Islam (Pre-610 C.E.). Part of the information provided here, however, describes the status of woman as late as the nineteenth century, more than twelve centuries after Islam.

Women in Ancient Civilization

Describing the status of the Indian woman, Encyclopedia Britannica states:

In India, subjection was a cardinal principle. Day and night must women be held by their protectors in a state of dependence says Manu. The rule of inheritance was agnatic, that is descent traced through males to the exclusion of females.

In Hindu scriptures, the description of a good wife is as follows: "a woman whose mind, speech and body are kept in subjection, acquires high renown in this world, and, in the next, the same abode with her husband."

In Athens, women were not better off than either the Indian or the Roman women.

"Athenian women were always minors, subject to some male - to their father, to their brother, or to some of their male kin.

Her consent in marriage was not generally thought to be necessary and "she was obliged to submit to the wishes of her parents, and receive from them her husband and her lord, even though he were stranger to her."

A Roman wife was described by an historian as: "a babe, a minor, a ward, a person incapable of doing or acting anything according to her own individual taste, a person continually under the tutelage and guardianship of her husband."

In the Encyclopedia Britannica, we find a summary of the legal status of women in the Roman civilization:

In Roman Law a woman was even in historic times completely dependent. If married she and her property passed into the power of her husband . . . the wife was the purchased property of her husband, and like a slave acquired only for his benefit. A woman could not exercise any civil or public office . could not be a witness, surety, tutor, or curator; she could not adopt or be adopted, or make will or contract. Among the Scandinavian races women were: under perpetual tutelage, whether married or unmarried. As late as the Code of Christian V, at the end of the 17th Century, it was enacted that if a woman married without the consent of her tutor he might have, if he wished, administration and usufruct of her goods during her life.

According to the English Common Law:

> *...all real property which a wife held at the time of a marriage became a possession of her husband. He was entitled to the rent from the land and to any profit which might be made from operating the estate during the joint life of the spouses. As time passed, the English courts devised means to forbid a husband's transferring real property without the consent of his wife, but he still retained the right to manage it and to receive the money which it produced. As to a wife's personal property, the husband's power was complete. He had the right to spend it as he saw fit.*

Only by the late nineteenth Century did the situation start to improve. "By a series of acts starting with the Married women's Property Act in 1870, amended in 1882 and 1887, married women achieved the right to own property and to enter contracts on a par with spinsters, widows, and divorcees." As late as the Nineteenth Century an authority in ancient law, Sir Henry Maine, wrote: "No society which preserves any tincture of Christian institutions is likely to restore to married women the personal liberty conferred on them by the Middle Roman Law."

In his essay The Subjection of Women, John Stuart Mill wrote:

> *We are continually told that civilization and Christianity have restored to the woman her just rights. Meanwhile the wife is the actual bondservant of her husband; no*

less so, as far as the legal obligation goes, than slaves commonly so called.

Before moving on to the Qur'anic decrees concerning the status of woman, a few Biblical decrees may shed more light on the subject, thus providing a better basis for an impartial evaluation. In the Mosaic Law, the wife was betrothed. Explaining this concept, the Encyclopedia Biblica states: "To betroth a wife to oneself meant simply to acquire possession of her by payment of the purchase money; the betrothed is a girl for whom the purchase money has been paid." From the legal point of view, the consent of the girl was not necessary for the validation of her marriage. "The girl's consent is unnecessary and the need for it is nowhere suggested in the Law."

As to the right of divorce, we read in the Encyclopedia Biblica: "The woman being man's property, his right to divorce her follows as a matter of course." The right to divorce was held only by man. "In the Mosaic Law divorce was a privilege of the husband only .... "

The position of the Christian Church until recent centuries seems to have been influenced by both the Mosaic Law and by the streams of thought that were dominant in its contemporary cultures. In their book, Marriage East and West, David and Vera Mace wrote:

Let no one suppose, either, that our Christian heritage is free of such slighting judgments. It would be hard to find anywhere a collection of more degrading references to the female sex than the early Church Fathers provide. Lecky, the famous historian, speaks of (these fierce incentives which form so conspicuous and so grotesque a portion of the writing of the Fathers . . . woman was represented as the door of hell, as the mother of all human ills. She should be ashamed at the very thought that she is a woman. She should live in continual penance on account of the curses she has brought upon the world. She should be ashamed of her dress, for it is the memorial of her fall. She should be especially ashamed of her beauty, for it is the most potent instrument of the devil). One of the most scathing of these attacks on woman is that of Tertullian: Do you know that you are each an Eve? The sentence of God on this sex of yours lives in this age: the guilt must of necessity live too. You are the devil's gateway: you are the unsealer of that forbidden tree; you are the first deserters of the divine law; you are she who persuades him whom the devil was not valiant enough to attack. You destroyed so easily God's image, man. On account of your desert - that is death - even the Sop of God had to die). Not only did the church affirm the inferior status of woman, it deprived her of legal rights she had previously enjoyed.

WOMAN IN ISLAM

In the midst of the darkness that engulfed the world, the divine revelation echoed in the wide desert of Arabia with a fresh, noble, and universal message to humanity: "O Mankind, keep your duty to your Lord who created you from a single soul and from it created its mate (of same kind) and from them twain has spread a multitude of men and women" (Qur'an 4:1).

A scholar who pondered about this verse states: "It is believed that there is no text, old or new, that deals with the humanity of the woman from all aspects with such amazing brevity, eloquence, depth, and originality as this divine decree." Stressing this noble and natural conception, them Qur'an states:

> *He (God) it is who did create you from a single soul and therefrom did create his mate, that he might dwell with her (in love)...(Qur'an 7:189)*
>
> *The Creator of heavens and earth: He has made for you pairs from among yourselves ...Qur'an 42:1 1*
>
> *And Allah has given you mates of your own nature, and has given you from your mates, children and grandchildren, and has made provision of good things for you. Is it then in vanity that they believe and in the grace of God that they disbelieve? Qur'an 16:72*

The rest of this paper outlines the position of Islam regarding the status of woman in society from its various aspects - spiritually, socially, economically and politically.

1. The Spiritual Aspect

The Qur'an provides clear-cut evidence that woman iscompletely equated with man in the sight of God interms of her rights and responsibilities. The Qur'an states:

"Every soul will be (held) in pledge for its deeds" (Qur'an 74:38). It also states:

...So their Lord accepted their prayers, (saying): I will not suffer to be lost the work of any of you whether male or female. You proceed one from another ...(Qur'an 3: 195).

Whoever works righteousness, man or woman, and has faith, verily to him will We give a new life that is good and pure, and We will bestow on such their reward according to the their actions. (Qur'an 16:97, see also 4:124).

Woman according to the Qur'an is not blamed for Adam's first mistake. Both were jointly wrong in their disobedience to God, both repented, and both were forgiven. (Qur'an 2:36, 7:20 - 24). In one verse in fact (20:121), Adam specifically, was blamed.

In terms of religious obligations, such as the Daily Prayers, Fasting, Poor-due, and Pilgrimage, woman is no different from man. In some cases indeed, woman has certain advantages over man. For example, the woman is exempted from the daily prayers and from fasting during her menstrual periods and forty days after childbirth. She is also exempted from fasting during her pregnancy and when she is nursing her baby if there is any threat to her health or her baby's. If the missed fasting is obligatory (during the month of Ramadan), she can make up for the missed days whenever she can. She does not have to make up for the prayers missed for any of the above reasons. Although women can and did go into the mosque during the days of the prophet and thereafter attendance et the Friday congregational prayers is optional for them while it is mandatory for men (on Friday).

This is clearly a tender touch of the Islamic teachings for they are considerate of the fact that a woman may be nursing her baby or caring for him, and thus may be unable to go out to the mosque at the time of the prayers. They also take into account the physiological and psychological changes associated with her natural female functions.

2. The Social Aspect

a) As a Child and an Adolescent

Despite the social acceptance of female infanticide among some Arabian tribes, the Qur'an forbade this custom, and considered it a crime like any other murder.

> *"And when the female (infant) buried alive - is questioned, for what crime she was killed." (Qur'an 81:8-9).*

Criticizing the attitudes of such parents who reject their female children, the Qur'an states:

> *When news is brought to one of them, of (the Birth of) a female (child), his face darkens and he is filled with inward grief! With shame does he hide himself from his people because of the bad news he has had! Shall he retain her on (sufferance) and contempt, or bury her in the dust? Ah! What an evil (choice) they decide on? (Qur'an 16: 58-59).*

Far from saving the girl's life so that she may later suffer injustice and inequality, Islam requires kind and just treatment for her. Among the sayings of Prophet Muhammad (P.) in this regard are the following:

> *Whosoever has a daughter and he does not bury her alive, does not insult her, and does not favor his son over her, God will enter him into Paradise. (Ibn Hanbal, No. 1957).*

Whosoever supports two daughters till they mature, he and I will come in the day of judgment as this (and he pointed with his two fingers held together). A similar Hadeeth deals in like manner with one who supports two sisters. (Ibn-Hanbal, No. 2104).

The right of females to seek knowledge is not different from that of males. Prophet Muhammad (P.) said:

"Seeking knowledge is mandatory for every Muslim". (AlBayhaqi). Muslim as used here including both males and females.

b) As a Wife

The Qur'an clearly indicates that marriage is sharing between the two halves of the society, and that its objectives, beside perpetuating human life, are emotional well-being and spiritual harmony. Its bases are love and mercy.

Among the most impressive verses in the Qur'an about marriage is the following.

"And among His signs is this: That He created mates for you from yourselves that you may find rest, peace of mind in them, and He ordained between you love and mercy. Lo, herein indeed are signs for people who reflect." (Qur'an 30:2 1).

According to Islamic Law, women cannot be forced to marry anyone without their consent.

Ibn Abbas reported that a girl came to the Messenger of God, Muhammad (P.), and she reported that her father had forced her to marry without her consent. The Messenger of God gave her the choice . . . (between accepting the marriage or invalidating it). (Ibn Hanbal No. 2469). In another version, the girl said: "Actually I accept this marriage but I wanted to let women know that parents have no right (to force a husband on them)" (Ibn Maja, No. 1873).

Besides all other provisions for her protection at the time of marriage, it was specifically decreed that woman has the full right to her Mahr, a marriage gift, which is presented to her by her husband and is included in the nuptial contract, and that such ownership does not transfer to her father or husband. The concept of Mahr in Islam is neither an actual or symbolic price for the woman, as was the case in certain cultures, but rather it is a gift symbolizing love and affection.

The rules for married life in Islam are clear and in harmony with upright human nature. In consideration of the physiological and psychological make-up of man and woman, both have equal rights and claims on one another, except for one responsibility, that of leadership. This is a matter which is natural in any collective life and which is consistent with the nature of man.

The Qur'an thus states:

"And they (women) have rights similar to those (of men) over them, and men are a degree above them." (Qur'an 2:228).

Such degree is Quiwama (maintenance and protection). This refers to that natural difference between the sexes which entitles the weaker sex to protection. It implies no superiority or advantage before the law. Yet, man's role of leadership in relation to his family does not mean the husband's dictatorship over his wife. Islam emphasizes the importance of taking counsel and mutual agreement in family decisions. The Qur'an gives us an example:

"...If they (husband wife) desire to wean the child by mutual consent and (after) consultation, there is no blame on them..." (Qur'an 2: 233).

Over and above her basic rights as a wife comes the right which is emphasized by the Qur'an and is strongly recommended by the Prophet (P); kind treatment and companionship.

The Qur'an states:

"...But consort with them in kindness, for if you hate them it may happen that you hate a thing wherein God has placed much good." (Qur'an 4: 19).

Prophet Muhammad. (P) said:

The best of you is the best to his family and I am the best among you to my family.

The most perfect believers are the best in conduct and best of you are those who are best to their wives. (Ibn-Hanbal, No. 7396)

Behold, many women came to Muhammad's wives complaining against their husbands (because they beat them)- those (husbands) are not the best of you.

As the woman's right to decide about her marriage is recognized, so also her right to seek an end for an unsuccessful marriage is recognized. To provide for the stability of the family, however, and in order to protect it from hasty decisions under temporary emotional stress, certain steps and waiting periods should be observed by men and women seeking divorce. Considering the relatively more emotional nature of women, a good reason for asking for divorce should be brought before the judge. Like the man, however, the woman can divorce her husband with out resorting to the court, if the nuptial contract allows that.

More specifically, some aspects of Islamic Law concerning marriage and divorce are interesting and are worthy of separate treatment.

When the continuation of the marriage relationship is impossible for any reason, men are still taught to seek a gracious end for it.

The Qur'an states about such cases:

When you divorce women, and they reach their prescribed term, then retain them in kindness and retain them not for injury so that you transgress (the limits). (Qur'an 2:231). (See also Qur'an 2:229 and 33:49).

c) As a Mother

Islam considered kindness to parents next to the worship of God.

"And we have enjoined upon man (to be good) to his parents: His mother bears him in weakness upon weakness..." (Qur'an 31:14) (See also Qur'an 46:15, 29:8).

Moreover, the Qur'an has a special recommendation for the good treatment of mothers:

"Your Lord has decreed that you worship none save Him, and that you be kind to your parents. . ." (Qur'an 17:23).

A man came to Prophet Muhammad (P) asking:

O Messenger of God, who among the people is the most worthy of my good company? The Prophet (P) said, Your mother. The man said then who else: The Prophet (P) said, Your mother. The man asked, Then who else? Only then did the Prophet (P) say, Your father. (Al-Bukhari and Muslim).

A famous saying of The Prophet is "Paradise is at the feet of mothers." (In Al'Nisa'I, Ibn Majah, Ahmad).

"It is the generous (in character) who is good to women, and it is the wicked who insults them."

3. The Economic Aspect

Islam decreed a right of which woman was deprived both before Islam and after it (even as late as this century), the right of independent ownership. According to Islamic Law, woman's right to her money, real estate, or other properties is fully acknowledged. This right undergoes no change whether she is single or married. She retains her full rights to buy, sell, mortgage or lease any or all her properties. It is nowhere suggested in the Law that a woman is a minor simply because she is a female. It is also noteworthy that such right applies to her properties before marriage as well as to whatever she acquires thereafter.

With regard to the woman's right to seek employment it should be stated first that Islam regards her role in society as a mother and a wife as the most sacred and essential one. Neither maids nor baby-sitters can possibly take the mother's place as the educator of an upright, complex free, and carefully-reared children. Such a noble and vital role, which largely shapes the future of nations, cannot be regarded as "idleness".

However, there is no decree in Islam which forbids woman from seeking employment whenever there is a necessity for it, especially in positions which fit her nature and in which society needs her most. Examples of these professions are nursing, teaching (especially for children), and medicine. Moreover, there is no restriction on benefiting from woman's exceptional talent in any field. Even for the position of a judge, where there may be a tendency to doubt the woman's fitness for the post due to her more emotional nature, we find early Muslim scholars such as Abu-Hanifa and Al-Tabary holding there is nothing wrong with it. In addition, Islam restored to woman the right of inheritance, after she herself was an object of inheritance in some cultures. Her share is completely hers and no one can make any claim on it, including her father and her husband.

"Unto men (of the family) belongs a share of that which Parents and near kindred leave, and unto women a share of that which parents and near kindred leave, whether it be a little or much - a determinate share." ((Qur'an 4:7).

Her share in most cases is one-half the man's share, with no implication that she is worth half a man! It would seem grossly inconsistent after the overwhelming evidence of woman's equitable treatment in Islam, which was discussed in the preceding pages, to make such an inference. This variation in inheritance rights is only consistent with the variations in financial responsibilities of man and woman according to the Islamic Law. Man in Islam is fully responsible for the maintenance of his wife, his children, and in some cases of his needy relatives, especially the females. This responsibility is neither waived nor reduced because of his wife's wealth or because of her access to any personal income gained from work, rent, profit, or any other legal means.

Woman, on the other hand, is far more secure financially and is far less burdened with any claims on her possessions. Her possessions before marriage do not transfer to her husband and she even keeps her maiden name. She has no obligation to spend on her family out of such properties or out of her income after marriage. She is entitled to the "Mahr" which she takes from her husband at the time of marriage. If she is divorced, she may get an alimony from her ex-husband.

An examination of the inheritance law within the overall framework of the Islamic Law reveals not only justice but also an abundance of compassion for woman.

4. The Political Aspect

Any fair investigation of the teachings of Islam o~ into the history of the Islamic civilization will surely find a clear evidence of woman's equality with man in what we call today "political rights". This includes the right of election as well as the nomination to political offices. It also includes woman's right to participate in public affairs. Both in the Qur'an and in Islamic history we find examples of women who participated in serious discussions and argued even with the Prophet (P) himself, (see Qur'an 58: 14 and 60: 10-12).

During the Caliphate of Omar Ibn al-Khattab, a woman argued with him in the mosque, proved her point, and caused him to declare in the presence of people: "A woman is right and Omar is wrong."

Although not mentioned in the Qur'an, one Hadeeth of the Prophet is interpreted to make woman ineligible for the position of head of state. The Hadeeth referred to is roughly translated: "A people will not prosper if they let a woman be their leader." This limitation, however, has nothing to do with the dignity of woman or with her rights. It is rather, related to the natural differences in the biological and psychological make-up of men and women.

According to Islam, the head of the state is no mere figurehead. He leads people in the prayers, especially on Fridays and festivities; he is continuously engaged in the process of decision-making pertaining to the security and well-being of his people. This demanding position, or any similar one, such as the Commander of the Army, is generally inconsistent with the physiological and psychological make-up of woman in general. It is a medical fact that during their monthly periods and during their pregnancies, women undergo various physiological and psychological changes. Such changes may occur during an emergency situation, thus affecting her decision, without considering the excessive strain which is produced. Moreover, some decisions require a maximum of rationality and a minimum of emotionality - a requirement which does not coincide with the instinctive nature of women.

Even in modern times, and in the most developed countries, it is rare to find a woman in the position of a head of state acting as more than a figurehead, a woman commander of the armed services, or even a proportionate number of women representatives in parliaments, or similar bodies. One can not possibly ascribe this to backwardness of various nations or to any constitutional limitation on woman's right to be in such a position as a head of state or as a member of the parliament. It is more logical to explain the present situation in terms of the natural and indisputable differences between man and woman, a difference which does not imply any "supremacy" of one over the other. The difference implies rather the "complementary" roles of both the sexes in life.

CONCLUSION

The first part of this paper deals briefly with the position of various religions and cultures on the issue under investigation. Part of this exposition extends to cover the general trend as late as the nineteenth century, nearly 1300 years after the Qur'an set forth the Islamic teachings.

In the second part of the paper, the status of women in Islam is briefly discussed. Emphasis in this part is placed on the original and authentic sources of Islam. This represents the standard according to which degree of adherence of Muslims can be judged. It is also a fact that during the downward cycle of Islamic Civilization, such teachings were not strictly adhered to by many people who profess to be Muslims.

Such deviations were unfairly exaggerated by some writers, and the worst of this, were superficially taken to represent the teachings of "Islam" to the Western reader without taking the trouble to make any original and unbiased study of the authentic sources of these teachings.

Even with such deviations three facts are worth mentioning:

1. The history of Muslims is rich with women of great achievements in all walks of life from as early as the seventh century (B.C.)
2. It is impossible for anyone to justify any mistreatment of woman by any decree of rule embodied in the Islamic Law, nor could anyone dare to cancel, reduce, or distort the clear-cut legal rights of women given in Islamic Law.

3. Throughout history, the reputation, chastity and maternal role of Muslim women were objects of admiration by impartial observers.

It is also worthwhile to state that the status which women reached during the present era was not achieved due to the kindness of men or due to natural progress. It was rather achieved through a long struggle and sacrifice on woman's part and only when society needed her contribution and work, more especial!; during the two world wars, and due to the escalation of technological change.

In the case of Islam such compassionate and dignified status was decreed, not because it reflects the environment of the seventh century, nor under the threat or pressure of women and their organizations, but rather because of its intrinsic truthfulness.

If this indicates anything, it would demonstrate the divine origin of the Qur'an and the truthfulness of the message of Islam, which, unlike human philosophies and ideologies, was far from proceeding from its human environment, a message which established such humane principles as neither grew obsolete during the course of time and after these many centuries, nor can become obsolete in the future. After all, this is the message of the All-Wise and all-knowing God whose wisdom and knowledge are far beyond the ultimate in human thought and progress.

6

STATUS OF WOMEN IN THE RURAL KHASI SOCIETY OF MEGHALAYA

INTRODUCTION

The issue of empowerment of women has been much discussed at various levels to find out the solution to age-old problem of gender discrimination, exploitation of women and for the upliftment of their status and position in the society. In terms of income women are poorer than men because more households headed by women fall below the income poverty line than households headed by men (HDR, 1997). Surveys of household consumption expenditure in many countries of North-South America, Europe and former CIS show the incidence of income poverty to be high among the female-headed households. In some countries like Indonesia, Morocco, Viet Nam, Zimbabwe however there is no difference between male and female-headed households in this regard.

Gender disparities exist everywhere in the world. Women are underrepresented in local and national decision making bodies. They earn less than men (as mentioned above) and participate comparatively less in wage employment and also remain mostly in low-grade jobs. In the poor areas even schooling of girl child is very poor and drop out rate is very high compared to men though one of the UN Millennium Development Goals is universalisation of primary education by 2015 (HDR, 2003). The target during 1990 to 2000 was achieved in this regard to reduce gender disparity in enrolment at primary level but looking at the gap in drop-out, income, work participation, social and political participation one can assert that there is a long way to go for the removal of gender inequality in education, economy and social status.

However, in most of the tribal societies even if poor, women always have an instilled special position and role they play in different spheres with great responsibility vis a vis their counterpart men. The Khasi society of Meghalaya is such a society, commonly known as matrilineal where authority, title, inheritance, residence after marriage and succession are traced through the female line. So it is presumed that they do not require any special effort to make them aware and get social, economic, political or psychological understanding and knowledge to establish their rights along with men in their society as they are automatically placed on an esteemed level. They are presumed to have free access to education, ownership of property, authority in their family and society; they are supposed to be the heads of their families and have the power to take decision what to be done or not etc. But a recent survey by us in the rural areas of Meghalaya shows that the number of families headed by the male is more than the families headed by the female (1.6:1). Also many of the families headed by females are due to compulsion as they are either widow, separated or deserted with small children.

Also in the political sphere, hardly anybody is there who is female and even in the Dorbar (similar to that of village panchayat of plain areas) females are not allowed to take part in the meeting or decision-making. But in most of the socio-economic activities, still now dominance on female is observed even though they are assumed to be physically weak. Also, even though some families are headed by males it may be that they are just to carry out activities with the guidance of their female counterpart who has better control over assets and therefore no fear of loosing anything even if they are deserted by their husbands. Therefore, a question may arise whether in Khasi tribe the status of women is ascribed or prescribed by the society. Also it is pertinent to enquire about the direction to which the position and status of women are moving with the development of the society.

This paper is thus an attempt to examine the *dynamics of status and role of tribal women in Meghalaya, especially of Khasi women in the rural areas.* It is examined through a number of social, economic, political, cultural, psychological and attitudinal indicators on the basis of the primary data on such factors collected from two villages in East Khasi Hills District of Meghalaya.

METHODOLOGY OF THE STUDY AND DATA:

Process of empowerment of women here has been studied through primary survey in two villages from East Khasi Hills District of Meghalaya. These villages are Ringkseh and Kynton-u-mon under Mawlyngknang block. The villages are chosen purposively on consideration of conveniences, such as access and communication, security, expenditure involved in survey etc. However most of the features of the rural Meghalaya have much in common in the aforesaid selected villages.

There are 257 households (119+138) in all in those selected villages. The ratio of male and female-headed families in the selected villages was found to be 1.6: 1 in Meghalaya. Though the society of Meghalaya is commonly known as matrilineal, more than two third of the families run by males and only around 1/3rd are headed by females. Then question naturally arises whether the society of Meghalaya is gradually approaching towards patrilineal or the dominance of female still has been prevailing in the same manner and the change has been just for the convenience without any major change in balance of gender distribution in any respect.

Then, we have stratified the families according to the characteristics of sex of family head, caste, occupation, education etc. and finally chosen 95 households; 37 out of 175 male-headed households and 58 from 82 female-headed households. Data have been collected, from the finally chosen households, on different aspects like family size, sex, education, caste, occupation, income and expenditure, mode of expenditure and also on their attitude/opinion towards social, political, cultural aspects i.e. on social, cultural, economical, political, religious and psychological aspects of the heads as well as other members of the families. From that information we tried to understand the process of empowerment by analysing the data. The study is mainly descriptive and exploratory.

OBSERVATIONS AND DISCUSSION

Basic Characteristics of Sample Households

From the table-1 we observe that out of 37 male headed households about 68 per cent of the heads are in the below 50 age group and over 43 percent are in the below 40 age group. Where as among the female headed households about 36 per cent of the heads are in the below 50 and around 20 per cent are in the age group of 20 to 40. On the other hand, around 22 per cent of male heads are in the above 50 age group and about 64 per cent of the female heads are in the similar age group.

Economic Status

Status can be earned due to the control over economic access and power. Thus here first of all, status is examined through the distribution of economic power i.e., whether the female household head is an earner or dependent, their holding of tangible and intangible assets, nature of inheritance of ancestral property and the nature of job opportunities in which women are involved as against their men counterpart. Also their status in the society can be known through the social position exhibited through the pattern of involvement in social functions and duties (organizer of functions, director, participants or just spectator etc), which provides dimension of respect earned from the general public. Also the position in the family is exhibited through their pattern (timing, quantity, quality etc) of nutritional intake that will be considered later. Of course in many Khasi families even if the men are breadwinner their wives become customary head. Table-4 described the percentage distribution of household according the earning and dependence of male and female heads across different age group as observed from the survey data.

From the table we observe that about 16 per cent of the all-family heads are dependent and over 84 per cent are earner.

In case of male heads about 92 per cent are earners and in case of female heads this percentage is about 79. Though the aged people (whether male or female) who are either retired or non-earner is found to be head in other societies, in Khasi society with the emergence of nuclear family earning became one of the principal criteria to be head of the family for both male and female. It indicates that now-a-days the male counterpart who contributes significantly to the family income gain command over their female counterpart.

Though females are prevalent in most of the socio-economic activities in Meghalaya over 20 per cent of the female heads are dependent and thus the criteria of earning is not essential for a female to be the head. Also, even if they do not earn and depend on the income of either husband or young children they can act as head and thus decision maker. Moreover, the deserted/divorced/widows also whether earner or not are the heads due to the condition of the family. In some cases of course, due to the death of wife or due to hesitation and influence of modern society some people announce the name of their senior most male member as the head of the family. However, the chance of becoming head of a nonearner female member is relatively more than a non-earning male member even in a joint family of the rural Khasi society.

If we look at the case of inheritance of property the traditional custom is to inherit ancestral assets primarily to the females especially the youngest daughter of the family. However the other daughters of the family also get the share of the ancestral property informally but not equal with that of youngest one and the settlement is done with the consent of the daughters' maternal uncle.

The data reveals that about relatively very less male heads (about 35 per cent) have received share of ancestral property while about 65 per cent does not inherit any property. Those male inherited property either due to the fact that there was no daughter of his parents or his parents through will inherited some property. But in case of youngest daughter the inheritance is compulsory. The data shows that 50 per cent of the female heads inherited property from their parents and the remaining

50 per cent did not as they were either not youngest daughter or their parents have nothing to inherit. However the overall fact is that though some of the males inherit parental property, the females had more privilege to inherit property.

The table-6 shows that monthly average per capita family income in case of female-headed household is much lower than that of male-headed household. Also average per capita expenditure on food, education, travel and other purposes (entertainment, drink, dress etc) are comparatively higher in case of male-headed household than that of female-headed household.

Only in case of health care and electricity female-headed household spends more than a male-headed household. But the coefficient of variation in income and expenditures across families are much higher in case female headed household than that of male-headed household. This is because many of female heads are either widow, deserted or separated with small children and hence has very poor income to spend. This indicates the disadvantageous condition of the rural females in spite of being known as matrilineal society.

In spite of all these one thing is clear that the management of families are better in case of female head than that of a male as they have a tendency of saving more and giving more emphasis on human development through education health care etc, which is clear from the table-7. The table represents the result of regression of the linear equation $Y = a + bX$. Where Y is either saving or educational expenditure or medical expenditure etc; and X is the income per head of the family. The regression is run separately for the male and female-headed households. The slopes coefficients are therefore represent the marginal propensities.

Table-7 reveals that marginal propensity to save, spend on education, health care is much higher in case female headed household than those of male-headed household. On the other hand, in case of other expenditures, the propensity is comparatively higher and significant for the male head than that of female head. For medical expenditure the coefficient is even insignificant in case of male head.

SOCIAL AND PSYCHOLOGICAL STATUS

First of all we have considered the understanding and feeling about male and female children. If we look at the composition of the families (not shown here), we find in both male and female-headed cases on an average, percentage of female children is more than the percentage of male children for all categories of sex and education of the head of households. The distribution of households according to their attitude towards the sex of children.

The table shows that most of the male and female heads express their independent attitude towards the sex of child. Of course, the percentage of heads prefers female child is more than the percentage of heads prefers male child and that increases with the level of education in both cases of male and female head. In Khasi society the dowry is absent and girls also participate in different socio-economic activities and that plays an important role for the non-discrimination between the sexes of child.

Also the nature and timing of food intake by the females shows their position in the family as well as society. Though customarily it is presumed that is out of love and affection the mother of sisters in the family take food after their husband, brothers or children. But in many cases it happens to be the fact that the wives wait even with hunger for their husbands to return from office, business or farm and take food after their counterparts. It however indicates the psychological position of the females in the family in the name of sacrifice. However the females in the Khasi families take food whenever they think it is necessary and in that sense they are more independent.

In the society if women can work and participate in different social and entertaining activities freely their position improves than if they cannot. In the backward traditional societies, normally women do not become member even of any such social organisation. In rural areas of Meghalaya also we find very few women especially the well educated one are member of similar organisation compared to men. Though most of the females are not the member of different social organisations or clubs, they can move alone freely and join any party, function or ceremony and mostly without the permission of senior or male members. The tendency is more for the more and more educated females and also with the increase in age. Therefore education makes the female to think independently and act without any fear even in the villages of Meghalaya.

Perception of male and female about whether the female would remain economically and non-economically dependent on men provides another indicator of status of the women in the society. Similarly the independence of the attitudes can also be known from the thinking of women about remarriage even after the death of their husbands. The male as well female heads think that the females would be independent of men economically and non-economically. Only a few (about 17 per cent of female heads) think they are much dependent on their male counterpart. Table-16 however indicates that there is no much difference between those who agree with the idea of remarriage after their husbands' death than those who do not. The percentage of agreement increases with the level of education. The implication is that even though the educated females acquire the ability to think better and earns the capability of economic independence, a major part of them do not want to remain in isolation of male counterpart. That may of course be because of future security.

POLITICAL STATUS

Though female in Meghalaya is much aware about their rights and position in the society, in political hardly any women actively participate. Even the society does not allow women to participate in political decision-making. Till now any woman Headman of a Dorbar is hardly found. Also they do not participate much into political discourses. Only recently women are allowed on a very limited scale to participate in Dorbar meeting. Though women in Khasi society are relatively free, still there are discriminations (social and psychological) as explained above, yet the women are not much interested into politics. Actually most of the rural women think even reservation of seat for the females in the local bodies or Dorbar is not beneficial to them. The opinion of both male and female heads in this regard is. Even some of the females do not bother about whether their name is in the electoral role or not. Of course most of the female exercise their franchise in the election and that percentage increases with the rise in educational level of the rural females as is observed.

INFLUENCE OF PRINT AND MASS MEDIA ON THE WOMEN

Women of even rural Meghalaya have some access to mass and print media and that plays an important role in raising awareness among them. Though relatively more percentage of male read newspaper the women are also not lagging behind. More than 66 per cent of women heads read newspaper daily or occasionally. Considering the percentage of illiteracy, relatively more females have access to newspaper. Though radio is also available in most of the families now-a-days relatively less percentage of people listen radio, which is true for both male and female. Although people are crazy about TV now-a-day, about 41 per cent of female head watch different TV programmes either regularly or occasionally in the sample areas. Where as about 70 per cent of male heads watch TV regularly or occasionally. Actually in our sample we have seen many female-headed household who are very poor and hence they do not have TV at home and hence less access to TV programmes. Moreover, they always remain busy for earning their sustenance and thus relatively very less time available for watching any programme of entertainment or other social relevance.

CONCLUDING REMARKS

Though Meghalaya is known as the matrilineal society, now many of the families are headed by the males. The tendency is increasing with the increasing involvement of male in the socio-economic activities, expansion of education, emergence of nuclear families etc. However in the family there is no discrimination among the male and female child. This is partly because of the economic independence of the females and their customary laws, which is still dominant in the rural areas.Though traditionally the women (especially the youngest one) are supposed to inherit ancestral property, men also inherit property under different circumstances. Though earlier female used to dominate in the field of various economic activities now-a-days male also involved in different activities. Relatively more females are illiterate than male. Data reveals that, now the high collar jobs are mostly occupied by the males and the income of the female-headed households are relatively less and associated with significant inter-family variation. Also incidence of poverty is more in case of female-headed household. Yet the female better manage the family and give more emphasis on the human development indicators like education, health etc. Women in the rural Khasi society are free from any limitation and can participate freely in any function of social and religious importance. Also they can move freely without the company of male or others and without the permission of male or other seniors. So there is very less insecurity problem unlike the other societies of plain areas. But psychological the rural women are not free and they feel much dependent on men.

Still now, the rural Khasi women are not well aware of their political rights or they may be reluctant to do so. To them political decision-making is not much important. Though local body like Dorbar is much powerful, their participation in such bodies also minimal. Even most of them do not believe in reservation in the local bodies or other constitutional areas that would help raising their status in the society. Rather they like to devote more on their social and economic activities for their welfare. It is however essential to adopt measures for the improvement of education, income of the females to fill the gap between male and female. As female manage family better they would be able to further the welfare of the family members and thus the society. Also the females may be pursued to take part in decision making democratically so that they can work in more organised way and empower themselves.

7

WOMEN'S STUDIES AND RESEARCH IN IRAN AND MUSLIM COUNTRIES

BACKGROUNDS

The basic sources of Islamic thought, contain substantial discourses on the commonalties and variations in women's and men's rights and obligations. Women's personal, family and social rights have been thoroughly covered in the Holy Quran , in Hadith and in the historical accounts of the Prophet's life and the life of other prominent religious leaders and Imams. However various factors in the history of Muslim nations resulted in a partial neglect of these rights and status. Among these factors, the influence of Jahilia culture and JiJdao-Christian prejudice against women and foreign domination, and colonialism were probably among the most consequential.

When a general renaissance and revival of Islamic thought occurred following the Islamic Revolution in 1979, a reconsideration of the status of the Muslim woman entered the agenda. The prospects of establishing an Islamic government with all the attributes and qualities ascribed to an Islamic state were promising only if the basic pillar of social justice and human dignity could be maintained. Islam was to be interpreted and applied to daily life in the context of its infallible principles on the one hand and in light of the evolving challenges and requirements of modern society on the other.

The issue of women's rights and status in Islam be ame a central theme in academic, religious and political circles. The interpretation and Ijtehad of Islamic principles in all areas of economic, social and political life became a prerequisite for the development of the Islamic government and its advancement in today's world.

As Imam Khomeini introduced his agenda for the Islamic Revolution, his particular emphasis on women's social and political participation in the context of a religious right and obligation became evident. Imam provided a strategy that would confront the thoughts and instigation of reactionary forces on one side and challenge the western models of women's liberation on the other. These discourses and the anti-Islamic bigotry of the western media against the Muslim woman created an ambivalent atmosphere in Iranian society which was quite favourable for the development of a serious academic debate on the conditions of women in Iran and the rights and status of women in Islam.

This milieu opened way for an integral approach to the woman's cause and for a serious consideration of the matter in cultural spheres initially and later in academic circles as well. Graduate Thesis in various fields in Humanities and Arts became increasingly inclined towards gender issues and women's concerns. Several women's studies centres were established to undertake research on the theoretical and practical aspects of women's issues.

This general national course along with the global trend for the advancement of women as reflected in international conferences since the 1970's created a favourable ground for establishing an academic course of women's studies. This degree program would identify the basic principles of Islamic thought concerning women in all spheres of life. The program would also provide a comparative analysis of existing notions on gender and women's rights with a particular insight on Islamic perceptions. The proposal of a religious paradigm for development that would take into consideration the concerns of women would be an inherent constituent of this program.

SIGNIFICANCE

While Women's Studies has been integrated into the undergraduate and graduate programs in many western universities, and some Asian universities offer the Course, very few, if any universities in Islamic countries have included women's studies in their degree programs. The academic approach to women's studies in Islam exists in a fragmentary form in theological schools and universities of Islamic countries.

In Iran, an undergraduate course on " Family Studies" was approved last year and has been included in the BA degree programs of certain universities. While the course is an important stride, many observers feel it lacks the necessary content to address women's issue~ at the fundamental level. The "Family Studies" course has a strong emphasis on the legal aspects of family rights and responsibilities in Islam.

Some university courses in western universities have begun to provide some information on women in religion and Islam which is also fragmentary and seriously biased with an orientalist approach to the issue. Objectivity on Islam is generally lacking in the west and this attitude becomes more serious when dealing with women in Islam and in an Islamic government like Iran.

At the national level ,it is generally appreciated that an academic approach to women's concerns and gender relations in society is necessary for the advancement of women and the society. The Islamic government is in need of policy makers, planners, implementers and advisors who understand gender issues and women's concerns and rights and can respond to the challenges facing the society. This degree program will not only provide academic centres with the necessary expertise on women's issues but will also train a new strata of professionals who can enter the government with necessary insights to the conditions of women in the Iranian society.

CONTENTS

The degree program has been designed to reflect the dimensions of Islamic ideology and the needs and requirements of the society. There is a strong tendency among academia in Iran to maintain and recognise the aspects of national identity and culture as opposed to the aggression of western culture through global mass media systems. This degree program has been tailored to fit the requirements of the graduate degree (Masters of Arts) in Iran. The program is interdisciplinary in nature and provides both a conceptual and a pragmatic approach to issues. Interactive lecture sessions accompanied with theoretical and field research are a constituency of almost every course.

The conceptual framework of women's status and rights in Islam and its manifestation in an Islamic society and government is one of the major trends of the Program. A study of the status of women in different religions particularly the monotheistic religions is provided as well.

The Women's Studies degree program also provides a particular insight into the rights, status and condition of the family and the position of the woman in this fragile human institution. The recent! global developments and trends in the field of the family and education are comprehensively undertaken and considered in the program.

The historical, political and social conditions of the Iranian woman and women in Muslim societies has been included in the Course. This covers an in-depth analysis of the tribal and ethnic variations which affect the Iranian woman. Women and gender in development are also the major orientations of this course. Religious academia discredit contemporary paradigms of development as incomplete and inconsistent with the requirements of human societies. The one-sided materialistic approach of present development concepts has failed to respond to the moral and spiritual dimensions of human life and have therefore created numerous dilemmas and problems for human societies parallel to the relative economic development.

A holistic and more systematic approach to development and the integration of women as actors of development as well as beneficiaries requires a serious consideration of religious, moral and spiritual values and parameters.

PROSPECTS

The evolution of religious thought and theory in all social dimensions becomes inevitable when religion undertakes the role of providing a framework for government and social development. In this light the conceptualization and ideologization of Islam in all aspects particularly in the fields of human rights and roles is necessary. An integrated academic approach to women's issues in Islam cannot be overlooked as Islam takes the position of a pertinent alternative way of thought and life in the contemporary era.

The establishment of this program in Iranian Universities is a response to the transformative role that the Islamic Revolution played in introducing a novel model of development and advancement for human beings and women in particular. The viewpoints and strategies that Imam Khomeini deliberately pursued concerning women and their role and status in an Islamic society will undoubtedly form the backbone of any theoretical discourse on women in Islam. While several political analysts and observers coined the past decade as the Khomeini Era, many academics and theoreticians believe the Khomeini Era of thought and contemplation is yet to come.

8

THE ROLE OF WOMEN IN AMERICA

It is clear that women in America enjoy much more personal freedom and independence than women in many other parts of the world. This freedom is something we hold dear and one of the things that define contemporary American culture. However, it is also clear that many immigrants, coming from very different-thinking cultures, view such women with at least suspicion and at most contempt. Acquiring a functional view of the women in America might take some re-thinking on the part of some immigrants who may have had little exposure to women in the workplace, women in charge, or even women operating on their own. It might give a more accurate view of the real character and status of American women if you think of them as "honorary men."

Different cultures espouse widely variant ideas of the proper role and place of women within a society. One coworker, from Egypt, informed me that women did not typically live outside of their parents' homes there unless they were married. There, a woman setting up "house" by herself is assumed to be setting up a place of prostitution. Why else would she leave the guidance and protection of her family? This way of thinking was completely new to me and would be to most Americans. Here, females, just like males, are expected to move away from parents' homes and set up on their own in order to prove themselves successful, fully functioning adults. True, a woman can more easily remain at home with her parents than a man can here, but past about age 25 others would begin to look at her askance. So expect the women here to live on their own, in apartments or homes that they own, and consider such a situation to mean simply that such a woman is an adult and that she can afford such accommodations.

Further, in many other places in the world, women are expected to hold marriage and children as their primary goals and interest. Here, women are generally more interested in these things than the men are, but they do not necessarily place them first on their "to do" lists. In America, a woman is just as likely to decide that her education, for instance, needs to be completed before she can consider marriage or family. She may decide that her career needs to develop to a certain point first. In short, an American woman may have the same kind of broad concerns about conducting her life that men have around the world. In the case of men, most folks would consider holding such priorities as prudent in preparing for life's challenges, but women can still come under scrutiny for the same priorities. Here, it should not be surprising to find women delaying marriage and family into their thirties, forties or even fifties.

Finally, many cultures associate a female's independence with evidence that she is morally and/or sexually slack. The title of this article is "honorary men" for a reason. It suggests that independent women in America should be viewed through the same lens through which most folks would view men. A young man, living independent of his parents, working on his education or his career, may be morally upright or morally depraved; he may be sexually chaste or sexually promiscuous. His status as an independent man cannot tell you these other aspects of his character. Rather, one would need to meet him and get to know him before one could make such judgments. This scenario is exactly the same for American women. A woman living on her own and conducting her own personal and professional business can run the whole gamut from dutiful, traditional and chaste to self-involved, nontraditional and sexually free. One would need to engage the indiv dual woman in order to find out the truth.

Similarly, American women tend to wear jewelry and make-up, and to many immigrants, too revealing clothing. Yet American women are typically dressing within the norms of social correctness (and beauty) that all women follow in their own cultures. American women of all types even dress more conservatively as they meet the requirements of various workplaces. The few women who violate such codes receive the same shocked and negative reactions from other Americans that they do from immigrants. So, despite the make-up and high-heels, the skirts and the hairdos, remember that these women are meeting the norms of the society. American's women's style of dress, then, has little to do with her morals or her character. In short, it might make more sense just to think of us all as honorary men, and proceed accordingly.

THREE VALUE SCALES IN MODERN WORLD

In modern world, values are measured on three coexisting scales: non-materialistic, materialistic, and postmaterialistic. The latter term was introduced by American sociologist R. Engelhart (Silent Revolution, 1997, and Cultural Shift in Developed Indus-trial Society, 1990). His studies are based on worldwide surveys of public opinion. The core ides is that material well-being of postwar period resulted in major shift in large populaces' perception of values. Engelhart calls former values "materialistic" and the new one-"post-materialistic". Respondents in the surveys were offered a wide range of values and should check those of them they perceived as their own.

"Materialistic" values included: "national-level order", "price regulations", "economic growth", "national defence", "stable national economy", "crime containment". "Post-materialistic" values included: "more public participation in government", "freedom to communicate one's opinion", more public participation in decision-making at community level", "improve public and environmental health", "make society more friendly and diversified", "make ideas overpower money".

"Post-materialistic" values, in Engelhart's sense, differ from their "materialistic" counterparts rather in quantitative than quality characteristics. To qualify the new system of values widely adopted today by modern western youths, it would take a combination of two words: "post-materialistic" (which is already in place) and "post-patriarchal" (which is not). In these terms, non-materialistic values are described as "patriarchal" (which is essentially the same). The term "patriarchy" was initially introduced by feminists to designate men's supremacy over women carried out through variety of public institutions. Today this term is widely used by all type of ideologists as reference to societies based on rigid hierarchy. "Post-patriarchal" society produced new values that can be described, according to a German sociologist H. Z. Betz, as "mixture of left-libertary and non-materialistic." It means that post-materialistic values should include all rights and freedoms of today's democracy-and that is the main feature distinguishing post-materialistic set of values from the non-materialistic set.

Non-materialistic values were placed in almost every culture throughout human history. These values included struggle, victory, unity, mutual support, unselfishness, honor and other concepts of the same row. Past cultures having shifted to materialistic values (Carthego, for instance) were usually renounced and sometimes demolished by their neighbors. Only with industrial revolution, Western Europe and USA made their final choice of materialistic values and eventually overruled non-materialistic values both at home and abroad. Materialism established new values: individual, his rights and liberties, personal benefit. It was materialism that gave start to concepts of equal rights for men and women, women's "entitlement" to artificial abortion, liberty to choose one's sexual orientation, etc.

"Post-materialists" plan to keep all these gains of democracy. For this reason, post-materialistic system of values is strikingly different from non-materialistic paradigm of the past. It can be argued that the idea of returning to pre-materialistic values is both attractive and repulsive for "post-materialists". Therefore, they check each value for its compatibility with emancipation trends. There seem to be no other explanation why one would protest against drugs being tested on animals and stand for artificial abortions at the very same time.

The same reasoning helps explain why patriarchal ethics is deemed "egotistic" by post-materialists. Whereas an individual feels that he belongs to his kind-be it a nation, a class, a tribe, or a family-he becomes a part of self-sufficient "collective ego", while true unselfishness, to their opinion, means belonging to entire humanity without any discrimination between human groups.

New values-either post-materialistic or post-patriarchal-are publicly promoted by so-called alternative movements (ecologists, ecofeminists, communitarians and some others). Their goal is to help evolve new political culture. Political culture is known to be always "stratified" to some extent. Today politicians operate in terms of traditional culture (based on concepts of authority, hierarchy, law and so on). However, other strata of political culture exist today within the global framework of the prevailing authoritative one. They are, for example, rural and community self-government culture, "guerilla warfare" political culture of left radicals, and others. Western "civic" and Eastern "patriarchal" political cultures cause abundant discussions. For post-materialists, however, these distinctions and deviations seem to not exist at all. They assert that what we have today is solidified "oppressive" political culture.

Therefore, they visualize future political culture to be "soft" and feminine as opposed to "hard" and masculine culture of today. Alternative movements associate crisis of the western civilization with dominance of masculine ethics and thinking. Masculine way of thinking is essentially dualistic in its perception of the world; hence, reality is fragmented into pairs of opposing concept: Nature/culture, body/spirit, manhood/womanhood, I/other, etc. Moreover, horizontally fragmented world is subjected to vertical classification by hierarchy, assigning elements the more importance and power, the higher their standing is. Values prevalent in masculine ethics are freedom, personal autonomy, equality, equity, etc. In addition, for all his life a man has to prove his sexual identity, and for this end he fervently competes with others of his like to confirm his standing.

Feminine culture and thinking may be generally characterized by the following features. First, it is integrated perception of the world inherent in women. "Femininity is determined through unity," writes Caroline Gillighan. Second, feminine ethical values are primarily those of mutual dependence, compassion and care. A female does not have to constantly prove her status (it is soundly based on her reproductive function); consequently she is not inclined to construct hierarchical chains and promote herself to higher standing in them. Third, women acquire essentially different socialization experience. Right from the beginning, they are taught how to care for others, make decisions that would incorporate others' interests, keep her family clear of conflicts, etc. Many think that with building-up women's role and representation at all levels of power a "bloodless revolution" may occur through gradual replacement of masculine "terror-based political culture" with feminine culture of universal care, pacifism, ecological thinking, etc.

If males remain prevalent at power any longer, the global catastrophe will follow inevitably, as Elizabeth Gray believes, because for male politicians "steadfastness is a cult." Male politicians are almost incapable of compromise, as their primary concern is to play self-assured winners.

Alternative movements' adherents largely agree that most women (not to say about men) are yet unready to accept most of "feminine" values. To spread new values, it will take a worldwide effort-"New Enlightenment" as it is often called. Of course, skeptics may say that all attempts to remold human psychology are utopian. The same label used to be attached to the Enlightenment ideas. Nevertheless, so prominent a sociologist as Alexis de Toqueville in his The Old Order and the Revolution acknowledges that it was enlighteners who had prepared the Great French Revolution, as the latter was grounded in abstract concepts, rather than in realities of that time. Apostles of new values openly declare themselves to be new enlighteners, and since the old ones succeeded in their mission, it's not improbable that their conceived inheritors will be successful too.

Education is the main tool to reengineer human mind and morale. From standpoint of new social values, school education systems that we presently have are "estrangement-producing machinery". Moreover, not only education system requires complete restructuring, basic principles of what and how is taught in school must be revised. That is why new schools are among major concerns of projects implemented by alternative movements. One of them (movement for humanistic education) entirely focuses on this problem. The movement sees its mission in opening schools of new type which would be deeply rooted in local communities. Children are brought up on entirely new principles, often contradictory to those practiced elsewhere. For example, children are taught to play new games that do not imply competition and winners, while unisex-style clothes prevent boys and girls from evolving "sexist templates" of how they should behave. As mentioned above, "non-materialistic" values do not imply "feminine" or "mild" political culture.

With the exclusion of "the golden billion", majority of earth's population keep on living with non-materialistic values (or rather pre-materialistic from European standpoint). Whereas collectivism, care for neighbors, and-to some extent-"femininity" (harmoniously combined with women's' secondary role) are natural attributes of the third world, it is absolutely free of any motives of liberation and emancipation. Moreover, there is no evidence that, on having achieved understanding of solidarity and collectivism as values to be unconditionally preserved in the future, these nations would want to adopt democratic values in their common sense (e. g., equality in face of the Law).

Most humans still live in communities that profoundly disprove materialistic values, including their manifestations in form of human rights and freedom so cherished in the West. Far more doubtful prospect is of political culture feminization, especially if looked upon from the standpoint of ethnic psychology. L. N. Gumilev wrote in his In Trouble of Illusion, that "history evolves not in itself, but in every particular ethnos... For universal human values to take possession of the entire humankind, multiple nations of today should merge into a single hyperethnos. However, as long as levels of passionate tension vary across superethnoses already present, as long as land-scapes and climates vary from country to country and require specific skills to adjust... chances for such merger are narrow..."

Though in somewhat peculiar (not in his days) language, Gumilev makes it clear that prevalence of feminine (care, peace, cooperation, security) or masculine (aggression, struggle, quest, self-assertion) qualities depends on age of an evolving entity-be it an individual or a nation. In this sense, Nietzsche was absolutely correct when he wrote that, in certain periods, "manly, belligerent, victorious instincts take over all others, such as 'happiness' instinct..." while at other times other instincts dominate, those of "contemptible prosperity of which minor shopkeepers... women and other democrats dream." Putting aside Nietzsche's disregard to shopkeepers' values, he was absolutely right about their feminine origin.

Getting back to Gumilev's terms, we see that whenever feminine values prevail in political life of "ethnos", it has already entered its "autumn" characterized by declining livelihood and overall sluggishness of the nation. In other words, we witness a nation that has passed its activity peak and is getting prepared for dissolution. At this stage, nations become peaceful; moreover, they seek harmony with the Nature. Iceland and Norway were the two nations Gumilev had chosen as examples of declining ethnoses. Today these two countries are at forefront of "feminine" political culture.

In this context, feminine domination is associated with rather pessimistic expectations for the future. Therefore, post-patriarchal values and political culture may be expected to spread only over those ethnic systems driven by inertia, while other nations will stick to masculine values at practically any cost.

As for Russia, most recent surveys reveal a bizarre picture: romantic elders oriented towards collectivism and pragmatic youths oriented towards individualism.

In 1995 survey undertaken by Russian Independent Institute of Social and National Problems, 93.4% Russian respondents backed the statement of "clean conscience and inner harmony" as a major human value; 90.7% supported "family and friends"; while only 35.4% mentioned "well-paid job", and 8.1%-"public cognizance and fame". However, of younger respondents (22-26 years old) only 89.2% the first statement, while elders (>60) were much more consonant (98.9%). Young vs. elder score in support of the three other values was: 89.8% vs. 91.8%; 38.1% vs. 25.2%; and 6.5%.

Separately stands the assertion that a person should "make his way into power, in order to have influence upon others". Among younger people this statement gained approval of 9.1%, while of older citizens it was supported by 0.0% precisely.

Obvious analogies may be drawed between this survey and "materialistic" and "non-materialistic" values. So far, a certain part of Russian young generation is quite happy with "materialistic" values which have already produced strong repulsion in their western counterparts (e. g., "competition drives development", "the strongest survives", "consumption above all" and other market-oriented values). All others (note, that they are not "elders" in American Medicare sense, for this group included everyone of 35 and above) simply reject these values as if they were non-existent, for experience of all their previous life suggests that these values are not actual values, but rather channels for fraud and corrupt behavior to take place of morality. In addition, middle-aged and elders had lucky opportunity to grow up while enjoying far better social and economic standards (which, in turn, theoretically means more openness to "post-materialistic" thinking).

Nevertheless, compatibility of "post-materialistic" values and Russian thinking is a thing that would take much insanity to believe in. Engelhart's evaluation method was developed for nations with developed market economies only. Having been applied in transition-market Russia, it produced the outstanding score, "Materialists-9 vs. Post-materialists-1" (while in Western Europe the average ratio is 4:3). What we observe, however, is rather non-materialism than post-materialism as opposed to "western materialism". Post-materialistic values depend on age of ethnos. Finally, they include libertary values which are understood as formal rights and negative freedoms (not to...). In Russian tradition, however, freedom is understood as positive "freedom of will", and rights are understood as a "gain for being rightful".

Despite of all, alternative movements exist in Russia. They attract persons of diverse (but always non-materialistic) orientation. As for post-materialistic values, they are inherent in a few-mostly representatives of intelligentsia with interests lying in fields of technical engineering, applied and natural sciences (for education in liberal arts always results in excessive self-esteem and lack of appropriate collectivism). Though unmistakable enemies of alternative values and movements include primarily those who constitute the bunch that has recently been designated as "the middle class in process of formation" (corrupt officials and businessmen who had finally attained/hope to attain western living standards). This powerful group is enthralled by gains of materialistic period and shows no sign of being bored of capitalizing.

It was back in 70's when certain social groups in the former USSR (primarily those who used to go in rounds with communist-future messages) silently adopted western values (while keeping on discrediting them in public) and began to practice excrescent consumption, unlimited (shadow) business development, private and public competition and so on. This phenomenon was then publicly labeled and disrupted as "veschism".

One point of this article is to assert that "post-materialistic values" are products of unprecedented growth of wealth resulting in incredible formal liberties that have evolved in the West. This unique process cannot be reproduced elsewhere on the earth (at least, in this and following generations). Therefore, standards of living that made western youths (and sometimes elders) to believe in "post-materialistic values" are non-attainable on the global scale. For this simple reason, "post-materialistic" values are doomed (at least, as they are today). Sooner or later, traditional non-material values that prevail in the most of human culture will take over (though with certain western-inspired modifications). Anyway, libertary impetus will never regain equal strength that we witness today in alternative movements. "New" Islam fundamentalism is, probably, one example of what future alternative movements will be like. While claiming to promote "true" Islam values, fundamentalists, in fact, have largely modernized tradition Islam to the extent that it might be as well designated as "post-materialistic religion". (After all, fundamentalism evolved as a substitute for Western values once so popular in the East.) For example, modern fundamentalists do not disclaim freedom and democracy; they just emphasize that they understand them differently. In this sense, new values may come into dominion over the world under any conceivable name.

WOMEN AS CONSUMERS AND PRODUCERS IN THE WORLD MARKET

Globalisation has had adverse effects on women in the South. As consumers, women are the targets for a host of dangerous products and a consumer culture which reduces them to commodities. As producers, they are exposed to work exploitation and occupational hazards. Health is humankind's most basic consumer need and the most precious possession, next perhaps only to life itself. Good health is particularly important to women because lack of it affects them for a variety of reasons.

As potential mothers requiring care and attention, women need specialised services related to the reproductive system. As mothers they become responsible for the health of their children and families. And as workers outside and inside the house, they often have to shoulder double burdens; consequently they are overworked, subject to poor working conditions and suffer undue overstrain and mental stress. They are more dependent on the health system than men, and are major consumers of health care due to their many roles.

In recent years many products related to women's health have been found to be dangerous or giving rise to illnesses which in some cases have led to deaths. Many of them have been banned or restricted in the developed countries although they continue to be marketed in the Third World.

Third World countries have become convenient dumping grounds for products and medicines peddled by the transnational corporations (TNCs). Most of these products do not meet the safety standards in their countries of origin in the North and many Third World women have become unfortunate guinea pigs and victims. Some of these products include dangerous contraceptives like Depo Provera, the Dalkon Shield and Norplant.

Not only have the TNCs affected the health of Third World women with their marketing of dangerous contraceptives, they have also introduced new food and new tastes at the expense of wholesome traditional nutrition. Many of these foods are hawked by the TNCs as fashionable items of consumption.

Across the Third World today can be found a wide array of costly beverages, packed in attractive cans and bottles, canned foods, frozen foods, fast food and processed foods which not only swamp supermarkets, but are also often prominently displayed in the remotest village shop.

The irony is that in most Third World countries, the basic needs of some two-thirds of the population are yet to be satisfied. Yet impoverished families have been persuaded by the sales tactics of TNCs to spend their hard-earned money on junk foods and products which they do not need.

Coca Cola is sold in every village shop and even the families of fishermen buy canned fish which is advertised on radio, television and in glossy magazines. Farmers who can hardly make ends meet are known to spend a third of the family income on cigarettes and alcoholic drinks thus siphoning off a valuable portion of their hard-earned money which could be used for family nutrition instead.

Bottled drinks and junk food have become essential items not only in the urban but also the rural areas and not only during festivals and celebrations but also in everyday living. In recent years, the American fast food culture has spread to many Third World countries, which are now savouring the delights of hot dogs, pizzas, McDonald's beefburgers, Kentucky Fried Chicken and A & W root beer.

In Third World countries when people with limited budgets are influenced by the prevailing culture to switch from traditional and nutritious foods to high-cost low-nutrition foods, there is an adverse effect on their health.

BOTTLE FEEDING OF INFANTS

One outstanding and well-known example of the detrimental influence of introducing new foods to replace traditional practices is the case of infant formula and sweetened condensed milk. Due to aggressive sales promotion by the milk companies, many poor mothers in the Third World have switched from breast-feeding to bottle feeding their babies. Because of this pressure from the milk companies and the prevailing consumer culture, women lose confidence in breast-feeding and themselves as mothers. Breast-feeding is no longer considered modern and a mother is led to believe that she is denying the best for her baby if she does not give the bottle. As a result, breast-feeding rates have been declining in the Third World.

The Tobacco Epidemic

With smoking declining in developed countries, the tobacco industry is shifting its operations to the Third World. Many Asian countries, including Thailand and South Korea, have had to open up to imports of foreign cigarettes in the name of free trade under pressure of Western governments and tobacco companies.

As a result, there has been a rise in the number of smokers, women included. Besides the adverse health effects, there is also a negative social impact. An ordinary worker or farmer smoking one packet of cigarettes a day may spend a quarter of his income on cigarettes.

In most Third World societies, when there is not enough food to go around, it is the women who have to give up their share. And when the men in the family are sick or die, it is again the women who have to bear the brunt of the family burdens and responsibilities.

The Image of Women in the Consumer Culture

The globalisation of culture promotes not only a Western brand of consumption and lifestyle, but also projects an image of women which is discriminatory, oppressive and male oriented. In this consumer culture, women have been reduced to mere commodities for mass consumption.

Women in most Third World societies have inherited the worst of both worlds. The concept in traditional feudal society of woman as the property of her husband subject to male authority in the family, is today made worse by the commercial exploitation of women in our consumer society.

This view of modern woman as a sex object is unprecedented in human history because it is only in our age and time that through the mass media and technology at its disposal the commodification of women has become so pervasive and insidious. This process is linked to a market economy where women are used as sex objects to sell products. This is seen time and again in advertisements where women are almost always depicted as vain and seductive, as sex commodities, dull-witted, in constant need of approval (almost always by men) and ultimately best left in the home or kitchen.

It is here that women are most exploited in terms of their sexuality and physical appearance. One has only to look at the advertisements flashing from cinema screens, billboards, bus stops, magazines and calendars to confirm this. Many of these portray scantily dressed women advertising motorbikes, cars or radios-products which bear no relation to the figure of the women in these ads. The commercialisation of the female body as an object to be feasted upon and consumed by eager male eyes, is seen in the semi-nude and nude pictures of women-in suggestive poses and revealing big breasts-on calendars advertising cigarettes, liquor, tractors, paints and machinery. This portrayal of women in mass media is but a reflection, albeit a distorted reflection, of how women are regarded and made out to be in a consumer society.

More important, consumer culture has created an image of woman in terms of her face and body. This in turn helps to shape women's views about themselves and how others view them. In our hearts and minds we begin to believe that the real woman, the meaning of 'femaleness' is the one we see so often in the beauty magazines or the models advertising beauty aids and women's products. Thus the real woman is all beautiful, all glamour, all seduction.

And in the process of trying to attain 'this real thing' women not only compete with each other to outdo one another in sophistication and seduction (for sexual attention from men), women also lose confidence in themselves and their true worth. In this manner, consumer culture manipulates and distorts the personality of women, destroying their self-confidence and makes all of them victims.

WOMEN AS PRODUCERS

In recent years TNCs have located some of their manufacturing plants and industries in the Third World. The main reason adduced for this is the abundance of cheap, hard-working and docile labour.

By this they mean women workers of course. The exploitation of women in this sector in terms of their low wages, poor working conditions, instability of employment, absence of employment benefits and oppressive laws which deny women workers their rights to representation, unionisation and compensation has been well documented in the literature.

This situation is also true in the plantation economy where women workers suffer double oppression and exploitation-working as coolies and labourers in the tea, rubber and oil palm plantations and working as beasts of burden for their other lord and master, the husband in the home.

Plantation society is an enclosed atrophied society. Workers here have almost no control over decisions affecting their lives. Perhaps it is only a little better than the slave plantations during the first wave of colonial expansion in the New World.

Hazards

One of the most serious forms of exploitation that women workers face is the hazards they are exposed to in the workplace. These hazards not only threaten their health, but that of their unborn children if they are pregnant. Although both men and women face hazards at work, women because of their dual jobs-one at the shop floor and the other in the home-have to shoulder more burdens and are therefore exposed to more hazards. Thus the fatigue and stress suffered by most women workers 'is a result of their 80-hour work week-40 on the job, 40 in the house, and 24 hours on-call duty to their families.'

Women workers face four types of work hazards-psychological, physical, biological and chemical hazards.

The most serious psychological work hazard is stress and a major source of occupational stress is job dissatisfaction. The majority of women work in occupations where wages are low and where they have no control over decisions affecting them. This coupled with shift work and poor working conditions result in stress, one of the manifestations of which is mass hysteria-a common occurrence among factory workers in Malaysia.

Physical hazards include noise, heat, ventilation and lighting, vibration, trauma and radiation, and biological hazards include exposure to bacteria, viruses, fungi and infections.

Chemical hazards are the most common. They include a wide range of industrial solvents, anaesthetic gases, heavy metals, dyes, inks, asbestos, shampoos, detergents, pesticides and radioactive materials. Women workers at home, in factories, hospitals and shops and whether they work as typists, agricultural workers, teachers or hairdressers are all exposed to these hazards.

For the female worker on plantations, her long and dangerous work as a breadwinner is further burdened by her household work. As a result, women workers suffer immense stress, hardship and strain and a general deterioration in their health.

WOMEN AS SELLERS

Many Third World countries are dependent on foreign trade. This is compounded by the fact that a large share of the exports of Third World countries consists of only a few commodities-raw materials which are more susceptible to price and demand fluctuations than manufactured goods. In the world market, both Third World men and women producers suffer from the low prices they are able to get for their produce. Their incomes are also reduced. And the industrialised countries dominate world trade.

This unequal relationship vis-a-vis the Third World means that industrialised countries (ICs) control the markets of both raw materials and manufactured goods. Third World countries have to take whatever price is being offered-both for their exports of raw materials and the imports of manufactured and industrial products from the ICs.

Thus, Third World countries have poor terms of trade for their commodities vis-a-vis industrial products of the developed countries. Their terms of trade have been declining in the past few decades and continue to do so.

Apart from the poor terms of trade for Third World commodities, a large portion of the export earnings of Third World countries goes to payment for freight, insurance, packing, marketing and shipping-services controlled by TNCs who, through their shipping firms, impose high and increasing charges for freight services.

Although this problem is not specifically related to women, women do suffer as they are also producers of commodities like rubber, tin, tea, bananas, cotton, coffee and sugar. Indirectly, they are also affected if their menfolk who are the primary bread-winners earn less income. With less money being brought home, the quality of life, health, nutrition and general well-being of the entire family is also affected.

SEX TOURISM

There is more insidious exploitation of women which is linked to world tourism. This global industry has given rise to the flesh trade whereby women and even children are made to sell their bodies for sex. Hundreds of thousands of women in Asian countries, forced by socio-economic circumstances, have been sexually exploited working as prostitutes, social escorts, dance hostesses and waitresses in nightclubs and cocktail lounges.

Sex tourism is the most dehumanised form of sex and economic exploitation of women. It has its roots in a Western decaying urban life, where society is alienated and deculturalised, and where the need to consume has become compulsive and devoid of any real meaning. Hence new stimulations, distractions and excitement have to be sought to give one continued satisfaction and what can be better than the fulfilment of sexual fantasies?

This barren existence is best typified by this young carpenter from Amsterdam who returns yearly to Bangkok on the sex tour: 'It's really unbelievable, all the gorgeous dames here. This is the third time I've come here and I swear that in all these times I haven't seen anything else except this bar. They drive you wild and for a few guilders you can pick the most beautiful of the beauties. This is something else, at least, than lying on your back in Spain to get a little tan. You're the king here and all for a few rotten pennies.'

This is also how much Asian women are worth. Through sex tourism, the industrialised countries export their sexual alienation and perversion to the Third World.

MARGINALISATION THROUGH DEVELOPMENT

The impact of the West which began first with colonial intervention and the development decades that followed have had adverse consequences on the role and status of women in traditional subsistence society.

The introduction of Western concepts of ownership of land has deprived women's usufructuary rights to cultivation and control of land. The introduction of cash crop production and Western male concepts of ownership have led to the exclusion of women in the cash economy.

The neglect of the food subsistence sector where women were confined, in place of export crops and the new technologies which were introduced in agriculture not only increased her burden but in many instances, led to her redundance in traditional agricultural activities. This has resulted in the increasing marginalisation of women in the traditional rural economy, reducing women to a position of dependence which was absent in the traditional economy.

This discrimination against rural women has led to a steady displacement of women in the traditional sector. Further displacement due to development projects like dam construction, mining activities, aquaculture projects and tourism development, forces women to drift to the towns and cities in search of wage labour. In the factories they are exposed to hazardous and stressful working conditions, sexual harassment and an urban culture and lifestyle.

Despite the various attempts of the UN and the International Agencies to highlight and alleviate the problems of women, a UNESCO study at the end of 1993 revealed that the status of women in the developing nations of Asia had actually deteriorated in the past three decades.

Hence the problems of women must be examined in the light of present development strategies. As such, the solutions to the problems have to be seen and understood within the context of the whole development process that is taking place both in the rural and urban areas.

THELYPHTHORIA OR EXPLOITATION OF WOMEN

The real meaning of sex, the relations of the sexes in the past and at the present time, and the influences that these relations have on the present condition of mankind, are questions that transcend all others in importance, and that have more to do in determining the present condition of humanity than all other questions combined. No more certainly does the race arise by generation than it falls by abuse of the generative powers and functions. So likewise with regeneration, which means literally a new birth. It means not only that the individual shall be born again, but it means that the generative functions, individually and collectively, must be re-formed. There is no human attribute in which man approaches so near to deity as in the power to generate human beings. Here he is a creator.

There is no power in man capable, when perverted, of dragging him so deep into hell, and through which he can degrade so hopelessly so many other human beings as through the sexual life. Neither England nor the "civilized world" have had time to forget the "Pall Mall Gazette's Secret Commission", through which a single glimpse was obtained of the ruined lives and horrible depravity caused by perversion and degradation of the generative power of man. It was as though the door of the bottomless pit had opened for an instant, so that the world could get a single glance and be stifled with one puff of the vapours of the inferno. All that Dante ever painted was as a pleasant dream to this. The inferno is no myth, nor is it in the bowels of the earth, it exists in the body of society, and is eating out the heart of humanity. The present writer has neither the purpose nor the power to paint this realm, this leprosy of society. It would be appalling to even name its departments.

The seduction, desertion, and prostitution of young girls ending in suicide; the most loathsome and demoralizing diseases, scarcely second to leprosy, if not the real cause of that terrible disease; infanticide, only another name for murder; rape with its lynchings, and murder in every form; the pouring out on humanity and in the pure air of heaven daily and hourly of a fathomless, conscienceless, heartless ocean of lust. It is as though there had been poured into the pure stream of life the very dregs of the bottomless pit, and then, as though to prevent a single effort at purifying the stream, the Prince of Darkness has tabooed the whole subject, and attempts to cover with odium everyone who utters more than a mild regret, or who dares to long for the pure waters of life. Ask any old physician, who has had opportunity to know the under-current of society, if the above category is overdrawn, and he will tell you that it is incomplete. Here at the very fountain of all, life is the root of all evil. We are now writing for theosophists, some of whom have expressed a desire for practical instruction, and here are a few hints only.

If the whole stream of life is corrupt, it can be purified only by commencing at the fountain-head. There is but one way in which any man can help to purify or benefit the world, and that is by purifying himself. The whole of humanity is sexually diseased. Only the grosser crimes have as yet been named in this connection. Legalized prostitution and perversion of the highest attributes under the sacred name and in the habiliments of Love have not yet been mentioned. The theosophic life and the highest human achievement has been often declared to involve absolute chastity-purity in thought, word, and deed; and with this condition, love has been declared to be the absorbing element, the crowning glory. Over against this statement stands the record of celibacy in the clergy, and to it may be added the results as ordinarily witnessed of male and female continence both in private life and in various societies, whether as a matter of choice or necessity.

The results desired have seldom flowed from these conditions, and hence the earnest student is often bewildered and left in doubt as to the real meaning and possible results of chastity. Beyond this there are young people greatly interested in studies called theosophic, beside many married persons seeking to know theosophic truths, and striving to lead theosophic lives. To these last-named individuals the present essay is particularly addressed. The reform of the world from the horrible abuses named is not herein attempted. The attempt is made only to throw a little light on this all-important subject, so that those who are really in earnest, and who desire the truth in order to use it and serve it, may receive assistance. Let those who talk of England and America as "Christian Countries", count up the number of prostitutes in the large cities alone; let them add to this the number of cases of seduction, rape, bastardy, suicide, and murder, including abortions, the latter largely among the upper classes, and when they have gone thus far with their statistics, let them pause and read the " Sermon on the Mount"; then if they are still ready to abuse and ostracise those who hesitate about attaching the sacred name of Christ to "modern civilization", we shall have nothing further to say in that direction.

If the wailing of the slaughtered innocents, the homeless waifs cast out on society, the despair and degradation of the poor prostitutes, and the shriek of the suicide as she rushes into the unseen world, do not blanch his face with horror and force him to cry, How long, O Lord! how long! argument would be wasted and words worse than useless. There are others again who do revere both the Sermon on the Mount and the author of it, and who hold the Bible and real Christianity in reverence, and who feel deeply the awful sarcasm of calling this or any present nation of the world, Christian. If these care to know the real bible doctrine on the subject under consideration, let them consult an old work bearing the title of this essay and printed in London in 1780. The following "memorandum" appears in the second of the three octavo volumes.

"The grand question to be tried is,-Whether a SYSTEM filled with obligations and responsibility of MEN to WOMEN, and of WOMEN to MEN, even to death itself, and this established by INFINITE WISDOM, is not better calculated to prevent the ruin of the female sex, with all it horrid consequences, both to the public and individuals, than a SYSTEM of human contrivance, where neither obligation nor responsibility are to be found, either of MEN to WOMEN or of WOMEN TO MEN, in instances of the most important concern to BOTH, but more especially to the weaker sex? " I have quoted the above as italicized in the original. The author shows the Bible doctrine to be beyond all controversy, that whether a man be married or single, he is "joined by God" to the woman with whom he is carnally intimate, and that "he shall not put her away all the days of his life", and as this necessarily involves polygamy and precludes divorce, the author faces the problem squarely, and shows, not by argument, but by Bible, that is "the law and the gospel". The present writer does not argue nor advocate this point either pro or con, but refers to it for the benefit of those interested in the subject from the Bible stand-point. The book can be found in many libraries, and can be occasionally picked up at old news-stands. One thing is very certain, and that is that the laws and practices of Christendom are widely at variance with the "law of God" as set forth in the Bible, and compiled and annotated in "Thelyphthoria, or a Treatise on Female Ruin".

Every careful student of religions, of occultism, or of theosophy, is aware that the symbols and the god-words of all-religions have a very close relation to sex. Not only Payne

Knight, and Inman, but hosts of other writers, have pointed out and abundantly illustrated this fact. The deity to whom was offered divine honours in the various religions, was sometimes male, sometimes female. The God of Christendom today is undeniably male, notwithstanding the fact that the original name in Hebrew is both male and female, and that to a specific degree. The Catholic Church, wise as a serpent, in this as in all other generations, recognises this androgynous God, and god-name, and has elevated a woman to the God-head. If our present civilization be claimed still as Christian, it cannot be called catholic in its treatment of woman, in its practice of abortion or infanticide, whatever may be said of other crimes in this direction. It would surprise most persons to learn to what extent the fast and feast days, and " all the ordinances of the Lord's house", conform to and are derived from the periods of time which are related to parturition, viability, and the like.

Suffice it to say that the mysteries of religion, like the mystery of life, are all involved in the mystery of sex. This fact no one having the least knowledge of the subject can deny, for the evidence is overwhelming. Furthermore, the degradation of religion and the degradation of life has everywhere, and at all times, gone hand-in-hand with the degradation of the sexual instinct, and has sprung directly from the sexual degradation of woman and the bestialization of man. On the other hand, pure religion, pure life, and pure men and women go together. In the degradation of the world, man has always taken the lead, and woman been the victim. Every student of history knows that no more correct measure of any age, or any people, can be made than that which is based on the position and estimate in which women were found at that time. The new age that is just dawning for the human race is called " the Woman's Age". For many centuries, at least, woman has not occupied the position which is open to her today, and it is doubtful if, since written history began, her opportunities have been anything like that which she may now enjoy.

True, this opportunity falls to the lot only of a favoured few. The great majority are still in darkness and bondage, the victims of man's laws and passions. The responsibility and the god-given opportunities of the favoured few are seldom appreciated. These favoured few, who, from larger intelligence or fortunate circumstances, are free to live pure and noble lives, seldom rise to the full stature of conscious liberty. We hear a good deal of the Brotherhood of man, but there is more pressing need of the Sisterhood of women. True the leaven of humanity is beginning to work. Yet, how many of these free and really noble women will pass a poor prostitute in the street without, almost unconsciously, gathering in her skirts for fear of contamination? How many will meet a girl in society over whose fair name has passed a cloud of suspicion, whether true or false, and not shrink into herself? And yet where are they who are so much in need of love and sympathy as these poor victims? To house these outcasts in asylums, feed them, clothe them, pray over them, thus marking them more indelibly as outcasts than even man has done, has seldom permanently reformed one. Ask your woman's soul, my noble sister, how it would regard these things were you to change places, and do not call yourself Christian till you have learned how Christ spake to these, and how he LOVED THEM. You can reform them but by love, and not by cold charity and self-righteousness.

Many of the students of the Higher Life are in every way unprepared for real chelaship, but they can place themselves in training if they so desire, but to begin by abandoning wife and children will be to train in the opposite direction. The very fact that they find themselves so situated is evidence of a needed development through these things, not away from them. Karma has placed them just here to learn, to consider, to overcome. If either man or woman imagines, when so situated, that he or she can draw away from companions and children, from friends and associates, leaving them to take their chances, and so develop the higher life, the first principle of theosophy has yet to be learned.

The nearness of your relation to these gives you the opportunity for helpfulness that no one else in all the world enjoys. There lies your work, you can make home a very paradise by learning the difference between lust and love. Love seeketh not its own but another's good. Love endures all, and bears all, and at last triumphs over all.

As even animal lust may create a human body, so divine love can regenerate a human soul. What we need in the world today is not celibacy, but happy homes in which love reigns, and love pure and simple will make these homes a tabernacle for angels. Husband and wife may so live together as to be a source of joy, of perpetual delight, nay, even of health and physical strength and continual inspiration to each other.

They may learn thus the very secret of love itself, and enter together the higher life, clad in raiments of purity and light, and they may help to uplift their children, and such children as the world sorely needs.

The fountain of life and the fountain of love flow from the same divine source. Both life and love are sexual, but in a sense that the world never even dreams of, and never will, till it learns to put aside the animal attribute egoism, and really exercise and base their whole lives on the principle of divine altruism.

How many men imagine they love the pure girl they "marry"? And how many of these have really down deep in their souls one thought beyond self? Ask the divorce courts of America and the unhappy homes of England. Reform the family, regenerate the homes, and from these will go out an influence that in time will reform the street, the brothel, and prevent at least the participation in these crimes and all the loathsome diseases and penalties of your own children.

If there is a young man or woman who is free from obligations, free to work for humanity, one who appreciates the opportunity, and values it above home or any personal advantage, or possible gain, the time for such an one has come. Their souls will be filled direct from the pure fountains of love, and they may be the blessed medium through whom the Divine Love is to reach the poor, the outcast, the unloved. Would any of tnese feel honoured and grateful to take orders direct from a Mahatma? to be the chosen medium between such an one and a society of theosophists?

The door is wide open. "Enter ye who will". Act as the messenger of love, of charity, of self-forgetfulness, of helpfulness to every ready soul, to the sinful, the degraded, no matter how low a criminal he or she may be, for by so much the more is help needed.

Do this modestly, patiently, persistently, and a new joy will come into your soul, and all mahatmas in all worlds will delight to do you honour, and whenever you need their help or their presence be sure it will not be wanting.

The writer, an humble layman, has tried this even in a slight degree, being trammelled on every hand; he has needed help, needed instruction many times, and it has never failed to come. It has come in its own way, often as though it came not. Yet there it was !

The first sentence in a book taken at random when thinking of something else, would perhaps answer a question that I deeply felt the need of knowing.

Be not anxious, be not disappointed, only be, faithful, silent, sincere, and patient. Do the duty that lies nearest at hand in the best way you can. Do it as though for love of the dearest one in all the earth; or, better, do it for the sake of Love. So the love-nature will expand and grow. The more you give out the more you will receive.

Love delights to flood the soul of the one who delights to pass it on. Love fills us full at all times; but what little dwarfed and deformed vessels do we present to the Goddess: she fills them full, and is poorer for this gift, for she is entitled to larger vessels and better measure, and less dross than we mix with the pure waters of love.

Love bargains not for return, receives nothing back, begs only the privilege of giving. Full-freighted soul! hurry on thy gifts, love waits without to renew thy store. Disappoint her not. Thy store of love will be like Egypt's bondsmen's quails and manna, not alone are the morrow, but in a moment, if thou restrain thy love. Dost thou desire the mysteries of love, to know how she creates, preserves, renews? Fill thy soul full of her, and thou wilt be love, the mystery thine. Shall not he who has the power of love have also the mystery? are these not one?

Where use reigns, mystery disappears. Love is the great revealer. Her neophytes walk in her presence as in a blaze of glory; ask what thou wilt in the name of love and it is done. Knowest thou the hierarchic name of love? the unwritten name, low-breathed from ear to ear? I'll give thee then a substitute till in some other fair degree the true Master's Word shall echo in thy soul.

'Tis self-forgetfulness, consideration for others, preferring to be burdened with nought else, that thou mayest be full of love, and only love.

Do this, and every zephyr of every wind that blows shall whisper in thy ear the name by which the fair goddess is known in realms elysian. Give all thou hast away but love, and then be quick to give love away: squeeze thy soul dry of love, and then with quick rebound thy love shall span all space, and sitting on thy throne shall be the fair goddess thyself, thy other self, now two in one, and One with all.

FREEING WOMEN FROM EXPLOITATION AND DESPAIR

Imagine a terrible plague—a devastating disease—descending on and ripping apart the fabric of your community, killing, crippling, or otherwise disabling half of your friends, family, and neighbors.

Beyond the human pain and suffering this would cause, consider the incredible impact it would have on your community's ability to thrive. How could the economy grow? How would societal institutions function? How stable could things possibly be? The world would be compelled to action.

Yet in far too many places around the world today, there is indeed a plague holding back many communities and keeping untold millions from reaching their potential. It is a plague the world must face, not only because it is the moral thing to do, but because the cost for ignoring it is simply too great. What is this plague? It is the systematic and violent exploitation of women. This exploitation takes many forms, depriving women of their most basic freedom, robbing them of their health, keeping them from the education they need and deserve, and condemning them to lives without economic opportunity.

No country can prosper when women's voices are silenced, their bodies exploited and their rights violated. Around the globe, the oppression of women goes hand in hand with failed societies. Nations, like women and their children, have the best chance to thrive where fundamental freedoms, human rights, and property rights are ensured for all.

The United States has been the world's leader in helping to free women from exploitation and despair. Guaranteeing the human rights of women and children is essential to the creation of stable, democratic, and prosperous societies. This is not only in keeping with the deeply held values of the American people; it is strongly in the United States' national interest as well.

As Americans, we take our rights for granted. We cannot conceive of being sold into sexual slavery, forced into an arranged marriage at age 5, subjected to female genital cutting as a rite of passage, systematically raped as a weapon of war, or killed with impunity in the name of honor—by a father or brother.

As the U.S. Ambassador to the United Nations Commission on the Status of Women, I have seen how women in many parts of the developing world, especially in regions of conflict, face these very threats today. It is inconceivable that in the 21st century so many women still lack legal protections for basic human rights.

PLIGHT OF REFUGEES

No group is in greater danger than the large number of women refugees and internally displaced persons. They are often single-handedly responsible for the survival of their children, even when their own survival is at stake. Every day provides challenges that increase the risk of physical danger: finding cooking fuel, carrying water (often for miles), obtaining sufficient food at distribution sites, and accessing primary health care for themselves and their families.

They are also exposed to violence at every stage in their flight. Secretary Rice has expressed deep concern with the rape of displaced women in Darfur when they venture out to gather food or firewood, a story brought to light in a July U.N. report.

Sexual violence and exploitation, associated psychological trauma, and the risk of sexually transmitted diseases, are among the terrible dangers confronting refugee women today.

Violence takes many forms—trafficking in persons, domestic violence, rape, and harmful traditional practices such as female genital mutilation and honor crimes. It shatters the most fundamental human right to which every woman is entitled: the right to be safe.

9

MODERN-DAY SLAVERY

The most egregious violation of human rights is the modern-day slavery of human trafficking, which affects hundreds of thousands of persons each year, mostly women and children, depriving them of basic freedom and inflicting unspeakable physical and emotional harm.

Ambassador John Miller, director of the State Department's Office to Monitor and Combat Trafficking in Persons notes that 80 percent of trafficked persons are female and nearly half are children. He states "Sex slavery... is the dominant form... then domestic servitude, both of which are largely women or girls. What was once a race issue has become primarily a gender issue."

Women are particularly vulnerable in post-conflict societies with economies in shambles. Faced with lack of opportunity at home, they are easily lured by false promises of well-paying jobs abroad. Many are then coerced into lives of prostitution, domestic servitude, or other types of forced labor.

As President Bush told the U.N. General Assembly in 2003, "Nearly two centuries after the abolition of the transatlantic slave trade, and more than a century after slavery was officially ended in its last strongholds, the trade in human beings for any purpose must not be allowed to thrive in our time."

The Bush Administration has provided more than $295 million to support anti-trafficking programs in more than 120 countries, including a special $50 million initiative that the

President announced at the U.N. This funding helps countries to develop laws, investigate cases, rescue and voluntarily repatriate victims, build emergency shelters, run awareness campaigns, and mount rehabilitation and vocational training programs.

Combating trafficking successfully requires educating people on prevention. One such program is run by the U.S. Agency for International Development. USAID/Ukraine's Trafficking Prevention Program has seven regional centers offering job skills training, hot lines, crisis prevention, and referral services to vulnerable women. More than 30,000 women have used the services provided by these centers.

We must remember that without buyers women could not be sold. That is why at the 2005 meeting of the Commission on the Status of Women, the United States introduced a resolution on eliminating the demand for trafficked women and girls. This was the first U.N. resolution addressing how demand—particularly for commercial sexual exploitation, or prostitution—fuels human trafficking. Certain countries do not want to acknowledge the important link between commercial sexual exploitation and trafficking in women and girls. However, the resolution was adopted by consensus with over 50 co-sponsors. Sadly, women are not just abused by strangers. On a trip to three Central American countries, I found that domestic violence afflicts an astonishing percentage of women and families. In a sample survey of over 300 women in Santiago and in Managua, reports of domestic violence reached 40 percent and 52 percent. I heard the same concerns from women in Latvia and the Republic of Georgia.

In many countries victims of domestic violence confront laws, or the absence of laws, that make it difficult or even dangerous to pursue justice. Many countries do not explicitly criminalize domestic violence, and even where they do, police and judges often treat it as a private or family matter and penalties are not enforced.

The United States funds education of law enforcement officers, judges, and medical personnel on the problem, trains attorneys in domestic violence prosecutions, and contributes funds for shelters and crisis centers for victims of domestic violence in many countries.

ATTACKING HIV, MUTILATION

Inequality and violence against women contribute to women's vulnerability to many things—including HIV/AIDS. Women who suffer at the hands of an intimate partner, who are raped during times of armed conflict and political instability, or are trafficked for sexual purposes are at high risk of contracting HIV. Women known or suspected to be HIV positive are especially vulnerable. They may be abused, abandoned, or even killed. Even when women are not living with HIV themselves, they bear the brunt of caring for those with the disease. Over half of the 42 million people living with HIV/AIDS today are women. Worse, among young people living with AIDS, nearly two-thirds are female. Over 2 million infected women give birth each year, transmitting HIV to newborns. Nearly 2,000 babies a day become infected with HIV during pregnancy, birth, or breastfeeding. Most of these children will die before their fifth birthday.

Because reducing mother-to-child transmission is a major U.S. priority, President Bush announced his $500 million International Mother and Child HIV Transmission Initiative, which dedicates funding specifically to prevent transmission of HIV from mothers to their newborns.

The United States' five-year, $15 billion program known as the President's Emergency Plan for AIDS Relief is working to prevent millions of new HIV infections, provide antiretroviral therapies to millions living with HIV/AIDS, and care for millions of HIV-infected individuals and AIDS orphans. The plan supports HIV/AIDS programs in 123 countries with a special focus on 15 countries in Africa, the Caribbean, and Southeast Asia representing more that half the world's infections. It also encompasses bilateral programs in nearly 100 other countries.

Women's health receives too little attention in the developing world. Each year more than 500,000 women (99 percent in developing countries) lose their lives to easily preventable complications of pregnancy and childbirth. Childbirth is the leading cause of death of women in Afghanistan, where the lifetime risk of maternal mortality is 1 in 15. The majority of maternal deaths are preventable through increased access to skilled birth attendants, antibiotics, and other currently available technology.

Last year I chaired a panel discussion at the U.N. aimed at increasing the political will so sorely needed to address this issue.

The United States has launched a $5 million initiative (REACH) to provide health-related accelerated learning and basic literacy training for women and girls in Afghanistan, including the training of midwives.

Worldwide, over the last four years, USAID has provided more than $475 million for maternal health, family planning, and reproductive health programs.

A harmful traditional practice that also threatens the health and violates the human rights of women is female genital mutilation or female circumcision, believed to prevent daughters from being unfaithful to their future husbands. Medically unqualified persons usually perform the practice—without anesthetic—on infants and girls. It may cause massive and fatal bleeding, and lead to chronic infections, sterility, and other complications.

USAID has supported activities to eliminate female genital mutilation in a number of countries. This includes training health care providers about the long-term implications of female genital mutilation and educating local communities to abandon this cultural practice.

VALUING WOMEN'S EDUCATION

Education is essential to addressing or averting every aspect of exploitation and despair, from reducing vulnerability to disease, maternal mortality, and violence to enhancing economic opportunity.

The ability to read and write is fundamental for life in today's world. Some one-sixth of the world's population is illiterate; two-thirds of the illiterate are women. Female education is strongly linked to economic development and health. For example, maternal and infant mortality is much higher—sometimes two to three times higher—among children of uneducated women compared with women with at least some secondary education.

President Bush has said, "Literacy and learning are the foundation of democracy and development. Indeed, educating women and girls raises every index of development." When you educate a man you educate an individual; when you educate a woman you educate a whole family.

Many cultures do not place value on education for women. Her value to her family is her "bride price." Parents contract a future marriage relationship for their very young daughters. A man, often much older, may pay a bride price to the family of a girl 5 to 7 years old, with a commitment to marry when she becomes "of age"—puberty.

The high dropout rate of girls in primary grades is partly explained by this practice of early marriage and pregnancy. It also encourages seeing the girl as property. Like human trafficking, treating women and girls as commodities is dehumanizing.

Some 120 million children, most of them girls, do not attend school, in part because of hunger or malnourishment. They are expected to stay at home, care for their siblings, and do household chores. Often the distance to a school poses a threat to girls' safety.

The United States leverages food aid to do more than reduce hunger. The 2003 McGovern-Dole International Food for Education and Child Nutrition Program provides children with nutritious meals as part of their education. In 38 countries around the world, this program feeds 7 million children at school. In countries where education for girls is not inherently valued, when schools provide nutritious meals, parents have more incentive to allow their daughters to be educated.

Some of the greatest education needs are found in post-conflict societies like Afghanistan and Iraq. Today, it is so hopeful to see young girls—who were forbidden by the Taliban to leave their homes unless accompanied by a male relative; who had to hide their books under their burkas—now studying math and science.

With U.S. support and the efforts of the Afghan people themselves, nearly 5 million Afghan children are enrolled in school. Of those schoolchildren, about 40 percent are girls—many more than at any point in Afghanistan's history. A new Women's Teacher Training Institute/Afghan Literacy Program, announced by our First Lady, opened in Kabul in September 2004. The Institute trains cadres of Afghan women to teach literacy throughout Afghanistan.

Similar progress is being made in Iraq, where the U.S. has renovated thousands of schools. Female attendance now exceeds pre-war rates, with girls making up some 45 percent of all primary students. U.S. programs are training teachers, and training Iraqi women in media, entrepreneurial, and democratic skills.

In 2002 President Bush launched the five-year Africa Education Initiative—to increase support for Africa's education programs by $200 million to provide 250,000 girls with scholarships and to offer teacher training.

The importance of education to securing women's rights was very evident during my recent visit to Côte d'Ivoire in West Africa. I went to train members of the recently formed Women Leaders Caucus of Côte d'Ivoire in leadership skills and the nuts and bolts of political campaigning. The women participating were well-educated professionals—professors, scientists, lawyers, pharmacists, etc., living in the capital city. They were highly motivated to run for political office and have an impact on the kind of society they live in.

By contrast, in what seemed like a time warp, we visited rural villages where the promise of education is an elusive dream. Women in these villages have little if any schooling, are married at 12 and 13, and live as little more than chattel. There, we found illiterate women hoeing fields, gathering firewood, and hunting clean water for their children. Picture women, babies on their backs, struggling under heavy loads of pineapples, water jugs, or baskets of firewood carried on their heads. Picture the dispossessed homeless widow with several small children in a culture that denies her the right to inherit her husband's property. These women—lacking education, ownership of property, or access to credit—can never be secure.

POLITICAL AND ECONOMIC RIGHTS

When women are educated, they are far less likely to fall victim to violence, poverty, or the scourge of AIDS. Women who have control over their economic assets are better able to avoid risky sexual and abusive relationships.

One key element in U.S. efforts to reduce women's vulnerability is promoting property and inheritance rights for women, which we do on the ground in many countries and in U.N. deliberations. In many ways we support entrepreneurship and women's integration into the mainstream of economic life. One of our greatest commitments is to micro-finance programs. Over the last few years our investment in these small loan and technical assistance programs—about three-quarters of which go to women—has topped $130 million. This simple tool—which may be a $100 loan to stock a stall in a market or acquire a sewing machine—gives millions of women the means to better their own lives, the lives of their families, and the economy of their countries. Huge gains for women can come from tiny investments.

To have an impact on the legal and social structures of any country, women must be a part of the political process. My own greatest accomplishment has been developing and leading negotiations at the U.N. General Assembly for a U.S. resolution urging countries to expand opportunities for women to participate in the political process. The resolution, passed by consensus with 110 co-sponsors, offers concrete steps countries and civil society can take to help reach this goal. Now I am helping to implement it in many countries.

President Bush has said, "respect for women is both a non-negotiable demand of human dignity and a foreign policy imperative of the United States."

In my work, I have seen things that have shocked and saddened me. I have met women who have energized and inspired me. And I am very proud of the work that the United States is doing to increase hope, human rights, and fundamental freedoms for women and their families.

Making the Harm Visible

At the end of the twentieth century, local and international forces have merged to escalate the sexual exploitation of women and girls. Policies, practices and crises are combining to increase both the supply of women and girls vulnerable to exploitation and the demand by men for women and girls to be used for their profit and sexual gratification. Sexual exploitation takes many forms, such as sexual harassment, incest, rape, child marriages, temporary marriages, female genital mutilation, pornography, bride trafficking, battering, sexual torture and prostitution. All of these practices violate women's dignity and autonomy.

Globally, one form of sexual exploitation, prostitution, is becoming more normalized and industrialized, with some powerful agents and institutions advocating for its widespread legitimization and legalization. As prostitution has increased, the demand for women and girls has resulted in widespread recruitment and trafficking to fill the brothels, bars and street corners.

In July 1997, a group of survivors, activists and service providers came together from Asia, Africa, Europe, South America, the Caribbean, North America and the Middle East to report on the situation for women and girls in their region and discuss efforts to combat sexual exploitation and provide services to victims. Participants in "Working With Women and Girls in Prostitution: Programs and Policies" focused on how sexual exploitation affects the physical health and mental well being of women and girls, and what obstacles prevent women and girls from escaping prostitution. Making the Harm Visible has its roots in that international meeting in New York City organized by the Coalition Against Trafficking in Women.

Making the Harm Visible is a collection of writings from women who are working to make the harm of sexual violence and exploitation visible. They speak out about their experiences, provide services to survivors, and create policies that force governments and communities to protect the rights of girls and women, not profit from their exploitation.

Women from every world region report that the sexual exploitation of women and girls is increasing. All over the world, brothels and prostitution rings exist underground on a small scale, and on an increasingly larger scale, entire sections of cities are informally zoned into brothels, bars and clubs that house, and often enslave, women for the purposes of prostitution. The magnitude and violence of these practices of sexual exploitation constitutes an international human rights crisis of contemporary slavery. In "Prostitution: A Form of Modern Slavery," Dorchen Leidholdt, the Co-executive Director of the Coalition Against Trafficking in Women, examines the definitions of slavery and shows how prostitution, and related forms of sexual exploitation, fit into defined forms of slavery.

In some parts of the world, such as the Philippines, prostitution is illegal, but well entrenched from providing "recreational services" to military personnel. In "Blazing Trails, Confronting Challenges: The Sexual Exploitation of Women and Girls in the Philippines," Aida F. Santos describes the harmful conditions for women and girls in prostitution in the Philippines, with problems related to health, violence, the legal system, and services. In other regions, such as northern Norway, organized prostitution is a more recent problem, stemming from the economic crisis in Russia. In "Russian Women in Norway," Asta Beate Håland describes how an entire community is being transformed by the trafficking of women for prostitution from Russia to campgrounds and villages across the border in Norway.

Political changes combined with economic crises have devastated entire world regions, increasing the supply of vulnerable women willing to risk their lives to earn money for themselves and their families. Aurora Javate de Dios, President of the Coalition Against Trafficking in Women, discusses the impact of the Southeast Asian economic crisis on women's lives in "Confronting Trafficking, Prostitution and Sexual

Exploitation: The Struggle for Survival and Dignity." Economic globalization controlled by a handful of multi-national corporations located in a few industrialized countries continues to shift wealth from poorer to richer countries. In her paper "Globalization, Human Rights and Sexual Exploitation," Aida F. Santos shows us the connection between global economics and the commodification and sexual exploitation of women and girls, especially in the Philippines. Structural adjustment programs implemented by international financial institutions impose loan repayment plans on poor countries, which sacrifice social and educational programs in order to service their debt to rich nations and banks. Fatoumata Sire Diakite points to structural adjustment programs as one of the factors contributing to poverty and sexual exploitation in her paper "Prostitution in Mali." Zoraida Ramirez Rodriguez writes in "Report on Latin America" that the foreign debt and policies of the International Monetary Fund (IMF) are primary factors in creating poverty for women and children. These forces leave women with few options, increasing the supply of women vulnerable to recruitment into bride trafficking and the prostitution industry.

Social problems such as sexual and physical abuse within families force girls and women to leave in search of safety and a better life, but often they find more exploitation and violence. Physical and sexual abuse of girls and women in their families and by intimate partners destroys girls' and women's sense of self and resiliency, making them easy targets for pimps and traffickers who prey on those who have few options left to them. These factors are evident in many of the papers from all world regions in this volume, such as Jill Leighton and Katherine DePasquale's, "A Commitment to Living" and Martha Daguno's, "Support Groups for Survivors of the Prostitution Industry in Manila."

Government policies and practices also fuel the demand for prostitution, as they legalize prostitution or refuse to enforce laws against pimps, traffickers and male buyers. In Making the Harm Visible, we see how countries with governmental structures and ideological foundations as different as the

Netherlands and Iran, both promote and legalize sexual violence and exploitation of girls and women. In "Legalizing Pimping, Dutch Style," Marie-Victoire Louis exposes the liberal laws and policies that legalize prostitution and tolerate brothels in the Netherlands. On the other extreme, religious fundamentalists in Iran have legalized the sexual exploitation of girls and women in child and temporary marriages and the sexual torture of women in prison. Sarvnaz Chitsaz and Soona Samsami document this harm and violation of human rights in "Iranian Women and Girls: Victims of Exploitation and Violence."

Global media and communication tools, such as the Internet, make access to pornography, catalogs of mail order brides, advertisements for prostitution tours, and information on where and how to buy women and girls in prostitution widely available. This open advertisement normalizes and increases the demand by men for women and girls to use in these different forms of exploitation. Donna M. Hughes describes her findings on how the Internet is being used to promote the sexual exploitation of women and children in "The Internet and the Global Prostitution Industry." In this milieu, women and girls become commodities-bought and sold locally and trafficked from one part of the world to another.

How do we make the harm of sexual exploitation visible? In a world where sexual exploitation is increasingly normalized and industrialized what is needed to make people see the harm and act to stop it? The women in Making the Harm Visible recommend four ways to make the harm of sexual exploitation visible: listen to the experiences of survivors, expose the ideological constructions that hide the harm, expose the agents that profit from the sexual exploitation of women and children, and document harm and conduct research that reveals the harm and offers findings that can be used for policy initiatives.

First, listen to the experiences of survivors. The contributors to this volume speak eloquently, passionately and urgently for the voices of survivors to be heard and used as the basis for a global movement against sexual exploitation. The power of survivors' testimony and their visible participation in political struggle is emphasized. The survivor testimonies of Jill Leighton,

Alexia, Christine Grussendorf and Jenny speak clearly about the violence perpetrated against women and children in prostitution. In her poem, "They Are Showing Your Face," Victoria Marinelli shows us the harm of media sensationalization, which further exploits the victims of sexual abuse and exploitation. The sexual abuse, exploitation and torture of women political prisoners is recounted by Ladan Pardeshenas in "Women's Activism for Freedom in Iran" and by Aida F. Santos in the Philippines in "Memories." Malka Marcovich, in "The Violence of Silence: Survivor Testimony in Political Struggle," calls upon her experience in interviewing the survivors of Nazi Germany's "final solution" to argue the importance of survivor testimony in a movement against violence. Angel Cassidy strongly and succinctly states the need to speak out about the violence and exploitation in "Never Be Quiet." And in "Not Sex Work," Victoria Marinelli gives us her manifesto against redefining sexual exploitation as "sex work."

Second, expose the ideological constructions that hide and excuse the violence, exploitation and harm. We are bombarded with misinformation and ideological constructions of prostitution and other forms of sexual exploitation that make the harm invisible, benefit the sex industry and provide cover for the men who buy and exploit women and girls. We need to expose the explicit and implicit rationales used to justify the sexual exploitation of women and girls. Contributors to Making the Harm Visible challenge the excuses men use for exploiting women and children, and call for everyone to do the same. The oldest excuse is the biological determinist one that men have to have sex. If they don't have a wife or available partner, then buying a woman or using a child is the only alternative. Men often escape accountability for the harm they inflict by this simple, but false, assumption. The same underlying thinking applies to men in the military, who supposedly need to buy women as part of "rest and relaxation." In the papers from the Philippines and Cambodia, the presence of military personnel is sited as resulting in increased sexual exploitation of indigenous women. In "Corregidor Tales," Aida F. Santos describes the underground remnants of cells where "comfort women" were kept in sexual slavery for Japanese military personnel during World War II.

Historically, patriarchal religious ideologies have justified the sexual abuse and exploitation of women and girls in many forms, including child marriages, temporary marriages, and women's lack of sexual autonomy. In the paper on Iran, several forms of sexual exploitation of women and girls have been legally instated under fundamentalist rule. In "Trafficking and Prostitution in Bangladesh: Contradictions in Law and Practice," Sigma Huda describes the no-win situation that girls and women face after being trafficked or prostituted. In countries to which Bangladeshi girls are trafficked, such as Pakistan, the victims face long prison sentences for illegal entry into the country, or under harsh Islamic law, can be stoned to death for fornication.

Liberal ideologies about sexuality also overlook the harm of exploitation by uncritically viewing all sexual activity, including prostitution, as forms of sexual expression that should be permitted and protected as individual choices and rights. This sexual liberal philosophy merges with the neoliberal economic policies and practices to rename prostitution as "sex work." This reconfiguration of sexual exploitation is condemned by numerous contributors to Making the Harm Visible.

The contributors to this volume also ask us to critically examine explanations of prostitution that search for the cause of "self-destructive behaviors" in girls or women's personal deficits and defects. Although women in prostitution often suffer from drug and alcohol addiction, several of the authors urge us to see this as a symptom of the harm of prostitution, not as the root cause. Although, several authors discuss poverty and economic crisis as factors in compelling women and girls into prostitution, they remind us that this is what is fueling the supply, but equally important is men's demand for women and girls they can buy.

Third, expose the agents that advocate for and profit from the normalization and legalization of sexual exploitation, whether they be individual men who buy women in prostitution, or governments and United Nations bodies that advocate for legalization of prostitution or the recognition of the prostitution industry as a legitimate economic sector. The Dutch government has legalized prostitution, legalized brothels and is putting into place a system of taxation to profit from the prostitution industry. The Netherlands is the leading advocate for the legalization of prostitution and redefinition of trafficking of women to include only those women who can prove they were coerced or deceived into prostitution. In "Human Rights: A European Challenge?" Malka Marcovich describes efforts to set new standards that will deprive women of their human rights in Europe as the European Union is being constructed. Mary Sullivan, in "Marketing Women in Australia" describes how Australia is incorporating legalized prostitution into its economic and tourism plan. In "Legalizing Prostitution: Legitimating Abuse," Donna M. Hughes argues against the legalization of prostitution in Eastern and Central Europe as a way to combat the trafficking of women from that region.

Fourth, document the harm and conduct research on sexual exploitation. The harm of sexual exploitation often remains invisible until someone focuses their attention on it and documents their findings. Often issues need to be theoretically reframed and different questions posed. Several women, Jill Leighton, Jenny, and Norma Hotaling, point out that even when there are visible signs of trauma in women's and girls' lives, no one asks the simple question: "What has happened to you in your life?" The contributors use their findings to describe and analyze the forces that compel women and girls into conditions of exploitation and, often, slavery. In "Strip Clubs According to Strippers," Kelly Holsopple systematically asks women about the verbal, physical and sexual violence that they were subjected to while working as strippers. Norma Hotaling reports on research she and others have done on violence against women in prostitution in "Women in Prostitution in the United States."

In "The Health Effects of Prostitution," Janice G. Raymond surveys previous research and reports on the multiple physical and mental health problems suffered by women in prostitution, many of which lead to shortened lives or death. The contributors to Making the Harm Visible urge us to ask different research questions about the demand from men to sexually exploit women and girls and the rationales that are used to justify this violence. The Research Project on Men and Prostitution in Japan provides us with a strong quantitative base and framework on which to examine men's use of women in prostitution. In "Why Men Buy Women in Prostitution," the findings from a survey of 2000 men on their use and attitudes towards prostitution are reported.

One of the most glaring problems in combating sexual exploitation is the lack of assistance for its victims. The need for services is poignantly evident in Minerva Kalenandi's testimony, "You Need Some Place to Escape To," in which she describes being turned away from a domestic violence shelter even though she had sustained serious injuries from a pimp. Compared to services for other victims of violence, there a few services for prostituted women, resulting in women receiving little or inappropriate treatment. Since prostituted women are viewed with prejudice, they are often treated disrespectfully in treatment programs. Also, since few mainstream service providers recognize the harm in prostitution, the trauma the women have suffered is not addressed.

Innovative programs for women escaping sexual exploitation that address the harm caused to victims, though few in number, have been created in many world regions. Numerous contributors to this volume report on the services they are providing to victims of sexual exploitation. They describe innovative work and share ideas on programs and projects to assist women and girls. The founders of these programs bring a feminist analysis to the multiple problems faced by women and girls in situations of sexual exploitation. The women and girls are treated with respect and care to restore their dignity.

In "She Let Me Talk and She Listened," Jill Leighton describes how the simple act of listening can save a life. The workers and volunteers in these agencies reach out to women and girls on the street and in jails. In "Phoenix Rising," Kathleen Mitchell relates how the plan for Dignity House was conceived while she herself was in jail after being arrested for prostitution.

Many of the service providers in this volume were themselves prostituted women who know first hand the lack of services for women trying to escape prostitution. In Phnom Phen, Cambodia, girls who have escaped brutality and slavery in brothels can find services at the Cambodian Women's Crisis Center. A representative from this newly found center writes about "The Sale of Women and Girls to Brothels in Cambodia."

The contributors describe model programs that provide services to women and girl victims of sexual exploitation and create a space for survivors to come to together to heal and find their voices to speak out and organize. In "Support Group for Survivors of the Prostitution Industry in Manila," Martha Daguno describes the first survivor's group to be set-up in the Philippines. Other agencies and organizations, such as BUKAL (meaning spring), and Women's Education, Development, Productivity and Research Organization (WEDPRO) are pioneers in developing services for sexually exploited women in the Philippines. Their efforts are chronicled by Aida F. Santos in "Blazing Trails, Confronting Challenges."

The involvement and leadership by survivors is emphasized in many programs. Working on an empowerment model these organizations work through peer educators. In "Casa de Passagem in Brazil," Ana Vasconcelos describes the empowerment and peer education model she uses with homeless street girls in Brazil. Norma Hotaling, in "First Offender Prostitution Program in San Francisco," describes their survivor run peer support program.

Women and girls trying to escape prostitution face fearsome odds. In "Breaking Free," Vednita Carter describes many of the obstacles the women face and their Afrocentric approach to providing services in Minnesota, USA. Pimps and perpetrators prey on the most vulnerable women and girls. Girls with disabilities are often targeted for exploitation because of their vulnerability. Claudia Vigil describes the work of the Homahi Foundation and its programs for mothers with special needs in "Prostitution and Mothers with Special Needs in Argentina." Services for victims of sexual exploitation receive little attention or support in most communities. Marlene Sandoval started the

Psycho-Social Rehabilitation Center in Chile in one room in a house with no running water. She reports on the work of the center in this volume.

Some services to women escaping prostitution are combined with community education and programs that confront men's harm to women. SAGE (Standing Against Global Exploitation) in San Francisco is the 1998 winner of the Harvard University Kennedy School of Government's Award for Innovations in Government for their cooperative work with the District Attorney's office to create a program commonly referred to as "the John's School." Norma Hotaling describes their original and successful work to reeducate men about the harm they cause in "The First Offender Prostitution Program in San Francisco."

Another important aspect to ending the sexual exploitation of women and girls is prevention. Zoraida Ramirez Rodriguez describes her education and prevention programs for schools and community organizations in "Preventative Action Against Prostitution in Venezuela."

Although the women in this volume come from all regions of the world, they share common goals and attitudes. They are survivors and visionaries who are not afraid to confront overwhelming problems and remain steadfast in their work. Most of them know that their goal of ending the sexual exploitation of women and girls is nothing less than revolutionary.

In "Surviving Sexual Slavery: Women in Search of Freedom," Chris Grussendorf writes graphically, with a searing analysis, about what is done to women in situations of torturous sexual abuse and exploitation in prostitution rings. She also forcefully proclaims the sustenance and aspiration of the women in resistance to sexual exploitation, "We stay alive because we are women in search of our lives; we are women in search of freedom. I stayed alive because my belief in something better than what they offered was greater than their hatred and destruction. I stayed alive because I wanted to be free, more than anything, I wanted to be free. I wanted to live in a world of respect." Organization and activism by women is essential to create change and end violence against women and sexual exploitation. In "Women United Can Make a Difference: The Situation in Spain and the European Union," Asuncion Miura describes how women working together changed public attitudes about violence against women and created services to assist victims of battering.

Sarvnaz Chitsaz and Soona Samsami relate the importance of women's leadership in political and social activism to end of women's oppression and usher in true equality for women and girls in the world. Women must undertake the work of organization and advocacy for women because it is not in the interests of men to do this work, although there are a few men willing to stand against the oppression of women. These writers understand that when the deepest forms of exploitation, violence and oppression are named, challenged and ended and all the victims healed, there will be a true social, economic and political revolution for women.

WOMAN'S CONSCIOUSNESS, MAN'S WORLD

The capitalist mode of production has penetrated farther and deeper than any other form of production. Geographically it has extended its technology in search of markets; politically it has devised the most ingenious methods of control in its own interests; economically it has created means of production, which are wonderful in their productive capacity and terrifying in their devastation. Its industry has devoured human labor power and human intelligence. In its search for raw materials it has laid waste the land and is beginning to exhaust even the sea. Worse, its version of itself has entered the souls and spirits of millions of men and women, so we no longer know what is our own and what is alienated to capital.

The antagonisms it generates produce the shifts and fissures that make the growth of new movements possible. In quiet times the hope of liberation grows lichenlike on inhospitable rock. In times of upheaval new growths can take root. In order to change capitalism we have to understand how it is made, how it moves, and how it came into being. We have to see how it is different from, or related to, other forms of production, how it is hinged together. It is a foxy old thing, wily at dealing with the opposition it brings into being, whether its opponent is the working class or movements for black or women's liberation.

The predicament of being born a woman in capitalism is specific. The social situation of women and the way in which we learn to be feminine is peculiar to us. Men do not share it, consequently we cannot be simply included under the general heading of "mankind." The only claim that this word has to be general comes from the dominance of men in society. As the rulers they presume to define others by their own criteria.

Women are not the same as other oppressed groups. Unlike the working class which has no need for the capitalist under socialism, the liberation of women does not mean that men will be eliminated. Sex and class are not the same. Similarly people from oppressed races have a memory of a cultural alternative somewhere in the past. Women have only myths made by men. We have to recognize our biological distinctness but this does not mean that we should become involved in an illusory hunt for our lost "nature."

The oppression of women differs too from class and race because it has not come out of capitalism and imperialism. The sexual division of labor and the possession of women by men predates capitalism. Patriarchal authority is based on male control over the woman's productive capacity, and over her person. This control existed before the development of capitalist commodity production. It belonged to a society in which the persons of human beings were owned by others. Patriarchy, however, is contradicted by the dominant mode of production in capitalism because in capitalism the owner of capital owns and controls the labor power but not the persons of his laborers.

In order to act effectively we have to try to work out the precise relationship between the patriarchal dominance of men over women, and the property relations which come from this, to class exploitation and racism. In order to understand the traces of patriarchy which have persisted into the present, it is essential to see what part patriarchy played in pre-capitalist society. The dominance of men over women in the past was more clearly a property relation than it is now. When a man married in a society in which production was only marginally beyond subsistence, he married a "yoke-fellow" whose labor was crucial if he were to prosper. Her procreative capacity was important not only because of the high infant mortality rate but also because children meant more hands to labor.

The family was a collective working group. The father was its head, but for survival the labor of wife and children was necessary. The introduction of individual wages and the end of the ownership of people in serfdom did not dissolve the economic and social control of men over women. The man remained the head of the family unit of production and he retained control over the ownership of property through primogeniture. Both his wife's capacity to labor and her capacity to bear his children were still part of his stock in the world. Moreover, the notion that this was part of the order of things was firmly embedded in all political, religious, and educational institutions.

Although capitalism temporarily strengthened the control over women by middleand upper-class men in the nineteenth century by removing them from production, it has tended to whittle away at the economic and ideological basis of patriarchy. As wage labor became general and the idea spread in society that it was unjust to own other people, although the exploitation of their labor power was considered perfectly fair, the position of the daughter and the wife appeared increasingly anomalous. Ironically, middle-class women came to the conviction that their dependence on men and the protection of patriarchal authority were intolerable precisely at a time when the separation of work from home was shattering the economic basis of patriarchy among the working class.

The factories meant that the economic hold of men over women in the working-class family was weakened. Machinery meant that tasks formerly done by men could be done by women. The woman's wage packet gave her some independence. Ideologically, however, men's hold persisted among workers and was nurtured by the male ruling class. Subsequently by continually reducing the scope of production, by developing the separation between home and work, and by reducing the time spent in procreation, a great army of women workers has been "freed" for exploitation in the commodity system. This integration of married women into the labor market has been especially noticeable in the advanced capitalist countries since the Second World War.... The result in terms of women's consciousness at work is only now beginning to be felt. While the dissolution of the extended kinship networks has produced in the nuclear family a streamlined unit suitable for modern capitalism, it has forced an examination of the relationships of man to woman and parent to child.

The struggle of the early feminist movement for legal and political equality and the assumptions it has bequeathed to women now, despite the degeneration of its radical impulse, have strained the hold of patriarchy in the capitalist state, though without dislodging it. The power of the working class within capitalism and the growth of new kinds of political movements recently, particularly for black liberation, have touched the consciousness of women and brought many of us to question the domination of men over women. This has taken a political shape, in the new feminism of women's liberation.

The development of contraceptive technology in capitalism means that ideas of sexual liberation can begin to be realized. The fact that sexual pleasure now need not necessarily result in procreation means a new dimension of liberation in the relation of men and women is possible. It also removes some of patriarchy's most important sanctions against rebellion. The right to determine our own sexuality, to control when or if we want to give birth, and to choose who and how we want to love are central in both women's liberation and in gay liberation. All these are most subversive to patriarchy.

However, although capitalism has itself eroded patriarchy and has brought into being movements and ideas which are both anti-capitalist and anti-patriarchal, it still maintains the subordination of women as a group. Patriarchy has continued in capitalism as an ever present prop in time of need. Although women are not literally the property of men, the continuation of female production in the family means that women have not yet even won the right to be exploited equally. The wage system in capitalism has continued to be structured according to the assumption that women's labor is worth half that of men on the market. Behind this is the idea that women are somehow owned by men who should support them. Women are thus seen as economic attachments to men, not quite as free laborers. Their wage is still seen as supplementary. If a woman has no man she is seen as a sexual failure and the inference is often that she is a slut as well. She also has to struggle to bring up a family alone, on half a man's income. This very simple economic fact about the position of women in capitalism acts as a bribe to keep women with men: it has no regard for feeling or suffering and makes a mockery of any notion of choice or control over how we live. It also means that women make up a convenient reserve army which will work at half pay and can be reabsorbed back into the family if there is unemployment.

Equal pay is obviously only the beginning of an answer to this. The inequality of women at work is built into the structure of capitalist production and the division of labor in industry and in the family. The equality of women to men, even the equal exploitation of women in capitalism, would require such fundamental changes in work and at home that it is very hard to imagine how they could be effected while capitalism survives. Our labor in the family goes unrecognized except as an excuse to keep us out of the better jobs in industry and accuse us of absenteeism and unreliability.

This separation between home and work, together with the responsibility of women for housework and child care, serves to perpetuate inequality. Women, as a group in the labor force, are badly paid and underprivileged. This is not only economically profitable to capitalism, it has proved a useful political safety valve. It is quite handy for capitalism if wives can be persuaded to oppose their husbands on strike or if men console themselves for their lack of control at work with the right to be master in their own home. Because production in the family differs from commodity production we learn to feel that it is not quite work. This undermines our resentment and makes it harder to stress that it should be eliminated as much as possible not only by technology, but by new styles of living, new buildings, and new forms of social care for the young, the sick, and the old.

In capitalism housework and child care are lumped together. In fact they are completely different. Housework is drudgery, which is best reduced by mechanizing and socializing it, except for cooking, which can be shared. Caring for small children is important and absorbing work, which does not mean that one person should have to do it all the time. But we are taught to think there is something wrong with us if we seek any alternative. The lack of facilities for children and the rigid structuring of work and the division of labor between the sexes again makes choice impossible.

Propaganda about our feminine role helps to make us accept this state of affairs. Values linger on after the social structures which conceived them. Our ideas of what is "feminine" are a strange bundle of assumptions, some of which belong to the Victorian middle class and others which simply rationalize the form patriarchy assumes in capitalism. Either way the notion of "femininity" is a convenient means of making us believe submission is somehow natural. When we get angry we are called hysterical.

Thus, although capitalism has eroded the forms of production and property ownership which were the basis of patriarchy, it has still retained the domination of men over women in society. This domination continues to pervade economic, legal, social, and sexual life.

It is not enough to struggle for particular reforms, important as these are. Unless we understand the relationship of the various elements within the structure of male-dominated capitalism, we will find the improvements we achieve are twisted against us or serve one group at the expense of the rest. For example, the wider dissemination of contraceptive information and the weakening of guilt about our sexuality have meant a major improvement in the lives of many women. However, the removal of fear alone is not enough because relations between the sexes are based on the ownership of property—property consisting not only of the woman's labor in procreation, but also of her body. Therefore, while class, race, and sex domination remain a constituent element of relations between men and women, women and women, and men and men, these relations will continue to be distorted. Sexual liberation in capitalism can thus continue to be defined by men and also continue to be competitive. The only difference between this and the old set-up is that when patriarchy was secure, men measured their virility by the number of children they produced. Now they can apply more "suitable" means of assessing masculinity in a use-and-throw-away society and simply notch up sexual conquests.

There are other examples of feminist reforms being distorted by the structure of capitalist society. We are far from the situation of baby farms and state-controlled breeding, but these are the lines along which pure capitalism, shorn of the remnants of earlier forms of production, would develop. Similarly, one group of women can be bought off at the expense of another, young women against old, middle class against working class. If we are ready to settle for a slightly bigger bite of the existing cake for a privileged section, we will merely create gradations among the underprivileged. We will not change the context in which women are inferior. For instance, in Britain there has been some discussion about giving women better jobs in management and promoting secretaries because they will work harder for less pay. Capitalism is not based on the organization of production for people, but simply on the need to secure maximum profit. It is naive to expect that it will make exceptions of women.

It is impossible now to predict whether capitalism could accommodate itself to the complete elimination of all earlier forms of property and production and specifically to the abolition of patriarchy. But it is certain that the kind of accommodation it could make would provide no real solution for women when we are unable to labor in commodity production because we are pregnant: socially helpless people protected in capitalism are not only treated as parasites who are expected to show gratitude, but are under the direct power of the state. Also class and race cut across sexual oppression. A feminist movement that is confined to the specific oppression of women cannot, in isolation, end exploitation and imperialism.

We have to keep struggling to go beyond our own situation. This means recognizing that the emphases that have come out of women's liberation are important not only to ourselves. The capacity to bring into conscious combination the unorganizable, those who distrust one another, who have been taught to despise themselves, and the connection that comes out of our practice between work and home, personal and political, are of vital significance to other movements in advanced capitalism. Similarly, the comprehension in women's liberation of the delicate mechanism of communication between the structures of capitalist society and the most hidden part of our secret selves is too important not to become part of the general theory and practice of the Left. Women's liberation has mounted an attack on precisely those areas where socialists have been slow to resist capitalism: authoritarian social relationships, sexuality and the family. We have to struggle for control not merely over the means of production but over the conditions of reproduction.

The problem about how a revolutionary theory can come out of a day-to-day practice defined by the existence of capitalism has long bedeviled revolutionary socialism. The concept of the Leninist party as the conscious embodiment of an alternative has become dubious because the party in reality will still express the viewpoint of sections which are the stronger within capitalism, most obviously men, for example.

Moreover, the party itself can become absorbed in the immediate problem of surviving within capitalism rather than in the task of exposing contradictions and seeking revolutionary transformation. The mobilization of new groups within capitalism against a specific form of oppression is thus very important, but more important still is the means of translating the experience of one group to another without merely annexing the weaker to the stronger. Thus it is not just groups that have a position of power at the point of production in the advanced sectors of the capitalist economy, but the organization of groups whose consciousness spans several dimensions of oppression that becomes crucial in a revolutionary movement. This is not an idealization of weakness. Women as a group are extremely vulnerable within capitalism, but because of our social situation we are forced to find the means of going beyond our own specific oppression.

The blocks against us are very real; male domination permeates every organization within capitalism including trade unions and revolutionary groups, and the problem of how to safeguard our autonomy while making a strategy of organizing with men is a persistent dilemma in the women's movement.

Nor is this an evasion of the urgent problem of making an offensive organization which is capable of overcoming the tremendous resources of the advanced capitalist state. The substitution of the women's movement for such an organization would be most evidently absurd.

Although we have the capacity to go beyond our own predicament, and although alternatives must be continually drawn out of our day-to-day struggle to defend women against capitalism, neither our structure, nor our politics, are the same as those of a revolutionary organization. We come into women's liberation out of our specific predicament as women, not as people who necessarily are committed to the creation of socialism. We are, moreover, essentially a partial organization representing a specific group.

There are no short-cuts. The making of a revolutionary socialist organization that is capable of taking the offensive without being either absorbed or smashed, which can at once safeguard the interests of the groups within it and not simply reproduce the structures of authority and domination that belong to capitalism, is a gigantic task. Autonomy and cohesive organization in the face of repression go uncomfortably together. The models of the past can help us, but do not fit the special problems of the modern capitalist state. However, the political process of making an effective movement for the liberation of women-which means a movement in which workingclass women are in the majority-is an essential part of this task.

FORCING MILLIONS OF WOMEN INTO THE SEX TRADE

A short play staged by a Filipino theatre group has become a popular feature on the international conference circuit, given the powerful message it conveys-women are abused when they are lured into the international sex trade by criminal gangs.

Written by Maria Paulin-Ballesteros, the play draws a parallel between women subjected to sexual exploitation and a chicken dish that is a favourite in the Philippines, 'lechon manok'. And Paulin-Ballesteros describes her work, titled We're Syndicated, Ma'am, as a 'fowl play'.

This Filipino human rights activist was inspired to write the play after attending an international forum, where three Filipino women narrated their plight after being forced into the sex trade in Nigeria. And the response the play has received-through its live performance or a videotaped account, in Asia, Europe and North America-has satisfied Paulin-Ballesteros.

'While Filipino consumers crave the lechon manok, male customers around the world are going crazy over their young women,' she told a Filipino newspaper in an interview. Paulin-Ballesteros' concern has been echoed by other human rights activists, who are equally worried about the rapid rise of women being transported around the world for the sex industry. Currently, according to available reports, close to two million women have been forced into 'sex slavery'.

In February, Regan Ralph, the executive director of the women's rights division of the United States-based Human Rights Watch (HRW), underscored the urgency for an international response to such abuse during his testimony before the US Senate's committee on foreign relations. HRW has been involved in documenting and monitoring this 'serious human rights violation' for many years, Ralph revealed. 'We have reported on the trafficking of women and girls from Bangladesh to Pakistan, from Burma to Thailand and from Nepal to India.'

In his view, the current trafficking in women is 'a slavery-like practice that must be eliminated', since it involves the 'illegal and highly profitable transport and sale of human beings for the purpose of exploiting their labour'.

He even exposed its prevalence in the United States. In August 1999, for instance, a trafficking ring was broken up in the southern state of Georgia that transported up to 1,000 women from several Asian countries into the United States and '(forced) them to work in brothels across the country'.

Similar evidence was presented in late February at a public hearing before the European Parliament. Close to 500,000 women are smuggled into Western Europe every year, experts said. According to researchers, nearly 60% of the women forced into the sex industry in some Western European countries are controlled by Russian and Albanian criminal networks.

NO CONTROL

The situation in Britain illustrates this scenario. According to research conducted by the University of North London's Child and Women Abuse Studies Unit, six out of 10 women in London's brothels have been 'trafficked' from countries such as the Ukraine. The study added that the 'criminal gangs trafficking prostitutes are not confining their activities to major cities'.

And once the women arrive in Britain, they are informed by the gangs responsible for their journey that they owe the gangs 'thousands of pounds for accommodation, fees to the brothel and advertising'.

In most cases, the manner in which women have been trapped into the sex industry hardly differs, say rights activists. The woman is approached with the promise of a good job in another country, 'and lacking better options at home, she agrees to migrate'.

Once overseas, however, she is delivered to her employer. In these new surroundings, the woman has 'no control over the nature or place of work, or the terms or conditions of her employment'. What is more, when the woman learns she has 'been deceived about the nature of the work', she finds escape 'both difficult and dangerous', given the coercive and abusive situations in the brothels.

Kevin Bales, a lecturer in sociology at the University of Surrey, in Britain, sees this explosion of 'modern slavery' as a result of many factors, among which are 'corruption' in governments and the 'silence' that has encouraged it.

In his book, Disposable People: New Slavery in the Global Economy, Bales argues that the international community needs to perceive the difference between modern slavery and slavery as it was known before the Atlantic slave trade of 200 years ago.

'If you insist on defining slavery as 'the legal ownership of one person by another' then slavery has pretty much disappeared. But the key to slavery is not ownership, but control through violence...(or its threat). Couple that with economic exploitation in which someone is paid nothing and you have a good working definition of the new slavery that encompasses about 27 million people around the world,' he says.

Human rights groups, too, have brought to light that aspect of the sex industry. The United Nations Office of the High Commissioner for Human Rights (UNHCR), for instance, defines trafficking as a situation where someone is persuaded, tricked or forced into leaving their country for the promise of a 'better life', only to end up in forced or slavery-like conditions.

But to guarantee the rights of these women, most rights groups feel that new international standards are required, including a broadening of the definition of 'trafficking', harsher punishment for those involved in the international trafficking of women, and guaranteeing that the victims have an opportunity to seek 'remedies and redress for the human rights violations they have suffered'.

And rights activists have stepped up their efforts to achieve such guarantees from the international community, given a projected UN convention that is due to be taken up this year-the UN Convention on Transnational Organised Crime. To end this cycle of human trafficking, they add, the language of this convention should not be watered down. For that would be 'extremely detrimental to women'.

Marwaan Macan-Markar is a correspondent for the Inter Press Service, with whose permission the above article is reprinted.

OLDER WOMEN'S HEALTH: FACING THE CHALLENGES

The health concerns of older women require special attention, especially in a changing social milieu in which there are fewer people around to care for them.

In a region where women continue to be valued less than men, older women's health reflects their life-long experience of discrimination, deprivation and neglect. The older women of Asia-Pacific today faced similar situations of poverty, malnutrition, poor health care, physical overwork and unhealthy work environments in their younger years. Along with high infant mortality rates, they faced high maternal mortality, maternal morbidity and reproductive tract infections.

To add to all these, few of them received immunisation as children or benefited from the public health interventions that have developed since. Consequently, the diseases of the older years such as maturity onset diabetes, Alzheimer's disease, osteoporosis, stroke, heart disease, arthritis and cancer are superimposed on an already compromised state of health.

These are acute issues facing the societies of the Asia-Pacific region. As life expectancy increases and fertility rates continue to decline, the region would see in the coming years more older persons, particularly older women, needing care and fewer people available to care for them.

Recognising this growing trend, the 1995 Beijing Platform for Action emphasised that older women's '...health concerns require particular attention. The long-term health prospects of women are influenced by changes at menopause, which, in combination with life-long conditions and other factors, such as poor nutrition and lack of physical activity, may increase the risk of cardiovascular disease and osteoporosis.

Other diseases of ageing and the interrelationships of ageing and disability among women also need particular attention.' In an effort to call for the non-marginalisation of older people, which includes older women, the United Nations declared 1999 as the International Year of Older Persons, with the theme, 'Towards a Society for All Ages'.

DIVERSE REALITIES, COMMON PROBLEMS

Traditionally, women gained value, status and authority within their family and community as they became older, for their wisdom and nurturing role as grandmothers. With modernisation and urbanisation, traditional families are giving way to nuclear families-a single set of parents, their children and a grandparent or two. In this setting and with the growing need for families to have multiple incomes to survive, grandparents, especially grandmothers, have become convenient babysitters whose medical needs are addressed within the economic constraints of the family. Such a responsibility comes at a time when these women expect to have the freedom to focus on their own needs and begin to experience a range of health issues related to ageing. Caring for young children is a demanding task that can isolate women, particularly women who lack financial and social resources to create a support network to maintain their physical and emotional well-being. These burdens would be particularly felt by older migrant women who do not speak the local language of the host country (e.g. older women sponsored by their children to enter and stay in a foreign country).

Longer lives coupled with the tradition of marrying older men means that more women will face the loneliness and vulnerability of widowhood. With a spouse's death, older women face a significant loss of economic security. Discriminatory inheritance laws regarding parental and spousal property greatly contribute to their vulnerable economic situation. Thus, widows bcome financially dependent on their children, while single older women may have no one to turn to but the state. In several South-East Asian countries, older women who came as migrants from other parts of Asia worked in the informal sector to support their families back home. Few of them had access to state pension schemes. Today, they have practically no savings and are financially helpless.

Older women are vulnerable to violence from bot' their families and society. The risk increases with their loss of independence. The violence is physical and emotional. Glorification of youth in the modern culture has created negative stereotypes of the elderly, particularly older women, and they are subjected to much abuse as a result of ageism. Widows may suffer from violence by their own children or by relatives. For married older women, they may have suffered a history of violence since their younger years.

ADDRESSING THE HEALTH NEEDS OF OLDER WOMEN

Clearly, the lack of health policies, programmes and services that address women's health needs from a life-cycle and holistic approach greatly affects their lives as they age. Special attention should be given to adequately meeting the specific physical, emotional and mental health needs of women aged 50 to 60, 70 to 80 and over 80. The views of older women are therefore important for any health policy and service development to be effective in addressing older women's realities. Mechanisms need to be put in place which would allow these women to be actively involved in the planning, design and implementation of health policies and programmes which concern their own health and that of their community. Care for older women must consider their pre-existing state of health and address their overall health-care needs instead of merely treating the immediate medical problem.

Due to their increased vulnerability in their later years, the issues of cost, quality and mobility or location of healthcare services would have to be considered carefully. Policies which promote parental care and support by the children need to be supplemented by appropriate support mechanisms (such as state-supported income security schemes), and high-quality affordable health and residential care for those older women who are unable to rely on family support. It is also imperative that boys and men are socialised into caring and nurturing roles so that the burden of caring for elders does not fall on women alone. Governments need to be committed to their social responsibility in the area of health and be ready to support effective community-based initiatives in meeting older women's health needs.

It is important to recognise that the ageing process, for some women, may be about declining health, frailty, emotional vulnerability and even senility. For other women, the ageing process may be a very positive experience. Nevertheless, decision-makers who plan policies and programmes for older women must recognise that active ageing will not circumvent the need for adequate care-giving, which can sometimes be intensive in nature. While it is true that older women have many contributions to make, their right to finally take a break from commitments and responsibilities in their old age should not be overlooked. Older women are not only survivors-they have made their contributions to society. In return, society should give them space to seek self-fulfillment.

10

THE TASK OF WOMAN IN THE MODERN WORLD

"The important thing for a country is that the men should be manly, the women womanly." This comment of Chesterton's embodies a fundamental principle of social order. In society, as in any organism, unity and order are achieved through the cooperation of very different members, each fulfilling his own functions and contributing his special qualities to the common good.

The deepest difference among human beings—far more fundamental than any difference of intelligence or ability, nation or race—is the difference of sex. "And God created man to His own image: to the image of God He created him; male and female He created them." This basic difference is not merely physical but also psychological, coloring the total personality. In the whole range of her being—her mind, her senses, her emotions, her will, her interests and reactions—woman differs profoundly from man.

It is obviously of the greatest importance that this difference find its proper expression in the social functions of the two sexes. Each has unique qualities to contribute to the enrichment of human life. It is essential for the full and harmonious development of society, and especially for a Christian society, that "the men should be manly, the women womanly." Man and woman are made to complement each other at every point. Man's capacity for theory, for forming an abstract and comprehensive view, is matched by woman's practical sense and her gift for detail. Man's ambition and self-assertion which spur him on to great achievement must be balanced by the creative power of woman's spirit of sacrifice and self-surrender. Man's ability for leadership and desire for power must be tempered by woman's spirit of love and selfless devotion.

The undue predominance of either masculine or feminine qualities creates profound disturbances which reverberate throughout the entire social structure, as we can see in our own culture. Western European civilization under the influence of Protestantism, rationalism, liberalism, and other secularizing trends, has become progressively more masculine in the last four centuries. Ours is a culture of the self-assertion of man: of man's reason and scientific method in the intellectual sphere; of man's will to power and conquest in business and world affairs; of man's independence of God in all aspects of life. In our time we need women with a vision of their great task as women who will help to restore the social equilibrium by creating a vital current of the great womanly virtues: the spirit of love, compassion for the suffering, generous self-sacrifice. As women our fundamental contribution to the new order lies in finding our proper role in society. Our most urgent task in the work of reconstruction is to face this problem: What is the function of woman in the social order?

THE UNIVERSAL MISSION OF WOMAN

Woman's essential mission in the world is to be for mankind a living example of the spirit of total dedication to God. To love God with her whole heart, her whole mind, her whole strength, and to radiate that love to the world—this is the universal task of woman. It is true that every human being is made for the love of God and is meant to be totally consecrated to His praise. In what sense, then, can we say that it is the particular mission of woman to be both an example and guide of man along the way of dedication?

There are two poles, two principles in human nature. Father Gerald Vann, O. P., in his recent book, "The Heart of Man," distinguishes these two basic tendencies as "man the maker" and "man the lover." Both principles are present to some extent in every human being, but man the maker is realized most perfectly in man; man the lover in woman. It is the maker who asserts, who imposes his idea and his will on the surroundings. The race takes its forward motion along the way of organization and invention from him. It is man the lover who gives, who yields his own will and gladly surrenders not only his will but his very self to the beloved.

Mankind has always recognized that love plays a far greater role in woman's life than in man's. Every woman when she looks into her own heart finds there the deep desire to surrender herself completely in love. Woman is by nature total in her giving; love absorbs her whole being. Byron was expressing the common experience of mankind when he wrote:

"Man's love is of man's life a thing apart
'Tis Woman's whole existence."

In relation to God, we must all fulfill the role of the lover, awaiting the divine initiative, surrendering completely to the divine will. As C. S. Lewis writes so beautifully, "Our role must be always that of patient to agent, female to male, mirror to light, echo to voice. Our highest activity must be response, not initiative. To experience the love of God in a true and not an illusory form is therefore to experience it as our surrender to His demand, our conformity to His desire." Christian tradition has often expressed man's relation to God in the beautiful phrase: the soul is the bride of Christ. But woman's nature has the greater innate affinity for the bridal role, for the act of loving surrender. That is why woman has been throughout Christian history a symbol and example of the spirit of complete consecration to God. Woman's natural capacity for wholehearted giving of herself in love is the basis for her glorious supernatural vocation. It is her function to help to lead mankind to God by becoming herself a radiant example of total dedication to His will.

The lover's surrender opens the way for the action of God's grace in the world. "The world can be moved by the strength of man, but it can be blessed in the real sense of the word only in the sign of woman," writes Gertrude von Le Fort. It is first of all to Our Lady that these words apply. In her, the universal mission of woman, the lover, was fulfilled most completely. Her "fiat" is the perfect expression of the creature's wholesouled surrender to the creator, and through her surrender the fullness of blessing entered into the world. These words may be applied, too, to the universal task of womankind, for it is the function of every woman to re-echo the "fiat" of Mary and thus to become a source of blessing to humanity.

WOMAN AS MOTHER OF MANKIND

Woman helps to lead society Godward by her direct service of mankind as well as by her example. Total dedication to God implies wholehearted service of man. A loving care for one's neighbor is but the necessary practical expression of a genuine love of God. In woman, the care for one's neighbor has the character of maternal love, with its warm personal devotion and generous sacrifice of self. Spiritually as well as physically, woman is the mother of mankind, the fountain and nurturer of life.

Through her relation to "man the maker" woman exercises a strong spiritual influence on the whole of a culture. Man leaves the imprint of his personality in the creations of his mind—works of science and art, monumental buildings and commercial empires. But woman's masterpiece is life itself. She is not interested in abstract or technical achievements but in persons, and in bringing persons to God. She stays in the background, the great inspirer, whose warm sympathy and encouragement spur man on.

Intuitively she perceives what is best and noblest in his proposals and helps to develop it. With her deep awareness of the sacramentality of life, she helps man to see matter as the image of spirit, inspiring him with her vision of the divine poetry of creation and the symbolism of human action.

In the life of every great man one finds this vital influence of a noble woman-Monica and Augustine, Paula and Jerome, Scholastica and Benedict, Clare and Francis, Blanche of Castile and King Louis, Clothilde and Clovis, Beatrice and Dante. Woman's influence is subtle and hard to define but nonetheless real. When she no longer fulfills her role as spiritual mother, culture becomes gross, materialistic, brutal, and loses grace and beauty.

THE THREE SPHERES OF WOMAN'S DEDICATION

Woman must needs fulfill her universal mission of dedication to God and loving service of mankind in some concrete set of circumstances. There are three spheres in which she can carry out her primary task: religious life, marriage, and single life in the world. In the designs of God's

Providence, some women in every generation, the "first fruits," are meant to consecrate themselves to God in religion; most women are called to dedicate themselves to Him in marriage; and very few are intended for the life of the unmarried woman in the world. But whether she becomes a nun, a mother of a family, or a single woman in the world, her essential function remains the same: to be a living example of the spirit of surrender and love, the spiritual mother of mankind.

The virgin consecrated to God by her vow of chastity has always been regarded with highest honor in Christian civilization. Consecrated virginity diffuses a fragrant atmosphere of purity and spiritual integrity throughout society, which contributes to preserve the sanctity of marriage and the dignity of womanhood. The greater the respect and esteem shown to virginity in a society, the higher the position of all women will be. It is significant that the Protestant revolt which has had so many unfortunate consequences for the position of woman began with Luther's attacks on virginity and his liquidation of convents and monasteries.

The topic of woman's contribution to society through the religious life, however, demands a separate article for adequate treatment. The present discussion will be confined to the role of woman in marriage and in the single life in the world.

WOMAN IN MARRIAGE

Woman's nature is admirably adapted to her functions as wife and mother. The responsibilities of the family develop her powers and mature her spiritually, mentally. and physically. Spiritually, a woman becomes mature through surrender, through finding the particular role in which she can accomplish her total dedication to God. The young woman who has found her vocation in life in marriage and is wholly given to her task of bringing her family to God is a mature person whatever her age. She will have that air of serenity and peace which are the sign of the basic fulfillment of her being.

The woman who has never surrendered wholeheartedly to any purpose outside herself remains immature all her life, like a bud which never unfolds itself. In marriage, woman can develop a spirit of selflessness which makes her dedication deeper and richer with the years. Her service to her family both expresses her love of God and increases her power of loving. The woman who has no outlet for her love, no one for whom she can spend herself, is apt to become hard, bitter, selfish, because she has no one but herself to consider. The woman who is constantly concerned with the needs of her family can unfold the qualities of love, tenderness, and unselfish devotion which make her truly great and truly happy.

Mentally, a woman's mind matures under the stimulus of the varied practical activities she performs for those she loves. In the concrete, living experience of the family, she can develop sound judgment and a keen insight into human nature. Lombroso's observation can readily be verified.

"The mother of a large family who has had no time to study, having been occupied with her children and her household, has more life, more breadth of ideas, than the old maid of the same age who has done nothing else than to potter about at universities and libraries." The responsibilities of her family life exercise all woman's mental powers. Her intuition and powers of observation are called into play constantly to discover the unexpressed desires of her family, particularly the needs of the helpless child. She has need of her intuition, too, as well as her tact, to help her solve the hundred problems of human relations and practical affairs that arise in the course of her day. Providing for the family helps to develop woman's natural ingenuity and inventiveness.

It is to the ingenuity of women intent on meeting the needs of their families that we owe the discovery of many of the most important arts: horticulture, for example; the creative arts of weaving, pottery, basketry; the domestic arts of food preparation and preservation; the uses of medicinal herbs in healing.

Physically, too, marriage and child bearing represent a development and completion for the normal woman, giving her new beauty and vitality. The mother of a large family experiences a physical fulfillment with the birth of each child which gives her fresh vigor and health.

Dr. Alexis Carrell observes that women attain their full development as a rule only after the birth of several children. He writes in "Man The Unknown": "Women who have no children are not so well balanced and become more nervous than the others. The importance to woman of the generative function has not been sufficiently recognized. Such function is indispensable to her optimum development. It is therefore absurd to turn women against maternity.

THE GIGANTIC TASK

In a well balanced society, where the family performs all its proper functions, the home is a society in microcosm, presenting all the problems of human relations, all the variety of human activities. The home is at once an economic and industrial center, preparing goods for family use; a school in which the young are introduced to the universe; a sanctuary for rest and relaxation; a temple dedicated to the praise of God. It is woman's function to organize and direct this complex undertaking, a role which demands intelligence talents and spiritual qualities of a high order. Chesterton describes the vastness of woman's task in the family in the following passage from "What's Wrong With the World":

"To be Queen Elizabeth within a definite area, deciding sales, banquets, labors, and holidays; to be Whiteley within a certain area, providing toys, boots, sheets, cakes and books; to be Aristotle within a certain area, teaching morals, manners, theology and hygiene: I can understand how this might exhaust the mind, but I cannot imagine how it could narrow it. How can it be a large career to tell other people's children about the Rule of Three and a small career to tell one's own children about the universe? How can it be broad to be the same thing to everyone, and narrow to be everything to someone? No; a woman's function is laborious but because it is gigantic, not because it is minute." One of the greatest of woman's responsibilities is her task as educator, transmitting the fundamental heritage of civilization, the traditions of culture and religion, to the new generation. The child receives his first introduction to civilization from his mother. The first formation of his mind and character belong almost entirely to her. She gives the child his first concepts of reality, his basic acquaintance with his mother tongue.

The child's ideas of God, of right and wrong, of repentance for faults, his first meeting with God in prayer—all come through the mother's teaching. She socializes the young human being, training him to honesty, courage, generosity, developing self-control, responsibility, and all those other virtues without which society cannot exist. She molds the men and women of the future. No other influence is as strong as the mother's in forming and preparing human beings for life.

Woman not only transmits the foundation of culture to the child; she is the great keeper of tradition in society, the custodian of manners and morals, conserving the gracious customs and fundamental standards of the race. She inspires and enforces the code of social behavior as, for example, the great chatelaines of the middle ages upheld the noble code of chivalry, and the hostesses of the seventeenth century salons cultivated the refinement of taste and manner. She keeps alive those religious customs and traditions in the home and community which link the daily life of man to God by so many intimate bonds. She is the guardian of the moral standard, especially in all that concerns the family. In this respect, as in so many others, the modern woman has abrogated her traditional role with tragic consequences for society.

It is impossible to exaggerate the importance for society of woman's achievement in the family. The family is the foundation of all the larger social structures, the basic cell on which all other agencies depend for the very existence and first formation of their members. A nation can flourish only to the extent that it is composed of healthy, flourishing families. But the family can endure only if the woman spends herself wholeheartedly to create a real home. If the woman looks down upon her function and neglects her task in the family, nothing can take her place; the family will disintegrate and with it the whole society. This should be abundantly clear to us when we see how powerless the most elaborate schools and the most advanced methods of social work are in the face of the rising tide of juvenile delinquents from neglected and broken homes.

It is superficial to think as women that we must be in the forefront of public affairs, politics, or business to influence the course of the world. "Not in the branches of a tree but in its roots do force and power reside," writes Gertrude von Le Fort. Woman is at the very roots of social life. If she keeps the sources of life pure and healthy, the entire social order will be renewed and reinvigorated by her effort.

WOMAN IN SINGLE LIFE

The other sphere through which woman can carry out her mission is the state of single life in the world. In normal times, only a few women are called to this vocation. But in our time, due to the war and to other abnormal social conditions, many women will remain unmarried. We should realize that this circumstance falls within God's Providence, and that He has destined the single woman to fulfill an important role in the modern world.

The task of the unmarried woman is, by her whole hearted surrender to God, to make virginity spiritually fruitful in the world. In embracing virginity, she should radiate purity and nobility of soul. Her very existence, like that of the virgin consecrated in religion, should be a strong positive influence upholding the dignity of womanhood and the sanctity of marriage.

By developing her capacity for spiritual motherhood, she should become a source of strength and comfort and inspiration to mankind. Never has the world been so full of misery, so desperately in need of the healing influence of woman's love. The mission of the unmarried woman in this time is to give the full riches of her maternal love and devotion to alleviate the sufferings and renew the hope of mankind.

In order to accomplish her vocation, the single woman must find an appropriate sphere in which she can carry out her dedication to God through loving service of human beings. She must strike out on new paths, searching for types of work in which she can use her womanly talents and develop her woman's nature. In the education and formation of the young; in agriculture, tending growing plants and animals; in the care of the sick, the weak, the poor, the helpless, woman finds fields of activity appropriate to her capacities as nurturer of life.

Unfortunately, work as it is carried on in these fields today often affords small opportunity for the use of woman's characteristic talents. In medicine, in education, in social work, we suffer from depersonalization, from too much large scale organization and mechanical routine, from too much concern with the physical aspects of the process. We need women to pioneer in these fields again, bringing with them their gift for warmly personal service and creating truly womanly occupations. We need women who will help to restore the emphasis on the spiritual, and who will make the work of healing, of teaching, of relieving the distressed a full expression of living charity between human persons.

HOW DID WE LOSE THE CONCEPT OF TRUE WOMANHOOD?

As we look over the modern world we may be tempted to echo King Solomon's cry: Who shall find a valiant woman? On every hand we see modern women turning away from this type of the greathearted woman. How does it happen that we have lost the concept of the woman of love and sacrifice and have accepted the ideal of the professional woman in its place?

Three major factors have contributed to the destruction of the womanly ideal: the Reformation, and the consequent secularization of western culture; the Industrial Revolution; the Feminist Movement. The Reformation was an ultramasculine movement with small regard for woman's qualities and woman's functions. As society lost its Catholic sense, it lost also the concept of total dedication, the understanding of the sacramentality of life, the regard for the sanctity of marriage—all principles intimately connected with woman's mission and dignity. At the same time, "the masculine desire to dominate the woman found expression in the law." Public opinion looked down upon woman's sphere. "Kirche, kuche, and kinderstube" ("Church, kitchen, and nursery") were linked together and treated with scant respect as fit only for women.

Along with the intellectual devaluation of woman's activities came the profound economic and social changes created by the Industrial Revolution. Seventy-five years ago the woman in the home was still the center of a variety of economic enterprises of unquestioned value and importance. But one by one almost all the activities through which a woman served her family, developed herself, and earned the esteem of society, have been lifted out of her hands and transferred to the factory. The sphere in which most women had found their means of dedication was severely curtailed. At the same time, economic necessity forced many women into the labor market to help support their families and thus led them further away from a womanly pattern.

The third influence which has contributed to the loss of a true concept of woman's function is the feminist fallacy. Feminism was born of woman's natural reaction against the depressed condition in which she found herself in a secularized, masculine, industrial culture. The feminists vociferously demanded equality, but unfortunately they conceived equality on a masculine pattern. Their whole struggle for woman's rights has simply helped to destroy the difference between the sexes and has worked to make the woman a slavish imitation of the man. Feminism is an abject surrender to the masculine ideal as the only ideal. The feminist has completely lost faith in herself as a woman. Her effort to prove herself "just as good as a man" betrays her insecurity and is a tacit admission of inferiority. Woman's struggle for freedom has led her deeper and deeper into a morass of conditions which frustrate her nature and her mission. Chesterton's bon mot is more than a witty pun: "Twenty million women rose to their feet with the cry: 'We will not be dictated to' and proceeded to become stenographers."

It is a summary of woman's situation in the modern world. Women rebelled against the confinement of the home; they find themselves now confined to the mechanical routine of the typewriter and the assembly line, rendered all the more monotonous for a woman because of its exceedingly impersonal character. Woman is made for marriage and motherhood; the modern woman in the name of freedom urges easy divorce and artificial sterility. Woman is well adapted to the universal activity of the home; her demand for freedom leads her to a narrowly specialized education and still more narrowly specialized career. Woman is made for love, for the giving of herself in personal, devoted service. In the modern world she has found her way to a position of lonely and selfish independence.

TOWARDS A SOLUTION

The problem of woman's role is fundamental and no simple, facile solution will meet it. It is not surprising that a society which has lost its sense for divine things and for man's own nature should have lost also the true concept of woman. The unnatural position of woman in our society is but one aspect of the disintegration of modern culture. Nothing short of an intensive and all-embracing renewal of the modern world in the Christian spirit will restore woman to her proper functions. What can we do as women to restore a true concept of womanhood?

(1) *Know Thyself*: As women, our first task is to regain our self-respect in the light of a clear concept of our nature and our role. We must grasp the full splendor of the divine idea of woman as it is revealed to us in the sacred writings, climaxing in the figure of Our Lady. If we have the courage to be ourselves and to follow our spiritual mission, then the world will once again recognize and reverence the immeasurable dignity of womanhood.

(2) *Restore the Christian Family*: We must strive in all ways to restore the family to its rightful dignity and full vigor as the basic cell of the social organism. The family must regain the entire range of its functions, the full scope of its gigantic task—religious, educational, cultural, economic. As women it is our particular responsibility to develop a new pattern of integral Christian life in the family, in which common prayer, work, study and recreation will build the bonds of unity and draw the family heavenwards.

(3) *Create Womanly Work*: If woman is to give the full benefit of her special qualities to society, it is of the utmost importance that we create, especially for the unmarried woman, many types of womanly work. We need pioneers of vision and imagination to take the lead in developing occupations which give woman the opportunity to mature and use her distinctive gifts. We must be alert to discover appropriate spheres of activity in which woman may realize her dedication to God in loving service of humankind.

(4) *Become Radiant Examples of the Spirit of Total Dedication*: Most important of all we must fulfill our primary mission to radiate the spirit of dedication in the world. Never has there been a period in the history of the race when the need for woman's spiritual mission was so great. At the root of all the disorders of our sad, sick world lies man's attempt to assert his independence of God. To bring tranquillity and joy into the chaos of modern society, the first necessity is a profound renewal of spirit, a wholehearted surrender of man to God, a humble and joyful acknowledgment of our complete dependence on Him. To light the way to this surrender is the spiritual mission of the women of the twentieth century, the task of woman in the modern world.

FAITH AND FREEDOM

Muslim women around the world see their future in democracy-and in Islam. To veil or not to veil is hardly the question. The fate of women's rights throughout the Islamic world today hinges on matters of far greater substance, from reforms of family and penal codes to new understandings of Islamic law and teaching. In these best and worst of times for Muslim women, it is perhaps not surprising that every promising bit of news seems to come with a disturbing counterpoint.

Take Shirin Ebadi, an Iranian lawyer and former judge, who in mid-October won the Nobel Peace Prize for her unceasing efforts to promote women's rights and democracy in her native land. In response to the jubilant reaction of Iranians throughout the Islamic republic, President Mohammad Khatami—a reformist, no less—dismissed it as "not worth all that fuss!" Several days after the Nobel was announced, Morocco's King Mohammed VI, who claims descent from the prophet Mohammed, proposed reforms in family law that stand to improve the lot of women throughout the North African kingdom. But long before he presented the reforms to the national parliament, Islamists had taken to the streets to denounce them, dwarfing a pro-reform demonstration by roughly 3 to 1. Also in mid-October, in an unusual instance of Bedouin perestroika, authorities in Saudi Arabia announced that the kingdom would permit the holding of municipal elections within a year—though it's still unclear whether women will be able to run for office or even vote. And at the end of September, in one of a dozen Nigerian states that have adopted sharia (Islamic law), a religious appeals court overturned the death sentence of Amina Lawal, 32, a Muslim woman accused of adultery. Yet while Lawal was spared the gruesome fate of death by stoning, at least five other women in Nigeria still face the same sentence.

Women's rights face an uncertain future throughout much of the Islamic world—though nowhere more pointedly than in the constitution-making efforts now underway in both Afghanistan and Iraq. In two nations widely viewed as test cases of the compatibility of Islamic and universal values, it remains to be seen whether and how the principles of sharia, or even the more general spirit of Islamic traditions, will inform their future laws. And behind those uncertainties loom even broader questions facing Muslim women everywhere. In particular, rights activists wonder, are the foundations of Islamic law and theology compatible with international standards of human rights in general and women's right in particular? And if so, what must be done to surmount the practical hurdles—including the crucial matter of who interprets the law—that stand in the way of reconciling Islam with universal principles of women's rights?

Muslim women themselves are already actively engaged with these issues. "When I talk with educated women from Morocco to Pakistan," says Ann Mayer, a professor of legal studies at the University of Pennsylvania's Wharton School and author of Islam and Human Rights: Tradition and Politics, "I find that they are much more inclined to evaluate their condition in relation to international standards of human rights. And they say that international standards only reinforce Islamic standards."

Confidence. That underscores one notable development of the past decade: a new confidence among Muslim feminists and human-rights activists that Islamic teachings and sources can support their efforts. This represents a sea change, says Amina Wadud, professor of Islamic studies at Virginia Commonwealth University and author of Qu'ran and Woman: Rereading the Sacred Text From a Woman's Perspective. As late as 1995, at the Global Women's Conference in Beijing, many feminists from Islamic countries insisted women's equality could be attained only by jettisoning religion, including the outward trappings of the faith, such as the veil.

Since then, though, an expanding reform movement within Islam, driven largely by increased literacy and an explosion of new media outlets, has led more Muslims to explore the sacred writings on their own. While this has often reinforced the patriarchal viewpoint of militant Islamists, it has also supported progressive and feminist interpretations. Wadud insists that it is unnecessary and even constraining to argue only on the basis of historical precedent, but she finds there is more in the sacred texts and traditions to support notions of gender equality than there is to deny them. She notes, for example, that in the period after Mohammed's death, women, including the Prophet's favorite wife, Aisha, played "key roles in preserving traditions, disseminating knowledge, and challenging authority when it went against their understanding of the Koran or the prophetic legacy."

Referring to the decision of Iran's mullahs to remove Nobel winner Ebadi from her judgeship on religious grounds, Wadud notes, "Nowhere is it said that women cannot interpret the law." Ebadi herself, in a recent interview with Iranian emigre author Amir Taheri, makes the same point in her words of advice to Muslim women: "Don't believe that you are decreed to have an inferior position. Study the Koran carefully, so that the oppressors cannot impress you with citations and interpretations. Don't let individuals masquerading as theologians claim they have a monopoly on understanding Islam."

Fine words, but have they yet had any practical consequences? The answer, many activists say, is a qualified yes. In that widely followed adultery case in Nigeria, for example, Amina Lawal's attorney, Hauwa Ibrahim, got her client exonerated, but on several technicalities that may not work for other women.

The real problem, says Mayer, is that Nigeria's version of sharia involves a "folkloric version" of Islamic adultery law. First of all, the rules of evidence spelled out in the Koran require either a freely gained confession from the accused or four eyewitnesses to the act of sexual penetration, neither of which was obtained in Nawal's case. Just as important, the maximum punishment for the crime is supposed to be 100 lashes, not stoning.

Illegal. Of course, even if the Nawal case and others did not involve a corrupted use of sharia, the punishments that Nawal faced would be in violation of both the spirit and letter of the U.N. Convention on the Elimination of All Forms of Discrimination Against Women (CEDAW), which Nigeria has signed and ratified. But appeals to international agreements have only limited effectiveness in advancing women's rights in the Islamic world. (Saudi Arabia is one of 50 out of the 57

Organization of Islamic Conference nations to sign and ratify CEDAW, but it explicitly stipulates that it will not observe any terms that contradict "norms of Islamic law.")

In some cases, appeals might even backfire. According to Wadud, the defense attorneys involved in another Nigerian adultery case had to send out word that any additional international pressure might actually sway the jurists on a religious appeals court not to overturn the verdict.

In a more general way, says New York University law Prof. Noah Feldman, the former U.S. adviser to the Iraqi Governing Council on constitutional matters, the United States faces a similar challenge in its efforts to guide Afghanistan and Iraq toward becoming democratic and rights-respecting regimes.

Feldman points out that as long as America is an occupying power, it can accomplish much "just by suggesting"—though, he promptly adds, the U.S.-led Coalition Provisional Authority had to insist on the appointment of several women to the 25-person Governing Council. "But at a certain point," Feldman cautions, "you cross the line to coercing people on how to run their lives."

Feldman prefers to stop short of that line, having disagreed openly with Sen. Sam Brownback and Rep. Frank Wolf's proposal for requiring explicit religious-freedom language in the Iraqi constitution. "Senator Brownback says if we allow the constitution to mention the word `Islam,' we'll have problems down the road, but I say if we don't, we'll have troubles immediately," Feldman explains.

That does not mean that he has little hope for women's rights. To the contrary, says the author of After Jihad, an argument for the future of Islamic democracy, "I am for promoting women's rights by saying they are compatible with Islam."

In Iraq, there are good reasons for thinking that Islam and women's rights can go together. Before the U.S. invasion, says Khaled Abou el Fadl, a visiting professor at Yale Law School, Iraq was one of the most progressive of Muslim nations in relation to women. Not only were there female jurists and lawyers, but there was a civil code that blended the best of French and Islamic laws. Among the latter, he points out, was a law allowing a woman the right to divorce her husband and sue for alimony and child support if he decided to take another wife. (A similar expansion of women's prerogatives is one of the reforms that Morocco's king has just proposed.) Like Feldman, Abou el Fadl worries that attempts to expunge Islam from Iraq's laws will only trigger a stronger urge on the part of many Iraqis to put more of Islam in—and that might mean the most sexist and partriarchal versions of Islam.

Which raises the most important issue: How can Muslim feminists and rights activists win the interpretive struggle against those mullahs and muftis who confuse partriarchal codes and customs with the core principles of the faith?

That is a major concern for Irshad Manji, a Canadian author and journalist. Like many other Muslim feminists, she sees the real problem of interpretation as one of overturning Arab traditions of honor that accompanied the spread of Islam and are now being recirculated throughout the world via the Saudi-funded Wahhabi religious establishment.

As Manji explains, within the Arab honor code, individual rights are secondary to one's status within the family or tribe. Women are reduced to "communal or tribal property." In Pakistan or Nigeria, she says, a man from one tribe or family may rape a woman from another as an act of communal retribution.

For Manji, who develops her argument in her forthcoming book The Trouble With Islam, one of the best solutions lies in women's growing participation in trade, commerce, and capitalism, all of which have been valued since Islam's founding. (Mohammed's first wife, Khadija, was an astute businessperson.) And the economic empowerment of women in the Islamic world is not merely theoretical. It is already underway even in the most Arab of states, Saudi Arabia. In Jidda and Riyadh, respectively, women own a quarter and a third of all businesses. And it is no secret among foreigners working in Saudi Arabia that women are the most educated, able, and productive employees in the kingdom.

By consolidating and advancing their economic position, Manji says, and by becoming tax-paying citizens, women can assert their standing as individuals. This emerging reality is hard to ignore, whether in Saudi Arabia or Iran. Already in Malaysia, Amina Wadud notes, women working through Sisters in Islam and other groups have helped reform domestic violence law by promoting what she calls a "nice blend of sharia and civil law."

Still, it is one of the sad ironies of Islam, Manji says, that a religion originally intended to transcend tribalism has, at least in many parts of the world, allowed the tribalist codes to reassert themselves. But Manji refuses to accept that irony as the last word on women's fate within Islam. And she is far from alone.

11

WOMAN'S FUTURE POSITION IN THE WORLD

To be strictly logical one should not treat of woman apart from the rest of the human race, for this is in a manner to admit that women are a distinct class, not affected by conditions, environment, etc., as men are. But we find a "woman question" actually existing. A great deal of discussion has been going on as to what is proper for woman, what her real nature is, and how many of the duties and privileges of man she should be admitted to. Women do not occupy the same position, socially, politically, economically, or intellectually that men do, and her powers are not equal to her brother's. She is daily reproached for trying to be other than she is, and reminded that her very nature forbids her presuming to climb out of the subserviency and inferiority which are now undeniably her portion. Thus a "woman question" is forced upon us whether we will or not. It is to discover, if possible, whether she may ever become equal to and like man without perverting her inherent nature, that this inquiry is made.

It is impossible to ascertain whether there ever was a time when woman stood an equally strong intellectual and physical being, on an equal footing with man, or not. If it ever existed, its memory is now very hazy. Yet there are writers who refer to it as a fact. August Bébel, in "Woman: Past, Present, and Future," refers to it thus: "We have no grounds for assuming that in this primitive state men were physically or mentally superior to women.... Certain savage tribes were governed by women instead of men owing to the superior strength of the former.... Primeval woman, although the equal of man in bodily and mental power, nevertheless became his inferior when periods of pregnancy, birth, and lactation forced her to look to him for assistance, support, and protection."

And in a more mystical sense Olive Schreiner refers to the time: "And he answered: 'Listen and I will tell you. Ages and ages long she has lain here, and the wind has blown over her. The oldest, oldest man living has never seen her move; the oldest book records that she lay here then as she lays here now. But listen! Older than the oldest book, older than the oldest recorded memory of man, on the rocks of language, on the hard baked clay of ancient custom, are found the marks of her footsteps. Side by side with him who stands beside her, you may trace them, and you may know that she who now lies here once wandered free over the rocks with him.'"

Matilda Joslyn Gage, in her "Woman, Church, and State," lays great emphasis upon the days of matriarchy, when women, as mothers of the race, ruled the people. But we have no evidence that any such period ever existed. Letourneau shows that cases have been where inheritances descended and relationships were determined through the women of the tribe. Accompanying this usage, a certain importance adhered to the mothers of the tribe. It is true, women attained powerful and prominent positions in the old civilizations that have come and gone. The mythical lost Atlantis was peopled with great women of divine aspect. There were queens in the days of Solomon; and the Helens, Cleopatras, and Hypatias of history dot the dark pages with glints of a glory to come. A matriarchy never existed; cases of matriarchy have been known. Woman never stood beside man his equal in all things; women have ruled in isolated instances.

Be that as it may, woman's subordination came to be complete. She was first knocked down, dragged away senseless, and made a slave. She was bought and sold, or traded; she became a thing, a piece of property, a bond slave. Her degraded position among men became a custom, then an institution, then a tradition. There were centuries of "dark ages for her, into whose gloom no ray of light ever pierced, and from whose depths little has come down to us to tell the sombre story." Slowly, very slowly man developed in intellect and acquired a rude knowledge of art. The woman in his tents could not remain very far behind him, and in time arose to some degree of companionship. That he treated her with a little kindness, and even appealed to her in times of weariness or perplexity for sympathy or counsel, was due, not to his traditions and creeds conceived in another grade of civilization, but to changed conditions and his own developed nature. There might even have arisen a "woman's rights question" in those old Mosaic days, had not the priests, who feared any loosening of their control over the people, issued a "Thus saith the Lord," and so riveted her chains for another three thousand years. "Thy desire shall be unto thy husband, and he shall rule over thee," settled the problem for the time.

"Economic dependence is the basis of all slavery," Bébel says; and he is right. All forms of slavery had their inception in some kind of economic dependence, but the slavery often exists long after the dependent condition has passed away. A thing, once established, once made an institution, is very apt to outlast the economic phase which determined its existence, and become a very troublesome matter. Institutions are crystallized ideas; they stand still: people grow—grow beyond and outside of them. Yet there they remain, unwieldy, mischief-breeding; to get rid of them at all is to tear them out by the roots at great cost of life and suffering. The bonds made ages ago, by economic conditions prevailing at the time, have become sacred; they bear another strength than that which they possessed when first formed. Though no longer with any economical basis for existing, they are even more effective in power than when first established.

Individually men are not to blame for the inferior position of women. They accepted a condition, a chain of customs, as they found them. Though long past the time when constant danger from without rendered it necessary that his whole family give him implicit obedience, the habit of expecting filial deference is fixed. Though the days of absolute property in wives have gone by, the sense of proprietorship in and responsibility for wives still prevails. That sentiment which played upon the superstitious fears of woman, setting a sort of mental watchdog to guard the master's property in his absence as well as when present, still exists in a modified form in the demand for perfect chastity in woman not expected man. The old feeling of ownership, which led men to seclude their women, has softened into that modern sentiment which would keep women guarded from the public gaze in every respect. The stern commands of old are toned down into "what is expected of womanly women," but that expectation is as binding as any chain or title deed to person could be.

Thus, through ages of subserviency, of which there were many grades, women have come to be what they are: emotional, since any prominent display of other faculties has been unnecessary in that "sphere to which it has pleased God to call her;" deceitful, since deceit has been her only weapon; illogical, since the encouragement of her reasoning powers would have often placed her in direct opposition to her master; vain, since her personal charms were long the only qualities for which she was considered; weak-minded, since strong brains were not desirable in that function to which man wished to limit her. So from long persisting conditions woman has come to be the creature she is.

But the change in woman's position and in the manner in which woman is considered during the last fifty years has been a remarkable one. We scarcely realize its greatness until we begin to compare the prominent women of today with women of the last century. It is perhaps correct to say that Mary Wollstonecraft began the modern woman's-rights movement. Her work, "The Rights of Women," written toward the close of the last century, is read more widely now than at the time of publication. It was many years before an organized effort was made to secure political equality for women. The movement, which has lasted through the lifetime of some of America's noblest women, though a little too narrow for modern sociological students, has been a great element in the remarkable change. Unconsciously it has builded better than it knew, and helped to widen the field and elevate the aspirations of women far more than the originators ever intended. The introduction of machinery has been the most potent factor in the transition. When the work of the world was done in the home, when the spinning-wheel, the loom, the soap vat, the "pig-killing," the bake oven, and the slender needle were institutions in every household, naturally "woman's place" was at home. But spinning-wheel and loom turned into great cotton and woollen mills; the pork-barrel became the vast packing-houses of our large cities; the needle was reserved for mending, and great clothing establishments took its place; the old lye barrel gave way to immense soap factories; and family ovens were relegated to the past, for the bakeries that now supply the staff of life.

It was no longer profitable to make these things in the seclusion of the home; and women followed the machines and went in great crowds to the factories. The demand for women's work came at a time when a new restlessness was pervading the inner sanctum of the home. Secluded and protected, kindly treated though they might happen to be, women began to feel that they were not living full, true lives. They felt that all their faculties were not being developed, that all their powers for giving and receiving happiness were not being called out. Though the duties of motherhood might for the time being occupy all their time and energies, it was also true that not all women were mothers of children, nor were the mothers always mothers of young children. A woman's life stretches over many periods, as does man's. In a lifetime she is capable of being much more than a mother, as man is expected to be much more than a father.

The restlessness was natural. Women came out into the world and became acquainted with each other and with their working brothers; they took a broader view of life; and something of that feeling of fraternity to which men had attained in their clubs, lodges, and unions, began to take lodgment in their breasts. For the "old" woman had no conception of the brotherhood of the human race. She loved her own passionately, and she loved her immediate friends; she loved her church and believed in a vague way that she "loved all men," as a good Christian should. But of the real solidarity of the human race, of the truth that "an injury to one is the concern of all," she had no conception. The "new woman" has a very fair realizing sense of this great social truth today. And therefore, though she may be more of a slave in the factory than she was in the narrow confines of home, she has come up higher. She has reached greater opportunities for full, well-developed existence; and though she makes some mistakes, she is far advanced in her evolutionary progress.

But as yet she is no happier, and men are not pleased. They think she has taken their places in the workshop, in the office, and at the business desk; they fear to lose the sweet, clinging, fragile, wheedling little creature they imagine they love; and they have not reached a conception of what the free, self-poised, capable, womanly woman of the future will be. They are not very well satisfied with the crude sample of the "new woman;" and they are in a manner drawing away from her in the consciousness of a lofty superiority which never needs a transitional stage.

Women themselves are not happy, because they are not yet accustomed to the new order—an order that is as yet chaotic and undefined. Just out from the unwholesome hothouse air of their old seclusion, the atmosphere of comparative freedom and independence strikes too harshly upon them, and they shiver. They cannot go back, and they cannot yet breathe easily. They can do wonders in adaptation, but they cannot find their equilibrium in half a generation of partial freedom. The adjusting process hurts; it always does.

What is it that woman wants? What is it she hopes to attain? What is it she lacks that men are not willing to give? It is no wonderful thing; nothing preposterous or presumptuous. She simply wants to be a human being, not a slave, not a toy, not a queen. She wants the equal personal liberty that every man demands in order to become a fully developed, well-balanced, happy, and useful being. Only this and nothing more.

With this emancipation—this "liberty to do whatsoever one wills so long as one [does not infringe] on the equal right of others to do as they will"—she needs not even the chivalry of old. Kindness, sympathy, love from equals she needs in common with man. She needs not that spirit of worship which some men who think they are "advanced" seem willing to pour out upon her; she needs not that undue devotion on account of her motherhood which many good people believe is right and just; she needs not that right which Robert Ingersoll declared she must possess when he said: "Women should have all the rights that men possess and one more—the right to be protected." The right to be a human being includes that right when necessary. If every individual in the world possesses an equal right to life, liberty, and the pursuit of happiness, the right of opportunity at nature's table, the right to develop to the highest she is capable of becoming, the rights of motherhood and womanhood are conceded. No better protection is needed than that which any enlightened human being will naturally give to another if circumstances make it imperative. A free woman will not choose to be "protected" in the old sense. Protection has ever been an implication of weakness and a willingness to occupy a subordinate position. Nations which call upon other nations for protection must needs give up for that protection some portion of their independence; and industries that can flourish only under "protection" create slaves in their turn.

A great fear seems to exist that if women were perfectly free to become whatever they see fit many dire calamities would happen. Woman would become "mannish;" she would lose her delicate sense of morality; and she might slight that one great duty to which she has been almost wholly consigned for so many ages. But why do we hesitate to trust woman free, when she has fulfilled so many precious trusts in bondage? I have no fear that motherhood and love is a great part of the sweetness of life, and free women are not likely to yield up any part of their happiness.

This one great fear seems to lie at the bottom of every objection to the full freedom and equality of woman—the fear that she will refuse to do her duty by the human race. It is the last prejudice, the last of the old traditions, that man is willing to let go. He will go so far as to admit the right of suffrage, to accept equal property rights, to grant equal opportunities in all the fields of human activity, but he cannot rid himself of that sacred old tenet: that a woman cannot be a good wife and mother if she have any other interest in life besides her home and children. Even very radical thinkers still at times declare that "woman's crowning glory is motherhood;" and only insist on equal opportunities and unequal consideration that she may be more fully and perfectly the mother. I am aware that I am proving myself a startling heretic to generally accepted ideas, but I most emphatically dissent.

I am aware that throughout the realm of nature the one blind impulse of every living thing is to reproduce itself. Everything else seems to be sacrificed to this one object. In the lowest living organisms individual identity is completely lost in the separation which creates two where one existed before. A little higher up in the scale extinction follows reproduction; and for many degrees in the ascending gamut the sole purpose of existence seems to be simply reproduction. But as the higher forms of life evolve, in both the animal and the vegetable kingdoms, more and more of life is utilized in other ways. Trees live to give shelter and shade, and they minister to our sense of beauty through many years; the higher animals have many uses, and many years of animal enjoyment, aside from the function of reproduction.

In the lower grades of human life the power of reproduction seems the most important part of existence. But as the race advances, develops, acquires knowledge, the existence of its members becomes rich and full with the wealth of life itself. The individual becomes an emphasized, distinct identity. It is something to the world that a bright, sound individual lives, acts, and thinks, even though it is never reproduced. The male portion of the race already feel as though fatherhood were a mere incident in their lives, and would be insulted were you to intimate that fatherhood should be the crowning glory of their lives. They know that they possess powers and capabilities that the world needs and appreciates, and that fatherhood, blessed though it be, is not the fullest and best manifestation of their existence. The idea is in every way as applicable to woman as to man. Why should all the faculties and energies of woman be turned to the fulfilment of this one function of her being?

It is flattering to man to think that it takes all of a woman's whole life to carry out her duty to him and his children. But if he only knew it, the entire devotion of her powers to this one purpose is the poorest preparation for wifehood and motherhood that can be made. Even the man himself feels a sort of undefined contempt for the woman who is nothing but wife and mother. A woman becomes morbid who simply retires within herself to brood over her fitness or unfitness for her "crowning glory." It is distorting, dwarfish, narrowing. Her child is unfavorably affected by this intensity of thought centred upon its embryonic existence. It is like that unwholesome "self-analysis" which has ever made up so great a part of the old religious creeds, and which still crops up in modified forms in the "new philosophies."

Let the woman live for herself, not for unborn children. Let her fill her life to the brim with happiness, knowledge, mental and physical activity; let lofty emotions and vigorous thoughts fill her being; let her whole existence expand to its fullest extent; let her forget her motherhood; she will be the better mother for first being a perfect woman. And to be this she must first be free. It will not do to ask what she will do with her freedom, to criticise, to judge; one must only wait. "The cure for the evils of liberty is more liberty."

Do not fear for the result. The trend of human evolution is upward and onward. The plant allowed to grow freely, in the sunlight, with warm rich soil and pure fresh air, will develop to its very highest possibilities. Cramp it, interfere with it, abstract either light or warmth, and it becomes a stunted, pale, sickly growth. Looking upon it, no one could tell what it might have become under proper conditions.

Do not fear that woman thus freed would become a poor mimicry of a poor sample of a man. To become "mannish" is in the eyes of conventional society worse than to commit a crime. But what do we mean by this term? If it is anything reprehensible, believe me, it is as bad in man as in woman. Does it apply to the manners, morals, or the intellect? It is very vague at best. For those qualities which we call "good" are as beautiful in man as in woman. We love bravery, self-poise, strength, honor, truthfulness in one as well as in the other. We love gentleness, kindness, sympathy, tact in both sexes. We see today timid men and brave women; weak-minded men and strong-minded women; deceitful men and truthful women; vain men and self-forgetful women. Under equal and similar conditions the virtues and vices would be diffused much more equally. For I hold another heresy: that there is no sex in intellect, sentiment, or morals. The same environment, the same treatment, the same teachings would result in a similarity of characteristics. There will never cease to be variety, but we should not find a greater tendency toward any particular group of faculties in one sex over the other.

True, some scientific scholars declare that it is a physical impossibility for woman under any condition to become man's equal in physical and mental strength, or to become free from her emotional disturbances and sensitiveness of nerves. The shape, size, and quality of the brain, they say, preclude this; her peculiar functions, the time and energy necessary to the bearing of children and the nourishing of them, prevent a change from her present nature. Nevertheless this is not a demonstrated truth; no one knows by actual experiment whether it is true or not. The fact that all human creatures are the subject of environment and of hereditary conditions signifies that woman is no exception. There is every reason to suppose that under like conditions with men, women would develop in a manner as men do. Woman's peculiar functions should not create the sharp distinctions now seen. Weakness, dependence, emotionalism, vanity, deceitfulness have been cultivated in woman; these traits have been considered her greatest attractions; tradition, custom, public opinion have fixed them upon her, and it will take long to eliminate them.

There is no reason why woman should devote more of her time and energies to motherhood than man does to fatherhood. Work, activity, interest in other things, both while carrying and nourishing children, are better than idleness. No special training, no particular occupation or exercise of one's faculties, or the cessation of activities, are necessary as a preparation for motherhood. The life which makes a woman all she is capable of being as a human being is the only one essential to the rearing of good children. So little is required of a mother that need interfere with ordinary duties and occupations, that it is difficult to see how motherhood should have, in itself, such a wonderful differentiating effect.

Woman has been considered too much as woman, and not enough as a human being. The constant reference to her sex has been neither ennobling, complimentary, nor agreeable. Either as slave, toy, pet, or queen, this ceaseless thinking of her sex instead of herself has been degrading. To finally arrive at her best she simply needs consideration as a fellow member of society.

Do not fear liberty. Just now the results of the beginnings of freedom do not seem very satisfactory. Woman seems to be an intruder; she cannot overcome at once the prejudices that had their inception in the time of her complete economic dependence. She herself is dissatisfied. She is not as lovable perhaps. She has lost some of the charm of clinging womanhood which at best man only heeded in his leisure moments, and has not yet gained the poise and individuality that will draw him to her as a companion. She is dissatisfied with the old gallantry, and has not yet attained the spontaneous recognition and respectful love she longs for. But this will come. There will be a time when men and women, equal human beings, clasping hands and looking each other in the eyes on a level—not leaning on each other, but upright—will feel a true fellowship; and mutual admiration and respect will exist between them. Then will love be sweeter, purer, more beautiful than the world has ever known.

12

WOMEN'S EMPOWERMENT

Wives are lonelier now than they ever used to be. In older, gentler times, when age still had its privileges, the old folks never harbored any guilt feelings about being a drag on the young. They either moved in, reasoning that it was high time they were supported for a change, or else they lived nearby. People moved less, and families stuck closer together. Grandma, never having become emancipated, was always around for advice and help. (Today grandma is likely to be off fund raising or taking courses at Columbia.) I know a Polish area in Chicago where everyone in the family lives within a few blocks of the others, and there are usually two generations in each house. They may have other problems, but loneliness isn't one of them.

The young college-educated mother with a medium amount of money is the one who reflects all the problems at once. In spite of her hopes for fulfillment through her children and contentment with woman's great career, she vaguely feels that she is frittering away her days and that a half-defined but important part of her ability is lying about unused; she is guilty about her feeling of futility because of her belief in the magic medicine of love. This is the housewife's syndrome, the vicious circle, the feeling of emptiness in the gap between what she thought marriage was going to be like and what it is really like.

Let's take a look at a fairly typical young mother. She married her husband because she loved him, and she still does. She has two children and is pregnant with a third. Whether in city or country, she is more or less surrounded by gadgets which free her from drudgery. If she is lucky, she has a cleaning woman once a week. She and her husband have enough money for a fairly comfortable life, but for time alone together are dependent on baby sitters and possibly a grandma who will help out in a pinch. If the young mother is in the country, the children play in the yard, and she watches them from the window; if she is in the city, she takes them out once or twice a day, pushing a carriage and pulling a tricycle. Talking to her friends on these outings is her solution to loneliness. Her day is full of a thousand pressures, some miniature, some large. Two of the main worries are illness and money. If everyone in the family is healthy for two weeks at a stretch, she counts herself fortunate. Every cold goes the rounds of the family, and she sometimes feels that she supports the pediatrician singlehandedly.

During the healthy periods she strives to improve her home, cook a new dish, do something about her looks, give a dinner party and a children's birthday party, go to the theater with her husband, catch up on her reading, have coffee with a friend. Her life vacillates between being very organized and completely disorganized, because she has the struggle of all women: to keep the house clean and in repair without being a shrew about people's messing it up. Because children are natural makers of havoc, she constantly strives to maintain the delicate line of balance. Usually, when the first child starts school, she is drawn into community or P.T.A. work of some kind. If she is normally conscientious, she feels she should do something, but if she is normally realistic, she knows she doesn't have time. So she does it anyway. Joining things as a virtue is a hangover from college, where well-roundedness and abundant interests were considered rungs on the ladder to heaven.

The demands of her family and community cause her to feel, as one woman put it, like a pie with not enough pieces to go around. Depending on whether or not she is gregarious, she longs for time to talk to her friends or time to be alone; I should say, the busier she is, the greater her urge to be by herself, to feel unique and separate again. Great numbers of friends are a luxury she can no longer afford; old friends often diminish in importance, which she is sorry about. But there is a limit to her capacity for giving affection, and maintaining old friendships at their original intensity requires an effort she hardly has the energy for. Besides, she is often forced into unwanted and demanding friendships with the next-door neighbor, the boss's wife, or the ladies' club chairman, and she must learn to cover up her real feelings. (To her surprise, she often ends by liking these women.) Another group of demanding relationships is required with her in-laws, and if she gets along well with them, she is lucky. If her husband now lacks the mystery and fascination of the wedding night, he is now more loved and appreciated. The occasions when they have time alone together are among her precious jewels.

In spite of this full life, the old illusions of what life was supposed to hold, the restless remnants, the undefined dreams do not die as they were supposed to. Probably every educated wife has found herself staring at a mountain of dirty diapers and asking herself desperately, "Is this all there is?" And at the same time she is embarrassed by her dissatisfaction; she, of all people, with her intelligence and realistic view of life, should be able to rise above it. But the paradox is that it is she who is least able to. She lives for a better day. Things will be easier when this baby is born, or that one toilet-trained, or the children are all in school; and she will have time to be pretty and intelligent and young again. The mistake is in thinking that everything is going to solve itself by magic. What our girl must do, as she stares at the diapers, is to accept some of the truths about marriage and motherhood that her education and society conspired to keep from her, and go on from there. And if she would appreciate what she has, she must do it now, not next year or five years from now.

The first truth is that marriage does not automatically equal security and contentment. An unmarried friend of mine told me once that she did not see how any problem in marriage could be as bad as one outside of it, because if you had your man, anything else could be easily straightened out. We had a long argument about whether the heart sank more over a sick child or a departed boy friend, and neither of us won. She is one of a good many girls who think that three dates a week, secretarial jobs, and the responsibility of keeping themselves clothed are a nerve-shattering, frantic business, and who look forward to marriage and motherhood as a long, relaxing rest cure. "Getting married and settling down" is a valid notion for men, as it has been throughout history, but not for potential mothers. The day the doctor confirms one's pregnancy is the day to start bracing oneself for the really hard work. (I cannot convince my unmarried friends of this, but, of course, that is as it should be, or many babies might never be born.)

The truth is that, with the birth of the first child, marvelous changes take place. From that moment on, mama is no longer the center of attention; the baby is. Mama and papa will give-and willingly-and the baby will take. They will assume responsibility, earn money, employ their energy, change their lives, if necessary-all for the baby. This is no light undertaking, but the business of life is starting now, and every day of mama's life proves it to be so. And here her struggle starts. She wants to give everything to the baby; she wants equally to hold on to herself, her intelligence and uniqueness, while the baby constantly tries her patience, her strength, her nerves, and roots out of her the deepest emotions she has ever known in her life. This is a whole new process, and not one that provides built-in security. It is a mistake to assume that marriage is a cure-all, a miraculous bit of psychiatry that is going to banish all the old problems overnight and, like phenobarbital, put disturbingly violent instincts to sleep. The benediction of church and state is not enough to still the quality of excitement that comes from strangeness and the idealization of a still-unknown experience. These things, after all, were part and parcel of sex before marriage, and half its value. Sex in marriage makes up in intimacy what it loses in mystery, but this does not mean that mystery is no longer attractive. The most embarrassing lust for the least likely person can exist in the best-adjusted P.T.A. member in town. Whether or not anything is done about it is another story, but probably most of the time nothing is. We take marriage very seriously; our Puritan heritage is still very much with us; and we fear the wages of sin. Besides, the communities of young married couples are built for decency and togetherness, and the woman who considers taking a lover simply has no place to go. All of the notions about peace being intrinsic in the state of marriage have to do with the happiness-togetherness cult, the great American dream, the return to the hearth. The peak of all earthly satisfaction is said to be found in the family, popping corn together in matching pajamas, not in hard work and self-denial, or even in the self-knowledge that came with the Freudian age. In our unending search for panaceas, we believe that happiness and "success"-which, loosely translated, means money-are the things to strive for. People are constantly surprised that, even though they have acquired material things, discontent still gnaws.

An Englishman said to me recently, "You Americans live on a much higher plane of expectancy than we do. You constantly work toward some impossible goal of happiness and perfection, and you unfortunately don't have our ability just to give up. Really, it's much easier to accept the fact that some things can't be solved." He is right; we never accept it, and we kill ourselves trying. The feeling of futility of the housewife is based on a history of high expectancy, a faith in external things, and an inability to see that the rewards are found within oneself. It is a paradox that the achievement of a home and family is so often regarded by women as the consummate solution for human ills, when actually the responsibilities it entails are enough to reduce some people to nervous wrecks. Marriage, entered upon maturely, is the only life for most women. But it is a way of life, not a magic bag of goodies at the end of the road.

The fact is that marriage and motherhood bring forth deeper and more staggering emotions than any experience before marriage. There is nothing soothing or secure about the feeling, familiar to all mothers, of wanting to murder one's child and really feeling capable of it, and then the next moment dissolving into the deepest love and repentance. There is nothing soothing about the insane annoyance that one can feel at some irritating habit of a loved one, or at loathing the knowledge of what he or she is going to say; one feels trapped by a total ability to see-mystery gone forever. It can be painful to find oneself isolated, in marriage, with problems that have always been shared with mother or girl friends, and to realize that there are some things that even one's husband cannot be told. This is the hard lesson of discretion. And there is nothing soothing to participants or onlookers about the spine-chilling habit of some couples who goad each other to a fever pitch of irritation, with repeated fingernail rasps on each other's well-known sensitive spots-all in the name of playful affection. It is frightening to see how close emotions are to the surface and how little it takes to make destruction.

And it is equally frightening to know suddenly how complete love is and how much one gives to it, to see how little one can really stand when someone in the family is sick, and to know how quickly one can be torn apart by nothing at all. A young mother said the other day, speaking of young mothers in general, "It always amazes me how vulnerable we are and how we, who are supposed to be so responsible, are such preys of our own feelings." In a family of love, one must become infinitely flexible to withstand the continuous jounce of emotion. This is the muscle that develops, not superefficiency or physical strength, and it is the weariness of this muscle that causes young mothers to want to run away and hide in a solitary place where nothing can jar the heart. The second truth is that a girl does not need a college education to take care of babies and keep house. I recall a lot of talk at college among engaged girls that bringing up children is a vastly complicated business which makes full use of a mother's brains and energy, and that no man on earth has a position as responsible and delicate as that of being totally in charge of the education of minds, souls, and bodies of two or three important human beings.

Well, for one thing, mother is not totally in charge, though she may like to think so. The influences of father, school, doctor, friends, neighborhood, city, or country are equally important. Besides, mother is not really in charge of herself enough to be in charge of her children. What the children learn is what mother is, not what she thinks she is. For another thing, the job is hardly complicated and delicate, at least at first. It is the simple, nerve-wracking, mindless, battering-ram process of trying to teach a savage to use a fork. It requires bloodless patience, a deadly will, enormous physical stamina, and a stable disposition, but no precision instruments. It takes strength and determination. For the fact is that motherhood makes the heaviest demands in what might be called the areas of least experience. I would be surprised if there were a single college-educated mother who has not been struck by the total uselessness of her liberal education when it comes to housewifery. Instead of distilling pearls of knowledge from a large body of facts, she must now master a whole new set of domestic facts: how to roast a chicken, remove gum from the rug, take a child's temperature, keep the shine on the Sheraton table, iron a blouse, or even change a tire or build a bookcase. Some of these necessities are positively shocking. The care of dirty diapers and the job of keeping the oven clean call for a strong-minded unfastidiousness; even more does the whole process of having a baby, which is certainly nature at its rawest. Learning all of these things calls for a day-to-day resourcefulness and is a new and rather frightening responsibility.

Choosing a house and everything that goes into it, and a school, and a competent doctor are decisions that the young mother makes without adequate knowledge, and she can ill afford mistakes. If her husband is sympathetic, he helps her with these decisions. If not, she gropes her way along and takes the blame when that lovely color for the living-room walls turns out to be bilious salmon pink in the sunlight. And this calls for a brand-new virtue, too; the ability to adapt oneself completely, in about thirty seconds flat, to an entirely new viewpoint. Around a house, no achievement is very permanent, and the day can turn inside out before one's eyes. The salmon-pink walls must suddenly be repainted, the baby sitter suddenly fails, the clean living room is no longer clean, the elevator in the apartment building breaks down, and mother and baby carriage are trapped for the day on the seventh floor.

BACKGROUND

The National Commission on Population which was set up to review, monitor and give directions for the implementation of the National Population Policy with a view to meeting the goals set out in the Policy constituted eight Working Groups on the following subjects related to population stabilization in the country:

I. Strategies to Meet Unmet Needs;

II. Primary and Secondary Education in relation to Population and Civilization;

III. Registration of Births, Deaths and Marriages;

IV. Media for Information, Education and Communication and Motivation;

V. Role of Panchayati Raj Institutions and Self-Help Groups;

VI. Mainstreaming of Indian System of Medicine and Homeopathy into the Health System;

VII. Task Force on Monitoring;

VIII. Advisory Group on Tribal Communities.

Four Sub-Groups have been constituted under the first Working Group on Strategies to meet the following specific unmet needs:

a) Sub-Group on Strategies to Address Unmet Needs of Contraception;

b) Sub-Group on Unmet Needs on Maternal and Child Health;

c) Sub-Group on Strategies for Unmet Needs for Public Health, Drinking Water, Sanitation and Nutrition; and

d) Sub-Group on Empowerment of Women, Development of Children and issues for Adolescents.

The Sub-Group met twice under the Chairpersonship of Smt. Margaret Alva, Member of Parliament and Chairperson of Parliamentary Standing Committee on Empowerment of Women. During the course of the deliberations of the Sub Group, two important developments took place-first, the provisional results of Census 2001 were published and National Policy for Empowerment of Women was approved by the Government. The Sub Group considered both the developments and deliberated on various issues of empowerment of women and development of children and adolescents in the context of the National population Policy.

The Sub-Group felt that the 'unmet needs' of empowerment of women and development of children and adolescents cover a whole gamut of issues which cut through the terms of references of all the Sub Groups and of the Working Groups and, therefore, there is bound to be considerable degree of overlapping in the terms of reference and deliberations of this Sub-Group. The issue of empowerment of women and development of children and adolescents is not a side or peripheral but a core issue for stabilizing the population growth of the country.

DEMOGRAPHIC TRANSITION

The demographic transition of the country in the recent years has brought the issues of women and children into the forefront of the country's development strategy. From a "high birth rate-high death rate" country of the pre Independence era, which provided fodder for the theory of Malthus, India had reached the stage of " high birth rate-low death rate" in the early fifties, which contributed to the high rate of growth of population. This continued till the beginning of the eighties, with a decadal growth rising to 21.51% in the fifties, from 13.31% in the previous decade, followed by 24.80% in the sixties and 24.66% in the seventies, despite all the national efforts made to contain this growth. The transition to the phase of "low birth rate-low death rate" has started at a very slow pace, with population growth sliding to 23.85% in the eighties and 21.34% in the nineties. If the goal of National population Policy of bringing TFR to the replacement level has to be achieved by 2010, the growth rate of population has to be brought down to 10.7% during the current decade, which is a very tall order and can not be achieved unless the issues of women, adolescents and children are brought to the centre stage of our development planning.

The changing demographic profile of the country indicate a few important trends which will have significant bearing on the position of women and children of the country. First, although the percentage of child population below the age of 14 has declined from 37.76% in 1991 to 34.33% in 2001, the absolute numbers of children are still on the rise. The population of children in the age group of 0-6 has increased from 150.42 million in 1991 to 157.86 million in 2001. Likewise the population in the age group of 7-14 is projected to be 170.34 million today as compared to 161.94 million in 1991. Together they constitute 31.9% of the country's population-a huge 328.20 million out of 1.02 billion-the largest number of children in any country anywhere in the world. The adolescents in the age group of 15 to 19 constitute another nearly 10% of the population. Together they constitute the most important potential human resource and it is the health, nutrition, education and well being of these children and adolescents that will determine the future of the country.

The second trend in the country's demography is the declining sex ratio. The overall sex ratio has declined almost consistently over the years-from 972 females per 1000 males in 1901 to 933 in 2001-although the numbers had improved marginally by 1 point in 1951, 3 points in 1981 and 6 points in 2001, but sliding by 5 points in 1961, 9 points in 1971 and 7 points in 1991. The decline of sex ratio have been particularly striking in the age group of 0 to 6 years in recent years. Census 2001 has registered this decline by 18 points-from 927 in 1991 to 945. This decline has been registered in all the States and Union Territories except Kerala, Mizoram, Sikkim, Tripura and Lakshadeep. The decline has been very sharp in prosperous States like Punjab, Haryana, Maharastra and Gujrat. In Punjab the gap in the sex ratio has widened to more than 200 per 1000 children. Unfortunately, the trend could not be arrested by rising female literacy during the decade. This is reflective of a deep seated prejudice against the girl child in the country. Countering this trend should be one of the priorities in the National Socio Economic Goals of the country.

While the female sex ratio among the children is declining, it is increasing among the aged, due to increased life expectancy among the females, leading to a strange gender asymmetry in the population pyramid of the country. With the gradual weakening of family based social security and absence of any strong alternate system, the care of the aged and particularly of the widows, is increasingly assuming the shape of a national problem to be reckoned with in the coming years.

The age pyramid of Indian population will swell in the centre in the years to come. At present 58% of Indians are in the age group of 15-59 years. This will increase to nearly 64% during the next ten years-from 596 million at present to 708 million by 2010, even if TFR reaches its replacement level. The implication of this transition in terms of additional needs of food, water, energy, health care, education and employment will be enormous. At the same time, the gradual increase in literacy particularly among the females on the one hand and the rise in the mean age of marriage of girls on the other, would mean that more and more girls will demand employment, particularly in the organized sector. New types of demands will be placed on the country's educational and training institutions for building capacity and skill of the workers and particularly of the female workers and of those who will be employed in the self employed and informal sectors.

The national demographic features often conceal substantial differences between States and between regions and sub regions within the same State in the achievement of basic demographic indices. These differences are conditioned by factors such as illiteracy, poverty, inadequate access to health and family welfare services etc, which often coexist and reinforce each other. At one end of the spectrum is Kerala with IMR and TFR comparable to many developed countries, but there are districts within the same State like ldukki and Malappuram where IMR and CBR are higher than the national average. At the other end are the States like Bihar and Uttar Pradesh (including newly created Uttaranchal an Jharkhand) which have the worst HDI indices in the world, but with districts like Almora and Ranchi with IMR and CBR much lower than the national level.

The co-relationship between various indices have also been conditioned by a complex web of 'other' factors which need to be studied in depth. Kerala and Tamil Nadu, for example, have achieved replacement level of fertility well before CPR of 60% was reached, whereas, in spite of a developed health infrastructure and CPR much above 60% Punjab is yet to reach that level. Inspite of low female literacy, Andhra Pradesh will be achieving replacement level of fertility much ahead of States with higher literacy rates. Maharastra, Haryana and Punjab have higher SDP than Kerala and Tamil Nadu, but are much behind the southern States in the rates of female literacy, infant mortality and fertility. These suggest that different strategic interventions are required in different States and in different regions and sub regions within the same States for reaching the desired goals of population stabilization. The Sub Group felt that concerted attention should be paid on 5 BIMARU States (Bihar, Madhya Pradesh, Rajasthan and Uttar Pradesh) plus Orissa which account for nearly 44% of the total population of India and which are anticipated to contribute 55% of the population growth in the next decade. Here again district and sub-district specific strategies and action plan should be worked out.

CONCEPTUAL ISSUES

National Population Policy has rightly looked at the issue of population stabilization not as a technical issue that has a technical fix. Population stabilization cannot be achieved by mere physical provisioning of contraception mix or emergency obstetric care. It is critical to involve people-and enable women in particular-to have a say in decisions relating to reproduction and livelihood. This brings in the issues of reproductive rights of women and of the larger conceptual issues of gender equality and of empowerment of women within and outside the household.

The linking of the issue of reproductive health with women's empowerment recognizes that underlying the issue of good health and nutrition for women, we need to examine the issue of power and the nature of gender relations between men and women within the family and community. Here the following conceptual issues need to be highlighted.

Defining Women's Health and Meeting Women's Health Needs: While there have been intense debates attempting to distinguish "women's health" as a more holistic concept than "reproductive health", the issue perhaps is to clearly define what is meant, for our purposes, by women's health and to locate the discourse within a framework of rights. While decision making linked to reproduction and regulation of fertility is important, meeting health needs of women through a system that is sensitive to the differential needs of men and women and their differential access to health care also needs to be taken into account. There are some aspects regarding organizational issues of health delivery which need to be specifically addressed. The division of the health delivery system in terms of two structures-family welfare and health-is not very conducive to a holistic approach to women's health.

Enhanced Awareness and Information: Linked to women's empowerment is the issue of raising awareness about rights-legal literacy, rights to education and health and enhancing information sharing about basic issues. Various studies have indicated that the knowledge of women and adolescent girls about their bodies, and reproductive functions is very limited. Substantial systematic efforts need to be made for enhancing women's and adolescent girls understanding and awareness about various issues.

Linking Health and Reproductive Rights to Other Issues Related to Human Rights: It is essential to recognize the connection between women's health and food security and other economic and environmental conditions. For example, lack of access to water impacts on hygiene, heavy load bearing leads to occupational diseases, lack of nutrition impairs productivity and so on. Therefore the issue of access to safe contraception cannot be delinked from the larger issue of access to food, water, shelter and the issues of sustainable livelihood and a safe environment.

Involvement of Men and Changing Power Relations in Family and Society: In view of the fact that we are laying emphasis on reproductive rights, informed choice and autonomy, it is important that attention is given to underlying social issues which relate to decision making and lack of choices at the level of the family. This involves the social conditioning of roles and responsibilities which one learns from one's 'culture'. It also means trying to address the structural/fundamental inequalities that exist and give rise to certain situations. For example, it is important that solution to anemia etc. is not viewed as a problem, which can be solved by distributing folic acid, but also as an issue of inadequate nutrition, which also has socio-cultural determinants.

Women's Participation: For an empowerment approach to be well integrated into health programmes it is important that women's participation is incorporated at each stage of the programme and issues regarding power structures are also dealt with. The entire conceptual shift from targeted family planning to reproductive health, which is based on informed choice, is to allow women to voice their preference and needs. However, for women to be able to speak out within the family and community social factors have to be taken into account and conditions create for an enabling environment which would allow this to happen.

STATUS OF WOMEN'S HEALTH

The experience of economic progress, political developments and social transformation of the last 50 years, indicate that although women of India have made major gains in terms of decline in maternal mortality and rise in life expectancy, increase in female literacy and employment, mobilization through self help groups and representation at the grassroots level democracy etc., large gender gaps still exist in almost every sphere of life, which do not empower women to have informed choices on their health and nutrition. India accounts for nearly 25% of the world's maternal deaths. Every year about 1,25,000 Indian women die from pregnancy-related causes many of which are preventable. Poor maternal health results in low birth weight and premature babies. More than 7% of the new born babies perish every year. Nearly 2.3% of the babies who survive the first year perish before they complete five years. The number is more in case of female babies.

The mean age of marriage at the national level is 19.5 years, but about 17.4 percent of girls are married below the age of 18 years. Corresponding rates show marked rural (20.3%) and urban (7.4%) difference. 8.3% of fertility in India is contributed by mothers below 19 years of age and this is also linked with pregnancy wastages ranging form premature death, still birth, neonatal deaths, low birth weight babies and maternal morbidity.

Micro Studies have indicated that women do not get adequate nutrition during pregnancy and lactation. The dietary intake of women in the lower economic group is deficient by 500 to 600 calories. In the above 7 years age group there are gender differences in consumption of cereals, pulses, and milk products. In the above 18 years groups, gender difference is quite prominent in the intake of energy rich food. According to an assessment of underweight and stunted growth of children (1997), in the age group of 1-5 years, almost half (49.1 %) of the girls were underweight and 20.3 per cent were severely underweight. Stunting was observed in 56 % percent of girls. The Body Mass Index (BMI) indicates that more women (36.1 %) than male (28.6%) are affected by various stages of Chronic Energy Deficiency.

Research has provided enough information on women's morbidity linked with the environment like indoor air pollution, iodine deficiency of soil/water, flurosis and arsenic related disorder, use of fossil fuels etc. The spread of Tetanus, Pneumonia, Dysentery, Typhoid, Cholera, Plague do not need any further research to prove their relationship with environment and sanitation. The brunt of all these fall disproportionately on women. Several domestic chores as also occupational work of many kinds affects the women and leads to an incurable state of health. This is true both at household level and at the work place specially in the unorganised industry sector where maximum number of women earn their livelihood.

Chronic Mental depression and neurosis in girls and adult females is quite wide spread, but the present health care delivery system and social attitude are ill equipped to tackle them especially in rural areas.

Studies have indicated that women are biologically and epidemiologically more vulnerable to AIDS. Male to female transmission of HIV is twice as efficient than female to male. Moreover, majority of Indian women being anemic, transfusion of blood during child birth is quite common making the women more susceptible to the contact. Besides social factors like lack of control over their own body, early marriage and repeated pregnancies, lack of information, poverty induced/forced prostitution, promiscuity of husbands etc. make them more vulnerable to this disease. The impact of HIV and Aids on women is also much more severe and critical. First, inter-generational transmission of the disease takes place through women. Secondly, the rejection and ostracisation of women and girls are much more than for males. Further, women and girls suffer disproportionately from the burden of the disease. The traditional gender role of women in caring for the sick make them more susceptible to the disease. Girls of AIDS affected families often have to leave the school to care for the sick.

Women are the victims of a whole plethora of violence committed against them-infanticide, torture, rape, molestation, battering, trafficking, prostitution, forced marriage, dowry death, custodial violence and so on. This is a reflection of the deep rooted 'gender ideology' of society. Often the crimes are committed by people who are close to the victims and are traditionally supposed to be their protectors. But the victims, especially the sexually abused girls and women, face the brunt of the act more than the abuser. Only a miniscule of the acts of violence committed against women are covered under legal provisions and the bulk of them go unreported. Complex and lengthy legal procedures, often involving substantial expenditure, poor rate of conviction and lack of support from relatives and community are the important reasons for under reporting of crimes against women. Even then the crimes committed against women in relation to the total crimes, has increased from 11% in 1996 to 13.5% in 1998.

Poverty in general, and extreme poverty in particular, has a significant gender dimension. Studies has been revealed that (i) the percentage of adult women exceeds the percentage of adult men below the poverty line, both in rural and urban areas; (ii) the percentage of children in the 0-4 age group in poor households exceeds that of non-poor households, and (iii) in both urban and rural areas, disadvantaged groups of women from Scheduled Castes and Tribes constitute a high proportion of the poor. Incidence of poverty is positively co-related with IMR-a poor couple perceives an additional child to be an investment, both as security against probable mortality of the surviving child and as a potential wage earner. Significant co-relation between spread of female literacy and decline of fertility has been observed throughout the country although there are regions where fertility has declined despite prevalence of illiteracy. A lot of gains have been made in the recent years in female illiteracy. For the first time the number of absolute illiterates has declined and rate of growth of female literacy has outpaced that of males. But still 45.84% of females in the age group of 6 to 50 are illiterates. The gap between male and female literacy is still as wide as 22 percentage points.

THE STATE OF INDIAN CHILDREN

India is to home the largest number of children in the world. Nearly one third of its population-328.20 million in absolute terms-is children below the age of 15 years. About 45% of its population are minors i.e, below the age of 18 years. The country had formulated a National Policy for Children in 1974 and ratified the United Nations Convention on the Rights of the Child in 1992. A National Plan of Action for Children (NPAC) was also drawn up in 1992, which had set goals for various indicators to be achieved by the year 2000. But most of these goals have remained unfulfilled, although significant improvements have taken place in all the crucial indicators like infant and child mortality rates, school enrolment ratios, drop-out rates, levels of mal-nutrition etc.

Infant mortality has remained around 72 per 1000 live births with no significant improvement in the nineties unlike in the eighties. This is much below the average of 6 in developed countries, 64 in developing countries and the world average of 59. There are significant disparities across States, within the

States and among castes, communities and other ethnic groups. Kerala for instance, has IMR of 13 per 1000 live births against 94 in Madhya Pradesh: The Infant mortality rate among Scheduled Castes is 24% higher than the national average. Like-wise, the rural and urban differentials also continue to be very high-46 in urban areas as compared to 78 in rural areas. The underlying reasons of high infant mortality are early marriage and childbearing, lack of birth spacing, inadequate maternal nutrition, inadequate antenatal care, and large proportion of deliveries lacking supervision by trained birth attendants.

The Child Mortality Rate (CMR) of India is also very high 25 children out of every 1000 who survive the first year die before they complete 5 years. India ranks 49 out of 189 countries in CMR i.e, if the worst is ranked 1, India is 49th. This reflects the inability of families to look after their young children. Despite efforts being made under the Integrated Child Development Services programme, malnutrition continues to remain a principal underlying cause of morbidity and mortality in under-5 children. This is because intrauterine growth retardation caused by inadequate nutrition during pregnancy cannot be corrected later on. It is an alarming fact that one out of three children are born in India with low birth weight (<2500 g). Coupled with unsupervised delivery and delayed complementary feeding, unhygienic sanitary practices and lack of access to safe drinking water, the average child succumbs to acute respiratory infections and diarrhea.

Malnutrition constitutes a major threat to the development potential of young children. Although surveys conducted by the National Nutrition Monitoring Bureau, Hyderabad have confirmed that there has been a declining trend in severe and moderate degrees of malnutrition amongst children, the micro-nutrient deficiencies, viz. Vitamin A, iron and iodine have been affecting children in various degrees. The national data indicates that although the proportion of nutritional blindness has reduced drastically, yet the sub-clinical deficiency of vitamin A still continues. Other health concerns of the children are vaccine preventable diseases, birth asphyxia, injury and disability,

Mother to Child Transmission (MTCT) of HIV and iodine deficiency disorders. While India has achieved great success with the Pulse Polio Campaign, reports indicate that this has affected routine immunization under the Universal Immunization Programme where the coverage has slipped in recent times. Birth asphyxia is linked to lack of resuscitation facilities during delivery. Many cases of congenital birth defects and mental retardation are caused due to neglect at the time of birth, which are preventable.

A growing incidence of HIV positive mothers in the general population suggests that problem of HIV infected children may soon emerge as a serious problem to be reckoned with. The rate of transmission from a HIV positive mother to her child varies between 15 to 40% with increased risk if the child is breastfed. A child infected at birth, unlike in the case of adults with HIV has a short window period of 3-5 years before the infection overwhelms the developing immune system of the child.

Education is a right of every child. The Directive Principles of State Policy enshrined in the Constitution of India require the State to provide free and compulsory elementary education to all children up to the age of 14 years. Although there has been a substantial increase in the enrolment of children at all levels of schooling, yet 100 million children are estimated to be out of school. Most of these children are vulnerable to neglect. The NSS survey of 1977 has indicated that child labour in the country has increased to 17 million as compared to 13.6 million in 1981 and 11.3 million in 1991. As many as 4.15 lakh children live on the streets in the mega cities of Bangalore, Mumbai, Calcutta, Delhi, Hyderabad and Chennai and are exposed to all types of exploitation.

ISSUES OF THE ADOLESCENTS

Adolescents comprise about a fifth of India's population, but they have so far not been recognized as a target of any strategy for development in the country. They are important human resource material, which can be effectively moulded and channelised for nation building. A bulk of population in this age group, particularly in the rural areas, are drop outs from schools and are vulnerable to exploitation of various sorts. The adolescent girls particularly are at high risk of anemia and mental and behavioral disorder. A three-fold strategy must be adopted for helping adolescents in the country. First, efforts should be made to retain them in the education system by progressively reducing the rate of dropouts from schools and colleges through improvement in educational facilities.

Secondly, vocational training and skill development for the drop outs should be organized in various traditional and non traditional trades, depending on their aptitudes and job opportunities, to prepare them to become self sufficient economically and responsible citizens of the country. Thirdly, the nutritional requirement of the adolescents, particularly of the adolescent girls, should be a matter of special concern, since they are the potential mothers and any investment in their health and nutrition shall not only empower them to be better women, but also be an insurance against the underweight and under nourished children of the future. Improvement of health of the adolescent girl is a definite way of breaking the inter generational cycle of malnutrition in the population. The adolescent girls need also to be protected from unwanted pregnancies and sexually transmitted diseases. Reproductive health services for adolescent boys and girls is particularly needed in rural areas where adolescent marriages and pregnancies are widely prevalent.

STRATEGIES FOR INTERVENTION

The intervention strategy for empowering women to have informed and effective choices on their health and nutrition and for the development of children and adolescents has to be multi-pronged.

CONVERGENCE OF SERVICE DELIVERY AT VILLAGE LEVELS

There are two main programmes in the Department of Women and Child Development, which aim at convergence of services delivery at the village level, namely, Integrated Child Development Scheme (ICDS) and Integrated Women.'s

Empowennent Programme (IWEP). The ICDS network through Anganwadi Centres reaches 85% of the villages and hamlets in the country. The IWEP (erstwhile Indira Mahila Yojana) which extends to 650 blocks operates through the self help groups of women. Both these programmes can be effective vehicles for the implementation of the National Population Policy. It is therefore critical that both the schemes are universalized.

Nutrition

The Supplementary Nutrition provided under the ICDS Scheme is one of the most vital components under Basic Minimum Service Programme aimed at eradication of the menace of malnutrition of children and women. The success of the programme however depends largely on adequate provision of funds to the States and UTs. An Action plan needs to be drawn up for taking up nutrition in a mission mode to cover infants, adolescent girls, pregnant and lactating mothers-the three critical links in the inter-generational cycle of malnutrition. One intervention that has successfully worked in improving nutrition levels as well as impacting favourably on retention of children in schools is the mid-day meal scheme. This has shown positive results in programmes like TINP and needs to be replicated widely.

Formation of Self-Help Groups

The formation of self-help groups as a basis for the social and economic empowerment of deprived and disadvantaged women has been found to be a successful mechanism for the organization, mobilization and self development of women. This has been tested through the IMY and Swa Shakti projects of the Department of Women and Child Development and is being replicated in a number of programmes of other Departments. These groups can facilitate the process of economic empowerment through thrift and savings, training and skill upgradation and access to credit and other productive resources. They can also be instruments of social empowerment through awareness generation and convergence of delivery of schemes. With the feeling of ownership and management of their own resources and savings, poor women have been able to choose their priorities and have even been found to cover the cost of additional nutrition and health gaps. The success of this approach has resulted in universalization of this mode of organization in all the southern States. There is a need to replicate this mode throughout the country.

Access to Resources

The issue of improved health and nutrition is intimately linked to access to and control over local, social, and economic structures. For women to be empowered we need to ensure

(a) equitable access and distribution of resources like land, credit etc.

(b) access to education.

(c) access to health/nutrition

(d) access to water and sanitation

This implies that resources should flow into these areas to bridge the gender gap and that systems be developed to plan, implement and monitor the 'bridging' of the gap. Various studies have shown that ownership of land tends to reduce fertility by providing an alternate means of security. Similarly education has its own impact on reproductive behaviour of both men and women. Improving the access of women/households in rural areas and urban slums to safe sources of drinking water will free them from the drudgery of fetching water and in decreasing the morbidity resulting from water-borne diseases such as diarrhoea and cholera. This will impact positively on the health and energy levels of women. Access to technologies which can reduce the drudgery of women on the various works performed by them both within and outside the household is also a very useful intervention for empowering the women.

Women's Component Plan

While the Planning Commission has already incorporated the concept of Women's Component Plan in the 9th Five Year Plan whereby 30% of funds/benefit on every women related sector actually flow to women, it is important that guidelines are finalized early so that this could be implemented effectively.

Development of Gender Disaggregated Data System

One of the constraints in the preparation, implementation and monitoring of plans for the development of women is the absence of gender segregated data on various indices of development at the State, district and sub district levels. This lacunae in our statistical system should be addressed on a priority basis.

Legislation

Laws should be gender sensitive and ensure equal provision and access to resources for men and women. Also there needs to be a much broader focus on implementation issues. Many of the existing statutes such as Indecent Representation of Women's Act, Minimum Wages Act, Equal Remuneration Act, and Pre-natal Diagnostic Act, Maternity Benefit Act, etc., are implemented more in their violation. A number of these Acts are under review in order to strengthen their provisions. The Maternity Benefit Act needs to be strictly implemented and expanded to cover women in the informal sector, along with provision of paid leave for a longer period.

Freedom from Violence

Women and girls face violence in various forms at various stages of their life cycle. This takes the form of female foeticide and infanticide, rape, dowry death and more indirect forms such as desertion or abandonment of older women. This calls for a multipronged strategy of implementation of laws, awareness, community sanctions etc.

Participation in Political Life

For empowerment, women need to have a voice in decision making and planning through adequate representation. Reservation of women in the rural and urban local bodies had enabled representation of nearly a million women at the grassroots who play a very important catalytic role in transforming the society. Similar representation in State Legislature and Parliament would further strengthen the process of empowerment of women.

Sustained Media Campaign

One of the most effective interventions that can take place to address the issues of attitude and mind sets of men and women, of the community and also of the functionaries of the government-the bureaucracy, police and judiciary is media campaigns. A sustained campaign through the print, electronic and folk media is necessary on various issues related to empowerment of women, health and nutrition, laws, value of the girl child, violence against women etc. As the Sub Group was deliberating on the issue of empowerment of women, the National Policy for Empowerment of Women (NPEW) was approved by the Government. The Policy makes a series of prescriptions for the economic and social empowerment of women and for mainstreaming the gender perspective in the development process. The policy has also enjoined upon all Central and State Ministries to draw up time bound Action Plan for translating the Policy into a set of concrete actions and measurable goals to be achieved by 2010. The Policy has also talked about identification and commitment of resources and responsibilities for implementation of the action plans and of development of suitable structures and mechanisms to ensure efficient monitoring, review and gender impact assessment of plans and policies.

National Socio Economic Goals

The objectives of National Population Policy have been conceptualised into three stages:

(a) *Immediate*-to address the unmet needs for contraception, health care infrastructure, and health personnel, and to provide integrated service delivery for basic reproductive and child health care.

(b) *Medium-term*-to bring the TFR to replacement levels by 2010, through vigorous implementation of inter-sectoral operational strategies.

(c) *Long-term*-to achieve a stable population by 2045, at a level consistent with the requirements of sustainable economic growth, social development, and environmental protection.

In pursuance of these objectives, the NPP has fixed a set of fourteen National Socio Demographic Goals to be achieved in each case by 2010. The NPEW has also urged that measurable goals to be achieved by 2010 have to be fixed in the Action Plan although these goals have not been stated in the Policy itself. Both the Action Plans of NPEW and of the medium term objectives of the NPP have taken the year 2010 as their time frame. There is urgent need therefore for operationalisation of the convergence of the two Policies through the Action Plans of the Governments at the national and State levels.

In other words, the fourteen National Socio Demographic Goals should inform the preparation of the Action Plans under NPEW and to that extent guidelines should be issued by the Department of Women and Child Development to all the State Governments and Union Territories. These fourteen National Socio Demographic Goals of NPP are:

(a) Address the unmet needs for basic reproductive and child health services, supplies and infrastructure.

(b) Make school education up to age 14 free and compulsory, and reduce drop outs at primary and secondary school levels to below 20 percent for both boys and girls.

(c) Reduce infant mortality rate to below 30 per 1000 live births.

(d) Reduce maternal mortality ratio to below 100 per 100,000 live births.

(e) Achieve universal immunization of children against all vaccine preventable diseases.

(f) Promote delayed marriage for girls, not earlier than age 18 and preferably after 20 years of age.

(g) Achieve 80 percent institutional deliveries and 100 percent deliveries by trained persons.

(h) Achieve universal access to information/counseling, and services for fertility regulation and contraception with a wide basket of choices.

(i) Achieve 100 per cent registration of births, deaths, marriage and pregnancy.

(j) Contain the spread of Acquired Immunodeficiency Syndrome (AIDS), and promote greater integration between the management of reproductive tract infections (RTI) and sexually transmitted infections (STI) and the National AIDS Control Organisation.

(k) Prevent and control communicable diseases.

(l) Integrate Indian Systems of Medicine (ISM) in the provision of reproductive and child health services, and in reaching out to households.

(m) Promote vigorously the small family norm to achieve replacement levels of TFR.

(n) Bring about convergence in implementation of related social sector programs so that family welfare becomes a people centred programme.

It may be seen that out of these fourteen goals the first seven relate directly to the women and children and the remaining seven concern them indirectly, although vitally. The Sub Group deliberated on each of these goals. Judging by the pace of progress achieved in the social sectors in the last fifty years, the Sub group felt that implementation of these goals during the course of a decade may become extremely difficult and challenging unless there is commitment of adequate resources by the Central and State Governments on the social sector, particularly in the fields of health, education and nutrition and unless there is strong and effective convergence of services at the grassroot level involving all the stakeholders and the functionaries of all the related Government agencies.

Reduction of IMR to below 30 per 1000 and of MMR to below 100 per 100,000 live births from 72 and 408 at present would require identification of the blocks (i) where IMR has already reached below 30 level, (ii) where it has reached a threshold level, (iii) where it would reach the mark during the decade given the normal rate of progress already achieved, (iv) where it would need additional input and (v) where it would require substantially additional input of both child and maternal care services. At present no scientific system of continuous grading and monitoring of ICDS services, according to the level of achievements of IMR and MMR, exists at the national level. Uniform guidelines and criteria are applied to all the ICDS blocks throughout the country, irrespective of the levels of achievement. This must be replaced by a block specific flexible approach with additional anganwadi centers and additional supplementary nutrition wherever required. This should be put in place immediately in consultation with the State Governments and other stakeholders.

Although there are marked differences in the level of IMR/ MMR between ICDS and non-ICDS blocks, such differences are very marginal in many blocks. In Uttar Pradesh, for example, average IMR in ICDS blocks is 86 per 1000 live births against 86.5 in non-ICDS blocks. This strongly suggests that the programme has not been properly implemented in certain States of the country. There is an urgent need for analyzing the causes of poor performance in some blocks and to take effective remedial steps for improving the level of performance in a time bound manner.

It is unfortunate that in the division of responsibilities between the Central and State Governments, Government of India have chosen the 'easy to manage' task of providing the cost administrative services and of medicines and learning materials, while entrusting the job of funding and arranging the nutrition items to the State Governments. Given the critical resource position of most of the State Governments, nutrition always remains a neglected priority for them. There are reports that the supplementary feeding programme in the States was not taken up for months together. Even the Additional Plan Assistance under Prime Minister's Gramodaya Yojana (PMGY) was not utilized for supplementary nutrition in many States. It is unfortunate that when the country is facing the problem of storage of surplus food grains procured by the Food Corporation of India, there are large number of infants and mothers who die every year due to lack of nutrition.

The country's achievement in food security must be converted into nutritional security by effectively distributing the surplus food grains at least to infants and mothers through the network of ICDS centers. This should be taken up in a mission mode, if the targets of IMR/MMR are to be achieved within the given time frame.

It is also unfortunate that the most backward areas of Bihar, Jharkhand and Uttar Pradesh, which have the highest incidence of infant and maternal mortality, have not yet been covered under the ICDS. These 450 blocks, which should have been the first charge on the programme, have been kept last in the priorities of the Government. The ICDS must immediately be extended to all the remaining blocks of the country and the unusual time lag between the sanctioning of the projects and the actual operationalisation must be reduced to a minimum. It is seen that the time lag is sometimes as high as two years, which cannot be justified by any means whatsoever.

The ICDS programme must also be effectively converged with the grassroot level programmes and infrastructure of Health and Family Welfare Departments, if the desired goals of IMR/MMR and of universal immunization of children against all vaccine preventable diseases are to be achieved. The States like Orissa and Gujrat, where such convergence has taken place, have done remarkably well, in a relatively short period of time. In most of the States the programmes suffer due to the lack of effective co ordination between the Department of Women and Child development and the Department of Health and Family Welfare. The village Panchayats and the community should also be involved more effectively with the functioning of the ICDS centers.

It is a matter of national shame that despite the Constitutional directive to the State to endeavour to provide within a period of ten years from the commencement of the Constitution, free and compulsory education for all children until they complete the age of fourteen years, more than 100 million Indian children either do not get admitted to schools or drop out.

It is high time that the Directive Principle is converted into justifiable Fundamental Right of citizens and a comprehensive package of incentives and disincentives are built into our national education system to make it a reality. The

Balika Samriddhi Yojana, which links payment of scholarship to girls to duration of school attendance should be implemented more vigorously and provided with adequate funds.

The average age of marriage at the national level has already reached 19.5 years and therefore achieving the target of 20 years by 2010 would seem to be an easily achievable task. But the average conceals significant regional differences. Child marriage is still a practice in many States.

About 20.3% percent of girls in the rural areas are married before 18 years. 8.3% percent of fertility in India is contributed by mothers below 19 years of age and this is closely linked with pregnancy wastages ranging form pre-mature death, stillbirth, neonatal deaths, low birth weight and maternal morbidity. Therefore, region specific strategies and action plans need to be worked out to achieve this national goal.

OPERATIONAL STRATEGIES

The Action Plan under NPP 2000 has outlined operational strategies for (i) empowering women for health and nutrition, (ii) child health and survival and (iii) adolescents. The Sub Group considered these strategies, but while broadly agreeing with them felt that the overwhelming emphasis placed on maternity and childcare services can not be taken as 'stand alone strategies'. Rather these should be effectively integrated with the overall perspectives, strategies and programmes for empowerment of women and of development of children and adolescents, as outlined in this report.

RECOMMENDATIONS

The Sub Group makes the following recommendations for the consideration of the National Commission on Population: The task of stabilization of population is not simply a question of birth control or contraceptives. It is intrinsically connected with the larger issues of alleviation of poverty, empowerment of women, changing mind set of men, women and community and of creation of opportunities and enabling environment of all round development of women, children and adolescents. There is a tendency to marginalize these 'strategic' issues in the belief that 'practical' needs are in some sense more immediate, urgent and easier to manage. Unless these practical needs of women are conceived within a long run and 'strategic' framework, there is a danger of losing sight of the essential inter connections between the two. In principle a long-run goal may well be achieved through a series of co-ordinated short-term strategies, but in practice these may turn out to be stand-alone pieces, which could be symptoms of a long run structural malaise. Defining 'short term' goals simply in terms of combating such symptoms would be tantamount to treating the symptom of the disease rather than treating the disease itself. Therefore, it is extremely important to design strategies for empowerment of women and for development of children and adolescents, keeping this disease in mind.

The long awaited approval of National Policy for Empowerment of Women which has closely followed the National Population Policy is a welcome development. It is understood that a new National Policy on Health and a National Policy on Youth are under consideration. The Government is also seized with the idea of declaring basic education as a Fundamental Right of citizens and formulating a Charter of Rights of Children. All these efforts should be integrated and the National and State Action Plans to be framed under each of these Policies should be effectively converged for the effective delivery of services at the grassroot level. The broad National Socio Economic Goals of NPP should inform the process of preparation of the Action Plans under NPEW.

The Planning Commission should make a commitment of adequate resources for the effective implementation of Plans to achieve the National Socio Economic Goals. At present less than 10% of the Annual Budget is spent on the social sector. There is a strong need and justification to substantially step up allocation to all these sectors, such as health, education, women and child development, rural development, social welfare etc.

Both the programmes on Integrated Child Development Services (ICDS) and Integrated Women's Empowerment Programme (IWEP) should be universalized covering all the development blocks of the country, but the design, content and guidelines of the projects under both the programmes should be flexible enough to meet the specific requirement of the blocks so that they are in a position to achieve the National Socio Economic Goals within the time frame prescribed in the NPP.

Larger number of creches/day care centers should be opened to encourage female participation in the economy and also to create a positive impact on enrolment and drop out rates of girl children.

The Kishori Shakti Yojana as a component of ICDS, which has been taken up in 2000 blocks needs to be reworked and restructured to have a developmental approach rather sectoral approach. It should have a gender centred adolescent nutrition and development programme and should aim at a high level of adolescent participation. It should meet the requirements of nutrition, training and education of the adolescent girls so that they can gain the knowledge and self-confidence to be informed and capable members of society. The restructured programme should be universalized to cover all the blocks in the country.

A strong focus on the adolescents should be built in various programmes and schemes to address their concerns related to health, nutrition, sexual activity and behivour, vulnerability to HIV/AIDS etc. Sex education is an area which needs to be specifically addressed.

The gains made by the country in food security should be converted into nutritional security of children and the mothers below the poverty line to completely eliminate nutrition related deaths within a given time frame. Here again block specific strategies need to be worked out in consultation with all the stakeholders.

The constitutionally mandated country wide Panchayat Raj Institutions with one third of its Members and Chairpersons from among the women, has the potential to co-ordinate various programmes of the government on women and children according to the needs and requirements of the micro level realities and to monitor the services to the community. If properly constituted and adequately empowered, they have the potential to ensure the highest degree of transparency and accountability at the grassroot level. Panchayats can also be used for initiating popular movements, as has been done in the context of the National Literacy Mission in a number of States. A nation wide movement on informed fertility control through the Panchayats can very well be initiated under the auspices of the National Commission on Population. Village Panchayats can become regular forums for discussions on village health issues, including issues of reproductive health and fertility control.

Capacity of elected representatives at the grass roots should be developed so that they will be in a position to design projects on health and related areas as appropriate to the needs and requirements of local areas.

Given the size and heterogeneity of our population and the power structure within the Panchayats, even the Gram Panchayats may still be far away from the community. Some NGOs have found it expedient to create intermediate structures between the Panchatyats and the village communities for more efficient processes of information and dissemination and better service delivery. But these local elected bodies are by and large the best instruments for implementing community programmes.

The self help groups of women have been found very effective in organizing and sensitizing women to various issues and empowering them socially and economically. The collaboration of Panchayats, NGOs and Self Help Groups at the grassroots level could become very effective for implementation of grassroot level initiatives in the social sectors. Depending on the strength of the stakeholders at the field level, different models of collaboration can be worked out for effective synergy of these initiatives, to transform the situation at the ground level.

The districts and blocks should be graded according to the level of achievements in the social sectors and block specific action plans should be framed for achieving the National Socio Economic Goals within the given time frame. Instead of uniform allocation of resources to blocks as is currently the practice in almost all the programmes, a more flexible and need-based approach should be taken. The segment of population and areas which have lagged behind in national development efforts, should be positively discriminated, so that they can be helped as quickly as possible to reach the minimum desired levels of standards and goals. But care should be taken to ensure that those blocks which have shown results do not feel discriminated against.

In order that district or block specific plans and projects can be prepared, implemented and monitored it is necessary to develop a system of gender segregated data on various indices of development at the district and sub district level at regular intervals. The absence of such data constraints the preparation of sound Women Development Plans at the field level.

The Medium Term perspective of 10 years should be adopted for the empowerment of women and development of children and adolescents. To that extent the National Socio Economic Goals of NPP should be accepted in the Action Plans for the Empowerment of Women and Development of Children and Adolescents. The achievement of these goals should be monitored on a quarterly basis and appraised on a bi-annual basis.

Involving the male is equally important for the empowerment of women and for stabilization of population. Reproductive decisions are typically taken within the family and hence promoting gender equality within the family has to be based on partnership and not on relationship of domination or subordination within the family. To achieve better understanding, every effort must be made to involve men in the promotion of reproductive rights. This is vital in order to change the societal perceptions about the contribution of women. This can happen only when women are seen by men-and by society-not as 'better halves' but as 'equal halves'.

There is a large unmet need for contraceptives and comprehensive information regarding their efficacy and usage. There has to be greater focus on male contraceptives as they are safer and easier to use. New contraceptives for women need to be carefully introduced with the fully informed participation of women. A system of incentives/disincentive for the functionaries as also the beneficiaries of various programmes should be developed to convey clear messages about the priorities of the Government regarding population stabilization of the country. However, in order to ensure that disincentives do not become a tool for harassing the disadvantaged, it is necessary to create an environment enabling the women to have self-determination in terms of their reproductive life.

The target of achieving 80% institutional deliveries by 2010 is a tall order, considering that more than half of the deliveries still take place at home at present. The idea of maternity hut in each village to be used as the village delivery room, with storage space for supplies and medicine, and equipped adequately with kits for midwifery, antenatal care and delivery and basic medicines, contraceptives and drugs and medicines for common ailments, is conceptually very sound but may be difficult to implement within the given time frame. A more realistic and practical alternative is to train and equip the village midwives to ensure 100% safe deliveries. This must be taken up immediately as a time bound national programme, to upgrade their skills.

In view of the shortage of trained medical personnel at the PHCs and dispensaries, it should be made mandatory for medical students in both Government and private medical colleges to go to designated rural areas for service for a period of 12 months after they complete one year of residency but before their final degree is awarded. Posting to rural areas for a minimum period of two years at a time should be legally binding for medical officers. Similar arrangements should also be made mandatory for nurses, pharmacists and other paramedical staff.

A Core Group of Women Functionaries at the village level such as ANM, AWW, lady school teacher and elected women Panchayat members could co-ordinate the various programmes on women and children at the village or hamlet level. They should meet once in a fortnight at a fixed place and date to discuss among themselves the progress of the implementation of the programmes and to sort out the problems and difficulties at the purely local level. Coordinating and an integrated approach rather than competition among the local functionaries is essential to ensure positive results. Common training and parity in salaries could ensure this.

Training and capacity building of field level functionaries, NGOs, SHG workers and PRI members are extremely important if they are to perform their desired roles for the achievement of National Socio Economic Goals. Role of Angan Wadi Workers (AWW) is very crucial for the success of the various grassroot level initiatives of the Government. Today the contribution of AWW is not limited to the ICDS only. Her services are required in other programmes also. But she is paid very little-even less than the minimum wage prescribed by the Government itself. Therefore, the honorarium of the AWWs should be enhanced suitably with incentives for results shown. But the AWW must be a local person who stays in the villages.

In view of unacceptable high neonatal and perinatal mortality a comprehensive package needs to be developed at block level concentrating on improving home based care through trained personnel, with adequate referral linkages.

Every infant and maternal death must be compulsorily audited, to have better understanding of the underlying factors for such deaths. Simultaneously, a system of accountability of every functionary must be put in place to fix responsibility for every action or inaction for causing or precipitating such deaths.

Certain clinical and medical interventions can result in immediate and significant improvement in the maternal mortality. Such interventions can also be very cost effective. For example, Tetanus Toxoid injections can prevent a significant percentage of maternal deaths. Such interventions can be taken as a campaign on fixed dates throughout the country, for which nation wide publicity can be given. The same occasion can also be utilized for the health check up of pregnant mothers.

The provisions of Pre-natal Diagnostic Act is not at all be effective in checking the practice of female foeticide, which have become rampant in many States. The requirement of prior permission of 'competent authority' before a case for violation of the provisions of the Act can be challaned before the court, has been found to be a hindrance for booking the offenders, since most of the States have designated the Director of Health Services as the competent authority and they have been found to be reluctant to take action against their colleague doctors. The Act needs to be reviewed thoroughly. More than that a concerted public opinion involving religious leaders and opinion makers from every field should be built up against this highly undesirable social practice.

A sustained, systematic, concerted and pervasive campaign in the print, electronic and folk media should be built up in support of the National Socio Economic Goals of NPP and on various issues related to empowerment of women, health related issues, value of girl child, rights of women, violence against women etc. Village melas and festivals, which bring people together, should be used to popularize these messages. The media budget of the entire social sector Ministries/departments should be pooled together for this campaign.

Network of IGNOU and other agencies should also be utilized for developing suitable packages and courses on health and nutrition education.

13

INTERNATIONAL CONFERENCE ON POPULATION AND DEVELOPMENT

DEBATE OVER POLICY

Many people involved in family planning policy and programs seek to balance a variety of concerns. Most agree that couples and individuals should be able to plan the number of their children and the timing of their births. They do not always agree, however, on how to prioritize the goals of family planning programs. Some focus primarily on reducing the rate of population growth; others, on the reproductive health needs of couples and individuals; and still others, on adhering to ethical or religious beliefs. In preparation for the International Conference on Population and Development (ICPD) in Cairo, September 1994, many voices have spoken up, advocating differing, but not always mutually exclusive, priorities.

Population Growth: Those concerned about rapid population growth emphasize that:

- Rapid population growth threatens the progress of all other efforts to improve the standard of living.
- Environmental resources are threatened by increasingly large populations.
- Family planning programs should provide services to as many people as possible as soon as possible.
- Family planning programs should focus first and foremost on providing contraceptive supplies and services.

Needs of couples and individuals. Those concerned about the needs of couples and individuals emphasize that:

- The preferences, satisfaction, and safety of current family planning clients should receive higher priority than increasing the number of contraceptive users.
- Family planning services should be part of programs that help women and men not only with avoiding pregnancy but also with a range of other reproductive health needs.
- Reproductive health care programs should devote more attention to improving the quality of care that they offer.
- Family planning programs should help women to achieve equity in society as well as to meet their reproductive goals and health needs.
- Environmental degradation and resource conservation should not be addressed primarily by emphasizing limitation of childbearing in developing countries.

Strongly felt ethical and religious beliefs underlie many people's differing positions on population and family planning issues, including the positions of people concerned about population growth or about the needs of couples and individuals. Some advocates, however, particularly identify themselves as speaking from an ethical or religious point of view.

Ethical Considerations: Those concerned primarily about ethical considerations emphasize that:

- All individuals and couples should have the right to make their own decisions about their fertility, free of coercion or pressure.
- Family planning programs should not set targets for numbers of new contraceptive users, incentives for contraceptive use, or field workers' quotas that might result in pressure on people to use contraceptive methods.
- Clients should be given an informed choice of contraceptive methods.

Religious beliefs. Some, but not all, who express a religious viewpoint emphasize their contentions that:

- Abortion is not acceptable.
- Only married couples should have access to contraceptive methods because sexual activity outside marriage is immoral.

Alone among major religions, the leadership of the Catholic Church objects to all contraceptive methods other than periodic abstinence. This position seems to have had more impact on policy-makers and the availability of services in some countries than on the attitudes of individual Catholics.

LABELS POLARIZE POSITIONS

Most policy-makers and advocates recognize that many of these viewpoints are legitimate and yet prioritizing program goals is necessary. In the public debate, however, labels are often used-sometimes unfairly and inaccurately-to imply that individuals and groups advocate extreme positions, ignore other points of view, or have malicious intentions. For example, those who focus on rapid population growth are sometimes labeled "population controllers" who disregard women, and those concerned with reproductive rights are sometimes portrayed as "radical feminists" who ignore the consequences of rapid population growth. As a result, positions have sometimes become polarized, focusing on disagreement rather than on the broader areas of accord.

Seeking Common Ground

In reality the serious debate concerns allocating scarce resources to achieve the multiple goals of meeting clients' needs, slowing population growth, and protecting the environment in ways that respect individuals' religious, ethical, and cultural beliefs. Can population policies both satisfy demographic goals and advance individual rights? A growing number of experts and policy-makers argue that conflicts, although they cannot be completely resolved, need not be as great as they sometimes appear. Suggested approaches include:

- Base national population policy on human rights as well as economic concerns. Policy often focuses on the economic benefit to all citizens of slower population growth. Policy-makers can emphasize more strongly, at the same time, that control over one's own fertility is a human right and that providing services that satisfy clients is as important a program goal as reducing total fertility rates.
- Focus on unmet need. Millions of women do not want more children, want to delay their first or next pregnancy, or need better reproductive health services. High-quality services that meet these people's existing needs would increase use of contraception, lengthen continuation, and in the process often reach demographic goals.
- Support public policies that indirectly reduce population growth. If policies support roles for women other than childrearing and make these roles socially acceptable and economically independent, some women may choose to have fewer children. Also, women who can provide for themselves and their children can better protect themselves from coerced sex and unwanted pregnancy. Changes that support more options for women include ending policies that encourage parents to favor sons over daughters, eliminating arranged marriages of young girls, enacting and enforcing minimum marriage ages, eliminating policies or tax provisions that favor large families, and assuring equitable male financial responsibility for women and children during marriage and after divorce.

FAMILY PLANNING-AN ASSET FOR WOMEN

Women want better lives for themselves, their children, their families, and their communities. They want to do their best in their current roles as mothers, wives, workers, and community members. Many women also want new opportunities in life-chances to learn, to make their own decisions, to have more say in the course of their own lives. Women want to have choices. Family planning is one important way that women can take control of their own lives and make more choices possible. Choices are essential to human dignity. Without choices and without opportunities, a person cannot hope for a better future. Without choices, a person can have little self-respect. A person imprisoned is punished by being denied choices; a person denied choices is punished even without being imprisoned.

Although poverty and lack of education often limit choices and opportunities for both men and women in the developing world, in general women's choices are especially limited. Social norms, often embodied in a husband, parent, or mother-in-law, prevent many women from having much say in their own lives or much autonomy to choose their own paths. Even if women were allowed to make choices, social and economic options and opportunities are often beyond women's reach. As a result, compared with men, women have less health care, less education, fewer choices of jobs, poorer pay, and less legal protection.

Family Planning Can Help

Family planning can help women meet their needs-both their practical need to perform conventional roles more effectively and their strategic need to find new roles and opportunities. By enabling a woman to control her own fertility, contraceptive use can help meet a woman's practical needs in several ways. Safe contraception contributes to good health: when women avoid unwanted pregnancy, they avoid the risks of childbearing or abortion. In the developing countries one woman in every 50 or so dies from causes related to childbearing. Also, birth spacing helps her children survive. In addition, contraceptive use may give a woman more choice in the use of her time by helping her avoid unwanted pregnancy, childbearing, and childcare. With better health and more control over her time, a woman may be able to do more in her customary roles for herself, for the children she chooses to have, and for her community.

Beyond meeting these practical needs, contraceptive use can help to meet women's strategic needs. Women who are healthier and have more control over their time are in a better position to take advantage of education, employment, or other opportunities if they are available. Also, by planning their pregnancies, women may find that they can plan more of other aspects of their lives.

Contraceptive use is often necessary but seldom sufficient to change a woman's situation in life. When a woman controls her own fertility, she may have more choice about the course of her life. Whether she can make changes in her life, however, depends on her personal circumstances, social norms, economic development, and law, among other factors. Changes in many households and throughout society will be needed before women can realize their full potential.

Family planning programs also can help meet women's needs, both practical and strategic. Of course, they do so chiefly because they provide contraceptive methods. In addition, programs can design high-quality services so that to some degree they may help women meet strategic needs. For example:

- Family planning programs can demonstrate to the community that women have a right to be informed and to have their decisions respected.
- Programs can help women recognize the value of their own opinions by seeking and heeding women's views and advice.
- Programs can help women practice making decisions in new areas and learn interpersonal skills needed to pursue their own interests.
- Programs can expand services to meet a broader range of women's reproductive health needs.
- Programs can help men both to play their part in contraception and to understand and appreciate women's new roles.
- Programs can provide women with income and skills by hiring, training, and promoting women and by offering them opportunities for leadership.

In these ways family planning programs help prepare women to make decisions and choices that formerly were not available to them. Of course, family planning programs cannot singlehandedly solve all the problems confronting women, but they can seek ways to help.

FAMILY PLANNING SAVES LIVES

Each year an estimated 500,000 women die of complications due to pregnancy, childbearing, or unsafe abortion. All but about 6,000 of these deaths occur in developing countries. Where poor health, frequent childbearing, and little access to good medical care are a way of life, an early death is too often a woman's fate. Contraceptive use can help protect women's lives and health by avoiding pregnancies. It is one of three crucial measures to improve maternal health: (1) reducing the number of pregnancies, (2) reducing the likelihood of complications during pregnancy, and (3) improving outcomes for pregnant women with complications. Reducing complications and improving outcomes require access to better obstetric care, more health care for poor and rural women, and improvements in women's living standards. Currently, emergency care often is unavailable.

Women who do not want to become pregnant can reduce their exposure to the risks of pregnancy and childbirth by using effective contraception. In this sense, using contraception is a strategy that women themselves can adopt to protect their health. Family planning and concern about maternal health have long been linked. The hope to relieve women's suffering and save lives inspired early advocates of contraception in both developed and developing countries. Now, worldwide, policy-makers recognize the importance of contraceptive use to women's health. The Draft Program of Action of the International Conference on Population and Development asserts that countries "should seek...reductions in maternal mortality through measures to reduce high-risk births, including births to adolescents, eliminate all unwanted births and all unsafe abortion, [and] expand cost-effective obstetrical and gynaecological care...". Answering a 1989 UN questionnaire, 62 of 67 countries wishing to modify fertility levels cited improving family well-being as a rationale.

CAUSES OF MATERNAL DEATHS

Pregnancy is the main reason that women of reproductive age die at higher rates than men. In Matlab, Bangladesh, the mortality rate for women ages 15 to 44 was 26% greater than for men in this age range. Some 30% of all women's deaths between ages 15 and 44 were related to childbearing. This study, conducted between 1976 and 1985, is one of the few long-term, detailed examinations of maternal mortality rates and causes.

The World Health Organization (WHO) defines a maternal death as "the death of a woman while pregnant or within 42 days of termination of pregnancy, irrespective of the duration and the site of the pregnancy, from any cause related to or aggravated by the pregnancy or its management but not from accidental or incidental causes." Behind the direct causes of maternal mortality-obstetric complications and unsafe abortions-lie the conditions of women's lives: inadequate care during delivery, chronic disease and malnutrition, poverty, isolation, and unwanted pregnancies.

Better care at childbirth and more access to that care would substantially reduce maternal mortality rates. Most maternal deaths occur among poor women who live in remote areas. Studies in Cuba, Egypt, Indonesia, Jamaica, Tanzania, and Turkey have demonstrated that maternal mortality is higher where access to a hospital is more difficult. When access improves, death rates drop. For example, in Oran, Algeria, the maternal mortality ratio fell 42% between 1971-75 and 1976-80 after fees for public hospital services were waived, a policy that greatly reduced the number of home deliveries.

Yet many women give birth without any trained help. For example, in 12 of 26 countries surveyed by the Demographic and Health Surveys (DHS) between 1986 and 1989, women had received no trained assistance in half or more of all births in the five years before the survey.

Chronic diseases and malnutrition leave many women unable to meet the physical demands of pregnancy. For example, anemia, often a result of poor nutrition, affects about 40% to

60% of pregnant women in developing countries excluding China-more than twice the percentage in developed countries. (By comparison, about 20% of men have anemia.) Malaria, sexually transmitted diseases, and infectious hepatitis also cause serious problems for many pregnant women and, unless treated, may kill them or their infants.

A woman's age and parity affect her chances of dying in childbirth. Health risks related to age and parity have been summarized as "the four too's"-too young, too old, too many, too close together. First births and births after the fourth are more dangerous than the second through fourth births. Women under age 18 and, more dramatically, those over age 35 face greater risk than women between these ages. Of course, age and parity are not risks in themselves; they stand in for the higher likelihood of specific risks associated with age and parity. For example, pregnancy can be dangerous to very young women because their pelvises are not yet large enough to accommodate birth. Many of these specific conditions can be managed if high-quality delivery care is available.

Some family planning programs have emphasized serving women in these high-risk age and parity categories, particularly older, high-parity women. The Mexican social security system found that this emphasis interested more doctors in family planning and thus helped expand contraceptive services. Still, the "four too's" do not justify overriding women's own informed decisions about whether and when to have children or to pressure them to use a contraceptive method that is not their preference.

Deaths from unsafe abortion. Many women resort to abortion to prevent unintended births. Because abortions are illegal in most developing countries, many women seek them clandestinely and undergo unsafe procedures. Even in some places where abortion is legal, poor-quality services put women at risk.

An estimated 10 to 20 million illegal abortions are performed worldwide annually, and an estimated 100,000 to 200,000 women die as a result-about one in every 100. These deaths account for 20% to 40% of all maternal deaths. In some Latin American cities abortions account for over half of maternal deaths. In Romania unsafe, illegal abortions were responsible for 86% of maternal deaths. After the procedure was legalized in 1992, the overall maternal mortality ratio fell in the first year to 40% of the 1989 level. Women who survive an unsafe abortion may suffer chronic pelvic pain, chronic pelvic inflammatory disease, and/or infertility. They face a greater risk of ectopic pregnancy, premature delivery, and other adverse health consequences in the future. The majority of deaths due to abortion can be prevented. Access to effective contraceptive methods reduces unwanted pregnancies. The procedure itself is safe if the practitioner uses safe techniques.

While contraceptive use can greatly reduce unwanted pregnancies, it cannot eliminate them. An estimated 25 million women become pregnant each year due to failure of their contraceptive method. Many women, especially young women, become pregnant as the result of forced sexual intercourse. A smaller number of women develop health conditions that make continued pregnancy unsafe. Many of these women will choose an unsafe abortion if they do not have access to a safe procedure.

INCIDENCE OF MATERNAL DEATHS AND ILLNESSES

While the number of maternal deaths is often estimated at 500,000 per year, the true number may be even larger. In many developing countries official statistics underreport maternal deaths, perhaps by one-fourth to one-half. Many maternal deaths go unreported. Others are attributed to other causes. Often deaths are reported but causes are not.

Even less is known about the extent of maternal illnesses in developing countries. A frequently cited estimate is 16 illnesses for each maternal death-a figure based on a 1980 study of one village in India. Applying this ratio to the entire developing world yields an estimate of eight million cases of nonfatal maternal complications every year. Such complications are often chronic and debilitating.

Maternal mortality is usually expressed as the maternal mortality ratio-the number of maternal deaths per 100,000 live births. The maternal mortality ratio measures the risk of dying that a woman faces each time that she becomes pregnant. This ratio is often mistakenly called the maternal mortality rate. (A ratio compares the numbers of two differing events; a rate compares a part to the whole.)

Maternal mortality ratios range widely, from an estimated 12 maternal deaths per 100,000 live births in North America to more than 700 per 100,000 in some parts of sub-Saharan Africa. For the developing world as a whole, maternal mortality is estimated at more than 400 deaths per 100,000 live births, while the ratio is below 30 per 100,000 in the developed world.

Due to poor health and poor health care, many women in developing countries face much greater risk in each pregnancy than most women in developed countries. They also face this risk more often because, on the average, they have more pregnancies. Thus the lifetime risk of maternal death-a statistic that reflects both the risk per pregnancy and the number of pregnancies-is far greater in most developing countries than in developed countries. Between one-fourth and one-third of all deaths among women in their reproductive years in developing countries are related to maternity compared with only one-half of 1% in the US.

In the developing world as a whole, any one pregnancy is, on average, about 16 times more likely to kill than in the developed world. And the higher fertility levels in developing countries double that relative risk over a woman's lifetime. Thus the average woman in developing countries is about 30 times more likely to die from pregnancy-related causes than the average woman in a developed country.

CONTRACEPTION CAN SAFEGUARD WOMEN'S HEALTH

While family planning programs should not be treated as a substitute for urgently needed improvements in delivery care, reducing the number of pregnancies that women have in their lifetimes also substantially reduces the risk of maternal mortality and morbidity, particularly where fertility rates are high and health facilities are poor or unavailable. The study in Matlab, Bangladesh, illustrates how fewer pregnancies results in fewer maternal deaths. In 1977 more intensive family planning services, including home visits by trained female family planning workers, were introduced in selected Matlab villages. In these test villages the percentage of married women using contraception rose from 8% in 1976 to almost 40% by the end of the study in 1985. In comparison areas, where services were not expanded, the rate rose much less, from 5% to 17%. By the end of the study, maternal mortality in the test villages had fallen to less than half of that in the comparison villages-even though there was no change in the risk of dying from any one pregnancy. Contraception and psychosocial stress. Lack of control over one's own life is a major cause of stress. Thus the use of contraception can improve women's emotional health by providing more reproductive control and greater choice about childbearing. Also, because using contraception, like other preventive health practices, reflects an orientation to the future, it can be an important step toward overcoming fatalism and lack of self-worth.

In some circumstances, however, obtaining and using contraception can itself be stressful, especially where modern contraceptives are not yet widely accepted. A woman may worry about visiting a family planning clinic and undergoing questioning or a physical examination. She may fear disrespectful treatment or negligent care. She may also fear that visiting a clinic or using contraception will provoke her husband's anger or will bring criticism from her family, her in-laws, or others. She may experience painful or worrying side effects from using a contraceptive method. She may hear frightening false rumors about the dangers of contraceptive methods. Family planning managers must recognize these possible stresses and develop strategies to relieve them. As contraceptive use becomes the community norm and as services improve, using contraception may become less stressful.

SPACING PREGNANCIES IMPROVES CHILDREN'S HEALTH

A child's serious illness or death is a common event in many places and a cause of great stress and grief. Couples can reduce their children's health risks by spacing births. Children who are born within 17 months after the preceding birth are about twice as likely to die before age 5 as those born 24 to 47 months after the preceding child. Even children born after an interval of 18 to 23 months are about one-third more likely to die than children born 24 to 47 months after the preceding child. In Brazil and Egypt the child mortality rate could be cut by up to one-third if all births were spaced more than two years apart.

Many women are having their children closer together than they wish. The World Fertility Survey (WFS) and Demographic and Health Surveys (DHS) indicate that 90% of women who plan to become pregnant would like to space their children at intervals longer than 24 months. More than one-third, however, have a second birth within 24 months.

Research also shows that children are more likely to die if their mothers are younger than age 18. According to the WFS and DHS, delaying the first birth until the mother is at least 18 years old reduces the risk of the first child's death by an average of 20%. In the Dominican Republic, Egypt, Mexico, and Peru, delaying childbearing at least until the age of 18 would reduce the risk of the first child's death by 30%.

Contraception use Helps Women Plan

Women who can decide if and when they will become pregnant are better able to plan other aspects of their lives. In the short term women who use contraception effectively may have more choice about the use of their time because they have fewer children. Women may be better able to make plans to take new educational, economic, and other opportunities. Also, in the long term society in general and women themselves may change their expectations of how women lead their lives. Young women probably benefit most from being able to control their own fertility.

The Changing Needs of Young Women

Young women's lives are changing. Almost everywhere in the developing world, more women are delaying marriage. In

29 of 36 countries that have conducted Demographic and Health Surveys, the percentage of women who had married by age 20 was at least 10% lower among women ages 20 to 24 than among the oldest women interviewed, usually those ages 45 to 49. As women delay marriage, they have more opportunity to complete their education, to develop remunerable skills, and to choose their husbands or to choose not to marry at all.

Avoiding unintended pregnancies is critically important to allow women to make these choices, especially in cultures where unplanned pregnancy precipitates marriage or where premarital births have particularly disastrous social or economic consequences. In Latin America and the Caribbean, the Young Adult Reproductive Health Surveys (YARHS) document that many women are sexually active before marriage but are not consistently using contraception. For example, in a 1985 survey in Mexico City, 13% of women age 15 to 19 and 44% of men reported premarital intercourse. Only 22% of the women and 31% of the men used contraception at their first sexual experience, however. Among unmarried women ages 15 to 24, half of all first pregnancies were unintended. Among married women in this same age group, 11% of first births were conceived before marriage.

Nevertheless, offering contraceptives to unmarried adolescents and young adults remains controversial. Some parents and policy-makers assume that the availability of contraception will lead adolescents to have sexual relations before marriage. This assumption is one reason that, formally or informally, many family planning programs refuse to serve unmarried young people.

In fact, data do not suggest that the availability of contraceptives encourages early sex. Most research on the subject comes from the US and other developed countries. For example, an international comparison found that sex education and contraceptive services were more available in Europe than in the US. Sexual activity among adolescents, however, was about as prevalent in the UK, France, and the Netherlands as in the US, while the US teenage pregnancy rate was much higher. Another US study found that teens who had a sexual education program in their school delayed intercourse and were less likely to become pregnant. Still other studies have found no link between the presence of contraceptive clinics in the schools and levels of sexual activity among students.

Contraception and Education

For many young women the most important fork in life's path is the divide between education and early pregnancy. It is true that many barriers stand between young women and an education. Some parents think that it is wiser to educate sons because there are more and better-paying jobs for men than for women. Also, some girls are taken out of school to work at home. Some families are not willing to educate girls if the school is distant or the teachers are male.

Still, once girls reach puberty, the greatest threat to their staying in school may be pregnancy. Students who become pregnant often drop out of school, or they are expelled by school authorities-a fate that does not befall male students who father children. In many African countries pregnancy is the most common reason that girls leave school and the main reason that the school-leaving rate is higher for girls than for boys.

To ensure that girls are not forced to leave school due to unwanted pregnancy, girls need to be able to refuse unwanted sexual intercourse and to have access to contraceptives, information, and counseling if they choose to be sexually active. Also, schools should help young women continue in school, not expel them, even if they are pregnant or have a child.

Policies that help young women avoid pregnancy and stay in school could help change attitudes in the long run. Parents and communities might be more willing to invest in girls' education if they had more confidence that their daughters would not become pregnant and leave school. Also, as more women complete an education, and as more women hold paying jobs, the perception of women's potential is likely to change, helping to break the vicious cycle that holds women back.

Some young women recognize that avoiding pregnancy protects their futures. For example, in a Kenyan study female students of high socioeconomic status viewed contraception favorably. Those who ranked in the top quarter of their class were nearly four times more likely than other female students to have used contraception at their most recent act of intercourse. These young women could afford contraceptives and recognized that an early pregnancy would endanger their chances for academic success and economic security.

Children benefit in various ways from their parents' use of contraception. Education appears to be one area in which women pass on the benefit to their daughters: Both sons and daughters from small families have better educational opportunities than children from large families. In a Thai community, in families with three or fewer children, 44% of the children went to lower secondary school, and 31% went to upper secondary school. By comparison, in families with four or more children, 24% went to lower secondary school, and 14% went to upper secondary school. In this study couples with small and large families were matched for wealth, religion, residence, parents' educational attainment, and parents' ambitions for their children's education. All couples had had access to modern contraceptive methods throughout their reproductive years. Similarly, in Matlab, Bangladesh, children in small families stayed in school longer because they did not need to care for younger siblings at home. Still, in both Thailand and Bangladesh parents provided more education for their sons than for their daughters.

Contraception and Employment

The relationships among women's status, employment, and childbearing are complex. Some statistical studies find lower fertility associated with more female participation in the labor force, while others find the opposite. Such inconsistency is not surprising, given the variety of jobs and occupations, demographic and household characteristics, cultural forces, and socioeconomic circumstances around the world.

While statistical research into women's labor-force participation and women's use of contraception has not produced clear findings, the conceptual links are clear. With eיective contraception, women are better able to work when they need to without the interruption of unplanned childbearing. Women also may find the burden of household work somewhat lightened. In addition to caring for children, women nurse the sick. Women in developing countries raise 50% to 90% of their families' food. In most rural areas women spend long hours carrying water, gathering fuel, and preparing and cooking food. How spacing and limiting births influence the daily lives of women working in the home also deserves research.

Wherever unplanned pregnancy would limit the types of work available to women, effective contraceptive use may help provide women with broader opportunities to obtain the economic security of a job. When a woman cannot be sure of avoiding pregnancy, her occupational choices often are limited. She may have to find employment that can be combined with childcare, that permits flexible hours, and that is easy to enter and leave frequently. Such jobs typically earn low, static wages. Most such jobs are in the informal sector of developing economies—for example, agriculture and petty trade. Even in the formal sector of developed countries, such jobs as nursing and teaching have been held mostly by women since employers did not care if pregnancy forced teachers or nurses to leave after a few years on the job. Seen as jobs that young women held until they had a family, these professions have commonly been paid less and offered less opportunity for advancement and less status.

More detailed studies, rather than large-scale statistical analyses of fertility levels and labor force participation, may offer a clearer view of how contraceptive use and employment are linked. For example, in Nigeria researchers found that young unmarried women out of school were using contraception in order to work longer before marriage. In one area studied, 75% of single women ages 18 to 25 were using contraception, more than five times the contraceptive prevalence of married women in the same age group.

Of course, many factors other than contraception affect women's employment. Women's autonomy within the family is one such factor. In some countries cultural norms call for women to remain at home no matter what their own preferences are. Also, some employers discriminate against women, partly because employers assume that women's commitment to their jobs is weaker than men's. Nevertheless, in modernizing economies women are an increasingly important part of the labor force. Where contraception is widely available and its use is accepted, employers can be more confident that female workers will not be forced to leave because of unplanned pregnancies. At the same time, however, the possibility that a woman may become pregnant is not legitimate grounds for denying her a job.

When women have access to contraception and new economic opportunities, many take advantage of both. In Bangladesh the Grameen Bank offers poor women small loans for income-generating projects. The women attend regular meetings at which they receive advice on their projects. They also learn the "Sixteen Decisions"-resolutions to make changes in their lives including planting vegetables, educating their children, and having small families. Women who have taken advantage of this new economic opportunity are more likely to be using contraception than women who are not receiving loans.

How can Family Planning Programs Benefit Women?

Contraceptive use protects women from the health risks of unwanted pregnancy and gives women more control over their own lives. Family planning programs help women primarily by providing contraceptive methods. What more can family planning programs do to meet women's needs? Women interact with family planning programs only briefly and infrequently. Still, in addition to providing contraception, those brief contacts can be designed to strengthen women's abilities to fulfill current roles and take on new ones. Program managers can seek to:

- Encourage respect for women,
- Provide a range of reproductive health care, and
- Design program activities to strengthen the skills that enable women to take new opportunities.

ENCOURAGING RESPECT FOR ALL WOMEN

By showing respect for women, family planning programs help women build self-confidence and self-esteem and thus strengthen their ability to make their own decisions and to act in their own interests. Also, showing respect for women as clients sets a good example for the community.

Family planning programs have an excellent opportunity to promote respect for women. Unfortunately, some programs have missed that opportunity-perhaps because program personnel share widespread social attitudes that denigrate women, because a program focuses on enrolling more clients rather than meeting clients' needs, because personnel are simply not aware that courtesy is important, or because service providers have too little time for each client. Program managers can encourage respect for clients in several ways:

- Ensure informed choice. Programs that help women make their own informed choices about their fertility show respect for their clients' right and ability to make decisions. To ensure informed choice, managers can see that clients are (1) offered a choice of methods, (2) given the information they want about each method, and (3) allowed to choose the method that they want, provided there is no medical reason to withhold it.
- Communicate respectfully. All personnel, no matter what their function, can act politely and in a respectful, friendly manner with all clients at all times. Program personnel demonstrate their respect for clients by paying attention to what clients say, answering their questions fully, never belittling their concerns and questions, and understanding and honoring their clients wishes. Also, programs must be sensitive to clients' modesty and preserve client-provider confidentiality.
- Train staff. Program managers can train staff to think of clients' needs and to communicate with clients. Staff also can learn how to communicate respect.
- Reward respect. Managers can reward personnel who treat female clients respectfully. They can measure the

success of programs and providers by client satisfaction rather than just by numbers of clients. To measure client satisfaction, managers can survey clients about the care that they received. Whether clients return for further services when needed also indicates whether they are satisfied.

- Improve staff morale. Family planning personnel may treat clients poorly if personnel themselves have to work with insufficient time, supplies, space, or pay. If so, managers can acknowledge the problems, remedy them if possible, and at the same time make clear that the staff's frustrations are not an excuse for treating clients disrespectfully. Also, public promotion that enhances the image of providers, along with training, improves morale and inspires staff to live up to their new image.
- Set an example. Managers are role-models for other program personnel. If they do not treat clients and staff with respect, they cannot expect their staff to do so.

Clients know when they are treated with respect. Among Chilean women interviewed at a family planning clinic run by the Instituto Chileno de Medicina Reproductiva (ICMER), "being treated like a human being" was the most frequently identified element in high-quality care. In a clinic run by the Bangladesh Women's Health Coalition, a woman commented on the care that she had received: "I'd heard about family planning before, but not this way. This is the only clinic where I was asked to sit down and where I was treated as an equal. If I knew about it in this way, do you think I'd have six children?"

People who are treated with respect develop self-respect. Brief contacts with a family planning program are not likely to revolutionize women's lives. Still, for some women, contact with high-quality family planning services can be a start; for others, a step forward; and perhaps for a few, a big step. A young mother in Chile credited a family planning service with improving her self-esteem: "I am valuing myself more. I am realizing that I am really worth something. I am a person, and I should take care of myself..."

OFFERING OTHER REPRODUCTIVE HEALTH CARE

A reproductive health approach to family planning services can improve women's health and therefore women's choices. Judith Bruce and Anrudh Jain define a reproductive health care approach as one that helps clients reach their fertility goals in a healthful manner. This approach focuses first on ensuring that clients receive high-quality family planning services and then on offering additional services to help women meet multiple health needs at the same time and place.

To attain high quality, family planning services require two components: respectful, helpful interaction between provider and client and technically skilled personnel. To assure high quality, family planning programs can (1) determine the services that they can offer, (2) develop locally defined standards of care, and (3) establish quality-monitoring procedures.

For example, those who counsel clients about contraceptive use must be trained to explain whichever methods are offered, to understand clients' needs, and to help them consider their options. Those who perform medical procedures need technical training. All training should raise providers' skills to a demonstrated standard of competence. Monitoring and supervision reinforce quality standards to assure that programs offer an informed choice of methods, hygienic care, and safe medical procedures. AVSC International has developed the COPE technique and the Population Council has developed the Situational Analysis approach to evaluate the quality of both client-provider interaction and providers' technical skills.

Many medical professionals favor a reproductive health approach because they see a visit to a family planning clinic as a rare opportunity to inform, screen, and treat women for a variety of reproductive health conditions, such as certain common sexually transmitted diseases (STDs) and conditions of pregnancy. Also, girls and adolescent women can be counseled about nutrition, anemia, and general health to help prevent later pregnancy-related morbidity and mortality. Some programs, too, may want the convenience of dealing with multiple health needs on one clinic visit.

Women often see little distinction among family planning, other reproductive health needs, and still other health needs, including their children's. When family planning personnel cannot help, some women feel that program personnel are not really interested in their health. In the ICMER clinic in Peru, women wanted a clinic visit to be an opportunity to learn more about their reproductive health and how to protect it. They preferred to discuss all their health problems with one provider.

Meeting a variety of needs encourages women to use services. For example, in Tunisia a family planning program recognized that new mothers have multiple concerns-about their new infants' health, their own health, and their ability to breast-feed. Therefore a clinic in Sfax began to offer neonatal, postpartum, and family planning services on one visit. Women are encouraged to come to the clinic on the fortieth day after giving birth, the traditional day on which a new mother first leaves the house. In 1987, 83% of postpartum women came for this visit, and 56% of these women adopted a family planning method. The approach is now being applied nationwide.

Not all women want all services, however. For example, some women may want a contraceptive method but not a pelvic exam or Papanicolaou smear. Requiring clients to accept services that they do not want could discourage them from getting any services at all.

In counseling women, programs also might broaden their focus beyond preventing pregnancy and disease. For example, women have a right to refuse unwanted sexual intercourse but often cannot do so. Helping women with such matters requires learning more about their private lives. Ruth Dixon-Mueller argues that providers cannot truly meet women's needs for contraception, disease prevention, or safety from violence without knowing something about how each client is sexually active. Providers may need to find out, for example, if a client has multiple sexual partners or is forced into unwanted sexual acts. Few family planning providers are prepared to elicit such information, which must be discussed in a sympathetic and reassuring manner. Training and a new way of thinking about the providers' role will be required. Of course, clients should not be required to disclose intimate information if they choose not to.

Weighing program options. Each program must determine its own ability to offer new services. Some programs may be strained to capacity, already serving as many clients as possible. For such programs, the scarcity of resources limits how much more they can offer. Other programs may want to attract more clients. For these programs, broadening services-and improving quality-may help. In choosing which services to add, each program has to assess clients' needs as well as program resources.

Still, some general principles apply to making these decisions. Elizabeth Maguire, Acting Director of the Office of Population, United States Agency for International Development, urges that family planning programs consider adding other reproductive health services "that will benefit the most women at an affordable cost and have the highest public health impact". Under these criteria a common, serious condition that is easily treated or prevented would have highest priority. Providers and other public health experts should involve clients in deciding which conditions are deemed serious, but without abandoning their professional judgement.

Many family planning managers are considering whether to offer services for sexually transmitted diseases. Adding STD services to family planning services can be appropriate because (1) many people need care, (2) combined services would be convenient for clients, (3) most STDs can be treated, (4) counseling could help women avoid STDs, and (5) most family planning programs offer condoms in any case.

Also, STDs are spreading and have serious health consequences. It is now known that infection with the AIDS-causing human immunodeficiency virus (HIV) is more likely in those with other STDs. Some family planning programs may find it difficult, however, to add STD services. Of course, family planning program managers can choose among several different levels of STD services: (1) prevention-information, counseling, and providing condoms and spermicides; or (2) in addition, initial screening and referral of suspected STD cases for diagnosis and treatment elsewhere; or (3) diagnosis and treatment as well as prevention and initial screening. The potential for impact and costs differs at each level.

Treatment after a septic abortion is also a serious need because so many women die from unsafe procedures. At the 1984 International Conference on Population in Mexico City, delegates urged governments to help women avoid abortion and to treat them humanely if they have had an abortion. Policy-makers can reduce the number of abortion deaths by improving treatment for septic abortion and by linking post-abortion care with contraceptive counseling and services. While offering contraception to all who want it, family planning programs can reduce abortion by reaching out especially to women at high risk of unwanted pregnancy, including adolescents, and by providing post-abortion counseling and family planning services in hospitals where women receive post-abortion treatment.

Around the world a variety of reproductive health programs are developing. For example, some affiliates of the International Planned Parenthood Federation (IPPF) in Africa and Latin America provide counseling and referrals for clients with STD symptoms. In Colombia the Asociación Pro-Bienestar de la Familia (Profamilia) offers contraceptive methods, screening for sexually transmitted diseases, sex counseling, clinics for men, AIDS prevention, and even legal services to low-income men and women.

In Bolivia a coalition of 18 public and private health institutions recently launched a national campaign to promote reproductive health services. The Bolivian National Reproductive Health Program encourages couples to use services that will improve family health including reducing the high maternal mortality rate.

These services include family planning, prenatal care, safe delivery and post-delivery care, breastfeeding promotion, and abortion prevention. To inform people about these services, the organizaticns, with technical assistance from Johns Hopkins

Population Communication Services (JHU/PCS), have developed a campaign logo, clinic signs, posters, radio and television spots, in-clinic videos, client-provider materials, and audio cassettes for play on buses. The campaign tells couples that they have the right and responsibility to protect the health of women and children.

STRENGTHENING WOMEN'S SKILLS

Women often need to build skills and self-confidence before they can take on new opportunities. Family planning program activities that strengthen women's assertiveness, communication, and decision-making skills can help prepare women to obtain fair treatment and to take new opportunities. In the process of delivering health services, high-quality family planning programs can help to build such skills by:

- Helping women learn to make informed choices in new areas of their lives,
- Supporting women's choices,
- Encouraging women to recognize their strengths and to build on them,
- Improving women's skills at communicating with their husbands and with people outside their families, and
- Creating new images and models of competent women and caring men.

These skill-building efforts do not necessarily require major new training, large new expenditures, or more staff. Much can be done in the everyday process of serving clients. A change of attitude and a change of emphasis can make a lot of difference.

Self-awareness can be the first step. Whether services meet women's needs can depend on providers' most basic assumptions about women and men. For example, if providers assume that women are solely responsible for contraceptive use, they may design services that make it difficult for men to obtain information and services. If, instead, providers assume that both men and women need services, they are more likely to design services that both men and women can use easily.

Making informed choices. Women make many decisions throughout their lives, but they may need to gain confidence in making new kinds of decisions, such as decisions to control their fertility or to seek new social roles. In a Mexican study young women with unplanned pregnancies seemed to be women with little awareness that they could make decisions for themselves. They were less likely than nonpregnant young women to know about contraceptives, to have discussed sex with their girlfriends, and to have aspirations and plans for the future. Women surveyed in parts of such countries as Bangladesh, Ghana, Jordan, Mali, Nigeria, Pakistan, and Tanzania say that they do not participate in decisions about having children. Many say that they obey their husbands' wishes or the will of God.

Reproductive health programs can help women make wider choices. By discussing reproductive needs and goals with clients, providers can give women practice in assessing a situation and making thoughtful decisions. Since making fertility decisions may be unfamiliar to some clients, the process requires skill and patience on the part of the provider. Ideally, the provider imparts information, listens attentively, encourages discussion, helps clients recognize their own needs, and answers clients' questions. The clients themselves make the decisions about whether and when to have children and how to carry out their plans.

Supporting women's choices. Respecting clients' wishes builds women's confidence in their own decision-making and their right to make decisions. For example, many women already know what contraceptive methods they want before they come to a family planning provider. Honoring a woman's preference is important to her satisfaction with family planning. In Indonesia, for example, 91% of women who were given the method that they chose were still using that contraceptive method after one year compared with only 28% of women who were given a method that was not their first choice. A 6-country IPPF study also found that women were more likely to continue contraceptive use when they received the method that they wanted.

Women's choices reflect their own needs. Providers cannot assume what women need or want. For example, in Peru some women in focus groups said that they preferred the rhythm method because it gave them the right to make choices about when to have sex. Also, its use implied the intelligence to take charge of one's life. Women chose this method because it requires cooperation between sexual partners, and that cooperation enhanced the relationship.

Therefore, to create the best services, managers can ask clients what they want and design programs and train staff accordingly. Even better, they can directly involve female clients and community members and groups in planning and monitoring services. Such a client-oriented approach is rare. Indeed, providers' biases often block access to contraception and to a choice of methods. Often because of misinformation about methods, providers may favor one method over all others or shun certain methods. Because of negative assumptions about clients, particularly about women, providers may deny clients a choice of methods or discourage use of methods that require clients to act-for example, using barrier methods at each act of coitus or taking an oral contraceptive tablet daily.

Recognizing women's strengths. Successful counseling helps women identify their strengths and build upon them in planning their lives. In India group leaders from the Institute of Health Management ask groups of women who is the most important person in their homes. At first, the women never mention themselves. Then the group leaders recite a list of household chores and ask the women who does each chore in their homes. The women repeatedly answer that they do the chores. When the leaders ask again who is the most important person in their house, the women laughingly answer that they are most important. Good counseling can help women recognize that they already plan their time, save money or grain, and care for their families and homes. Building on these skills, women may learn to plan other aspects of their lives, including their reproductive lives, in which they may have depended previously on others. Recognizing their own managerial role in the home, women can have more confidence applying these skills elsewhere. A manual prepared by the United Nations Educational, Scientific, and Cultural Organization (UNESCO) suggests an exercise to help women build their self-esteem: Women list their skills, such as planning their time and organizing their families. Then they say how those skills would help them in a business situation.

Improving communication skills. Family planning programs can help women speak up on matters that concern them. In particular, programs can encourage and enable women, and men, to talk about contraceptive use and reproductive health. Women's discussion groups have been the approach most widely used to help women bring up and discuss these issues.

To help women learn to talk about family planning, a program in rural Bangladesh designed with assistance from JHU/PCS organizes volunteer discussion groups. The program was set up to reach more people than family planning field workers could reach in home visits and because women were isolated and unaccustomed to discussing family planning with each other or with their husbands. The discussion groups, called Jiggasha ("to enquire" in Bangla), are formed for men and women separately. Leaders and meeting places are chosen to take advantage of the existing networks of communication in the community.

The Jiggasha meetings have encouraged women to discuss and use family planning. About 65% of participants report that, after attending several meetings, they have discussed family planning with their husbands or with other women in the group, and about 50% report talking to people outside the group or to a family planning field worker. Some 30% of the women began to use a modern contraceptive method, and 20% visited a health clinic.

In Bolivia in the early 1990s client-provider materials produced to improve the quality of reproductive health services and counseling contributed to communication between spouses. Before-and-after surveys found that significantly more clients had talked with their spouses about family planning after seeing and receiving the materials—95% compared with 84% before they had seen the materials in clinics. By comparison, the increase among those who had not seen the materials-from 83% to 88%-was not statistically significant. Later a video drama entitled Hablemos en Pareja (Let's Talk Together) was produced and shown in clinic waiting areas to help clients overcome barriers to communication between spouses.

Couples may find talking about family planning and reproductive health easier if they have discussed the subject first with someone of their own sex. Programs such as Jiggasha can help. For example, women in a rural area of northern India could not talk to their husbands about sexually transmitted diseases, even though they feared that their husbands might infect them. Health advisors organized the women into groups that discussed the problem and decided how to approach their husbands. After practicing the conversation in groups, the women were better able to talk with their husbands.

Family planning providers can help couples communicate better if they are aware of social conventions. For example, in Mexico a survey revealed that couples thought it immodest for the wife to start a discussion of family planning. These couples said that husbands should start such discussions and decide whether the couple uses a family planning method. In response, family planning providers designed counseling services for men and women advocating that women start discussion and that the couple make a decision together.

Strengthening communication skills is important to women and men who want their partners' support and cooperation in planning their families and protecting their reproductive health. For some, discussion may be a necessary step to taking an action they desire. For example, according to DHS data from six African countries, women who approved of family planning were more likely to use a modern contraceptive method if they had discussed family planning with their husbands in the year before the interview than were women who approved of family planning but had not discussed it. Studies in Java and South Korea have found that the more often couples discuss family planning, the more likely they are to use a contraceptive method.

Discussion between partners may make continued contraceptive use easier, too. In the IPPF 6-country study, women who thought that their partners agreed with their use of a family planning method were significantly more likely to continue using that method than women who did not know that their partners approved. Although studies link spousal communication with contraceptive use, the nature of the link is not obvious. It is not always clear whether more communication leads to more contraceptive use or, instead, couples talk more about contraception because they already use or plan to use a method. Also, some couples may not have an immediate reason to discuss family planning-for example, the woman is pregnant, the couple wants a child, or they have no access to contraceptives. New images of women and men. It will be easier for women to take new opportunities when society respects them as strong and competent. Men will find it easier to help women when they see positive images of men who support those qualities in women. Family planning communication can provide these images by portraying competent women and caring men in radio drama, videos, films, advertisements, and users' testimonials.

ENCOURAGING MEN'S COOPERATION

Women's situation will improve faster if men help. Protecting reproductive health particularly requires commitment from both men and women. While a woman can control her fertility without a man's cooperation-and many do-men's understanding and help make contraception and family planning easier and widen the choice of methods that a couple can use. Also, to prevent sexually transmitted disease, a woman must have the cooperation of her male sexual partner, who must remain faithful to her or use condoms. What can family planning and reproductive health programs do to encourage men's cooperation?

Changing Times and Changing Attitudes

Encouraging men's cooperation can start with understanding men's points of view. Many men approve of family planning and contraception. Even where few people use contraceptives, such as Burundi, Ghana, Kenya, Mali, and Pakistan, at least half of men surveyed approved of contraception.

Still, many men have negative attitudes about women choosing and using contraception. Some men fear that contraceptive use will make their wives independent of their control. They fear that their wives will have sex with other men if they no longer risk pregnancy. Some men may be unwilling to have their wives adopt family planning because they themselves know little about it. Some do not want their wives talking with strangers about sex and reproduction. Some worry that contraceptive use will harm their wives' health or their own (3). Some oppose contraceptive use for religious reasons. Some men think that large families reflect their masculinity or their wives' faithfulness in serving them.

These male attitudes about contraceptive use are part of some men's broader fears. Traditional social norms often have required men to maintain the honor and position of their extended family, village, religious group, or other social organization. Therefore men feel responsible for the behavior of their wives and children and think that women have no right to make decisions for themselves.

Men are not alone in imposing limits on women. Many mothers, even wealthier, better educated women, prefer sons and take better care of them (1, 374). In some places women dominate their sons' wives, pressure them to have many children, and even physically abuse them.

Paternalistic traditional norms are no excuse for the mistreatment of women, however. Violence against women, including violence from their husbands and other family members, can be condemned by religious and political leaders and prohibited by law, and the law, enforced. Also, legal changes in a variety of areas affecting women's well-being can be the catalyst to changing community norms.

Economic and social changes, too, are requiring couples to be more flexible about gender roles. More and more, both partners must produce income to support the family. As a result, men are finding that a wife with many skills can help support the family. In 1990 women made up 42% of the paid labor force in the developed world and 33% in the developing world. The need for women to earn income has changed gender roles. In the US some husbands and wives are arranging to work different hours, and more men are caring for the children. In 1991, 20% of children under age five were cared for by their fathers at home while their mothers went to work.

Some men find that they have gained through improvements in their wives' status. For example, in Colombia the Instituto Colombiano Agropecurio provides poor women with small loans and on-going help with planning and decision-making. The women and their husbands have worked together to make their enterprises succeed and to take care of their homes. Both husbands and wives said that they benefited from the project. The women became more self-confident and knowledgeable about dealing with local institutions such as schools and markets. Their new confidence made them better advocates for the family. In Zimbabwe and other areas of Africa, husbands report that their wives' employment as family planning field workers enhanced the prestige of their family. These men support their wives in their new positions even if the women do not bring in additional income.

ENCOURAGING MALE RESPONSIBILITY

Reproductive health programs can help men cooperate with their sexual partners to avoid unwanted pregnancies and to prevent sexually transmitted diseases. Specifically, programs can:

- Inform men about family planning, reproductive health, and contraceptive methods,
- Encourage and improve communication between spouses,
- Design convenient services for men,
- Provide contraceptive choices for men, and
- Promote images of male role-models who cooperate with women both in the family and in the community and who share the burden of ensuring reproductive health.

Informing Men: Many men want to know more about contraception and family planning and to be more involved. For example, in Malaysia, Nigeria, and Turkey, most men surveyed wanted to learn more about family planning. In Peru men in focus groups complained that false stereotypes of dominating men (machismo) limited their opportunities to obtain information about sexuality and family planning. In Tunisia men often accompanied their wives to the family planning clinic but then waited outside, talking among themselves. When asked, some said that they would like to be more involved. Men commented, "We are made to feel like strangers." "We are pushed aside...," and "From the way we are treated, one would think that this doesn't concern us."

Women, too, want men to have information. In Chile women asked that men be allowed to come to the classes at the clinic. One woman said that her husband did not always believe her and that she would "love to have him come to some of the talks."

Men need information about contraceptive methods for women as well as about those for men. Well-informed men can use a method themselves or support their partners in using a method. Well-informed men also can talk with their wives and cooperate in assessing their needs and choosing a family planning method.

Men especially need information about sexually transmitted diseases since men play a big role in the spread of sexually transmitted diseases including AIDS. Although there is much variation among cultures, except for female prostitutes men are likely to have more sexual partners than women. Men have more control over condom use. Men are more likely to control the frequency of sexual relations and the possibility of abstinence within a relationship. To reduce risk, men can: (1) reduce the number of sexual partners, (2) use condoms, and/or (3) practice sexual fidelity or abstinence.

Encouraging Communication between Spouses: Men can support women's choices better when couples can talk about reproductive health and family planning. But surveys show that even men who approve of family planning do not always discuss it with their wives. For example, in Burundi 94% of surveyed men approved of contraceptive use, but only 48% had discussed it with their wives in the preceding year. Family planning communication campaigns can change men's role in contraceptive decision-making. The Zimbabwe Male Motivation Project in 1988 and 1989 sought to inform men, promote more favorable attitudes, increase contraceptive use, and promote male involvement and joint decision-making. The project appeared to increase condom use particularly. Its impact on men's attitudes about decision-making was ambiguous, however. Men who heard the campaign radio soap opera, attended a lecture, or saw a pamphlet were more likely to say that the man alone should make the decision to practice family planning. At the same time, these men also were more likely to say that the couple should decide jointly how many children to have. Researchers concluded that future campaigns should put more emphasis on joint decision-making and discussion between spouses.

Some family planning programs welcome husbands and wives who seek family planning counseling and services together. While counseling a couple, a provider can encourage the woman to ask her own questions and express her own opinions. The provider also can encourage the man to understand and respect the woman's opinions and choices. Program managers seeking to improve women's situation need to make clear, however, that the program also welcomes women and men who come alone, does not require a husband's permission before serving a woman, and keeps the names of clients and all information about clients confidential, even from spouses.

BIBLIOGRAPHY

Augustine, P.A.: *Social Equality in Indian Society*, New Delhi, Concept, 1991

Benjamin, J.: *Socio-religious Status of Girl Child in India*, New Delhi, Ashish Publishing, 1991.

Bowlby, J.: *A Secure Base: Parent-child Attachment and Healthy Human Development*, New York, Basic Books, 1990.

Bruce, J.: *User's Perspectives on Family Planning: Some Operational and Research Issues*, New York, Population Council, 1983.

Erikson, E. H.: *Childhood and Society*, New York, W. W. Norton, 1993.

Forbes, Anna: *Kids with AIDS*, New York, Rosen Pub. Group's Powerkids Press, 1996.

Gordon, L.: *Women and Health in America: Historical Readings*, Wisconsin, University of Wisconsin Press, 1984.

Kegan, R.: *In Over our Heads: The Mental Demands of Modern Life*, Cambridge, Harvard University Press, 1994.

Mahler, Margaret: *The Psychological Birth of the Human Infant*, New York, Basic, 1975.

Medawar, J.: *The History of Family Planning in Britain*, England, Penguin, 1971.

Otsea, K.: *Progress and Prospects: The Safe Motherhood Initiative 1987-1992*, Washington, D.C., World Bank, 1992.

Piaget, J., & Whelder, B.: *The Psychology of the Child*, New York, Basic Books, 1964.

Ross, J.A.: *Family Planning and Child Survival Programs as Assessed in 1991*, New York, Population Council, 1992.

INDEX

A

Audiences, 43, 44, 46, 50, 51, 52, 54, 55, 56, 57, 60, 66.

C

Collaboration, 232.
Company, 4, 88, 103.
Consumers, 57, 64, 119, 164.
Crop Production, 126.
Cultural Hegemony, 58, 59.

D

Developments, 107, 208, 214.
Distribution, 11, 22, 23, 59, 96, 97, 100, 137, 222.
Diversity, 46, 73, 97.

F

Foundations, 147, 185.

I

Industry, 5, 6, 11, 49, 121, 125, 147, 148, 149, 151, 153, 155, 159, 164, 165, 166, 215.
Institutions, 40, 53, 70, 75, 81, 112, 135, 145, 147, 157, 192, 203, 217, 225, 246, 252, 270.
Insurance, 125, 220.
International Conference, 237, 243, 260.

M

Management, 5, 6, 12, 16, 99, 161, 221, 226, 244, 263.
Marginalisation, 126, 167.
Mass Media, 49, 106, 122.
Mechanisms, 12, 169, 224.
Methodology, 3, 5, 96.

O

Observations, 50, 97.

P

Performance, 164, 227.
Political Status, 101.
Politics, 14, 53, 56, 59, 63, 73, 74, 75, 77, 101, 163, 179, 185.
Production, 44, 53, 126, 155, 156, 157, 158, 159, 160, 161, 162.

T

Technology, 1, 2, 9, 11, 16, 17, 122, 144, 158, 169, 172.

U

Universal Mission, 172, 174, 175.

□□□